Poor

Kid

~~Page 24~~

P. 24

HYMNS

CHURCH OF JESUS CHRIST
OF LATTER-DAY SAINTS

PUBLISHED BY THE

CHURCH OF JESUS CHRIST OF LATTER-DAY SAINTS

SALT LAKE CITY . UTAH

Printed in the United States of America

The Deseret News Press

PREFACE

Within a few months of the organization of His restored Church, the Lord directed that Emma Smith, wife of the Prophet Joseph Smith, should make a selection of sacred hymns for use by the Saints in their worshipping assemblies. "My soul delighteth in the song of the heart," said the Lord in this revelation. "Yea, the song of the righteous is a prayer unto me, and it shall be answered with a blessing upon their heads." Since those early days the singing of sacred hymns has been an important part of the meetings in the Church of Jesus Christ of Latter-day Saints.

Among members of the Church were inspired hymn writers. Many of their songs were sung in times of joy and sorrow, cheering the Saints in their pioneer journeys, and strengthening them in their trials and tribulations. They became characteristic of the missionaries of the Church who traveled far and wide, and were a source of faith and consolation, encouragement and strength. Today as they are sung they add fervor to our meetings and provide inspiration for all who sing them or hear them sung.

From time to time since the days of Emma Smith, various compilations of hymns have been made to meet the changing needs of the Church. This present book is the latest and probably the most complete yet made for general use among the Latter-day Saints. It is planned that this volume will be used for all adult gatherings in the Church. Another book is provided for young people and children.

In this collection, in addition to arrangements provided for general congregational singing, special arrangements of many of our favorite songs are included for choirs, for men's voices and for women's voices.

The work of compilation was done by the General Music Committee of the Church, under the guidance of the First Presidency and the Council of the Twelve. An effort was made to include all of the hymns which have become favorites with the members of the Church down through the years. In addition, a number of new songs, both words and music, were written especially for this book. New settings have been provided for old words in some cases. A study was likewise made of great hymns used in the world at large, and some of these have been included in the volume. The entire work, including the preparation of the index, has been done with a view toward simplicity, in the hope that the book would meet the varied needs of the greatest number in the Church.

The wide use of this book is earnestly recommended. It is hoped that these songs will provide a means whereby faith, devotion, prayer, and other principles of the restored gospel may be taught. It is for that purpose it is provided. Musical directors, choristers and organists generally are urged to keep this purpose in mind as they prepare music for our religious services, and plan such music as will contribute to an increase of faith among the people.

DAVID O. McKAY
J. REUBEN CLARK, JR.
HENRY D. MOYLE
First Presidency

FOREWORD

The hymns in this book are in four general classifications: for congregation, choir, men's voices and women's voices. Except for those in the congregational section all hymns are designated as for "choir," "men's voices" or "women's voices" under the hymn title.

In the hymns arranged for men's voices, the tenor, or C clef, is used for the two upper parts. In this clef middle C is found on the third space and the parts should, therefore, be played and sung one octave lower than if they were written in the treble clef.

It will be noted by the index that many hymns are found in more than one arrangement. For this reason care should be taken that the organist uses the same arrangement as the singers and that the proper arrangement is used for the type of group singing it. For example: "women's voices" would be used for Relief Society, or other groups of women; "men's voices" for Priesthood gatherings; "congregation" and "choir" for use as indicated.

SECTIONAL INDEX

———

1

Come, Rejoice

Tracy Y. Cannon

Tracy Y. Cannon

Joyously ♩=50

1. Come, re-joice, the King of glo-ry Speaks to earth a-gain.
2. An-gels, mes-sen-gers from heav-en, Come to earth once more;
3. Great, oh, great, is Christ our Sav-ior. None can stay his hand.

Glad-some words ring out from heav-en, Joy-ous, won-drous strain.
Bring to men the glo-rious gos-pel; Price-less truths re-store.
Now he brings to us sal-va-tion, Cheer-ing ev-ery land.

Truth bursts forth in ra-diant light, Show-ing all the path of right,
Let all hear who live to-day! This is life, 'the truth, the way.
Sing, re-joice, the King of love Speaks to earth from heav'n a-bove.

Shout ho-san-na to his name, One and all his might pro-claim.
Shout ho-san-na to his name, One and all his might pro-claim.
Shout ho-san-na to his name, One and all his might pro-claim.

Abide With Me; 'Tis Eventide

M. Lowrie Hofford

H. Millard

Reverently ♩=69

mp

1. A - bide with me; 'tis e - ven - tide! The day is past and gone;
2. A - bide with me; 'tis e - ven - tide! Thy walk to - day with me
3. A - bide with me; 'tis e - ven - tide! And lone will be the night,

The shad - ows of the eve - ning fall; The night is com - ing on!
Has made my heart with - in me burn, As I com - muned with thee.
If I can - not com - mune with thee, Nor find in thee my light.

With - in my heart a wel - come guest, With - in my home a - bide;
Thy ear - nest words have filled my soul And kept me near thy side;
The dark - ness of the world, I fear, Would in my home a - bide;

O Sav - ior, stay this night with me; Be - hold, 'tis e - ven - tide!

O Sav - ior, stay this night with me; Be - hold, 'tis e - ven - tide.

A Mighty Fortress

Martin Luther   **Martin Luther**

With great dignity ♩ = 54

A might-y for-tress is our God, A tower of strength ne'er fail - ing. A help-er might-y is our God, O'er ills of life pre-vail - ing. He o-ver-com-eth all. He sav-eth from the fall. His might and pow'r are great. He all things did cre-ate And he shall reign for-ev-er-more.

4   All Creatures of Our God and King

Francis of Assisi

With exultation ♩=72

1. All crea-tures of our God and King, Lift up your voice and with us
2. Thou rush-ing wind that art so strong, Ye clouds that sail in heav'n a-
3. Thou flow-ing wa-ter, pure and clear, Make mu-sic for your Lord to
4. Dear Moth-er Earth, who day by day Un-fold-est bless-ings on our

sing, Al-le-lu - ia! Al-le-lu - ia! Thou burn-ing sun with gold-en
long, Al-le-lu - ia! Al-le-lu - ia! Thou ris-ing morn, in praise re-
hear, Al-le-lu - ia! Al-le-lu - ia! Thou fire so mas-ter-ful and
way, Al-le-lu - ia! Al-le-lu - ia! The flow'rs and fruit that in thee

beam, Thou sil-ver moon with soft-er gleam, Al-le-lu - ia! Al-le-
joice, Ye light of eve-ning find a voice, Al-le-lu - ia! Al-le-
bright, That gives to man both warmth and light, Al-le-lu - ia! Al-le-
grow, Let them his glo-ry al-so show, Al-le-lu - ia! Al-le-

lu - ia! Al-le-lu - ia! O praise him! Al-le-lu - ia!

5   As Swiftly My Days Go Out On the Wing

Smoothly ♩.=45

1. As swift-ly my days go out on the wing, As on-ward my bark drifts
2. Dark sor-row may come with man-y a sting; Stern tri-als in life my
3. Till an-gels of light my sum-mons shall bring, Till up-ward with joy my

o - ver the sea,
por - tion may be,   O Fa-ther in heav'n, this song will I sing: The
spir - it shall flee,

rock of my ref-uge is Thee, The rock of my ref-uge is Thee.

Rock of my ref-uge so sure,   Rock of my ref-uge so strong; O
    so sure,   so strong;

hide me there-in From dan-ger and sin, While here I am sing-ing my song.

Beautiful Zion for Me

turn to Back

Charles W. Penrose

J. R. Thomas
Arr. by Evan Stephens

Swinging movement ♩. = 60

1. Beau - ti - ful Zi - on for me Down in the val - ley re -
2. Beau - ti - ful queen of the west Reign - ing o'er moun-tains and

clin - ing, Mem - o - ries sa - cred to thee,
val - ley, Host of the pur - est and best,

Close round my heart are en - twin - ing, Clasped in the
Un - der thy stan-dard shall ral - ly, Robed in the

moun-tain's em - brace, Safe from the spoil - er for - ev - er,
gar - ments of peace, Vir - tue the crown of the glo - ry,

Beautiful Zion for Me

Chased are the tears from thy face, Joy shall de-part from thee
God shall thy king-dom in-crease, An - gels de-light in the

nev - er, When from thy pres-ence I roam.
sto - ry, When through the wide world I roam.

'Midst the world's gran-deur I see Naught like my own moun-tain
Naught on the land or the sea Charms like my own moun-tain

home, Beau - ti - ful Zi - on for me, Naught like my
home, Beau - ti - ful Zi - on for me, Charms like my

own moun-tain home, Beau - ti - ful, beau-ti-ful Zi - on for me.
own moun-tain home, Beau - ti - ful, beau-ti-ful Zi - on for me.

Behold! A Royal Army

Fanny J. Crosby

Adam Geibel

Martial ♩=84

1. Be - hold! a roy - al ar - my, With ban - ner, sword and shield,
2. And now the foe ad - vanc - ing, That val - iant host as - sails,
3. Oh, when the war is end - ed, When strife and con - flicts cease,

Is march - ing forth to con - quer, On life's great bat - tle - field;
And yet they nev - er fal - ter; Their cour - age nev - er fails;
When all are safe - ly gath - ered With - in the vale of peace,

Its ranks are filled with sol - diers, U - nit - ed, bold and strong,
Their Lead - er calls, "Be faith - ful!" They pass the word a - long;
Be - fore the King e - ter - nal, That vast and might - y throng,

Who fol - low their Com - mand - er, And sing their joy - ful song:
They see his sig - nal flash - ing, And shout their joy - ful song:
Shall praise his name for - ev - er, And this shall be their song:

CHORUS *Voices in unison*

Vic - to - ry, vic - to - ry, Through him that re - deemed us! Vic - to - ry,

Behold! A Royal Army

vic - to - ry, Through Je - sus Christ our Lord! Vic - to - ry,

vic - to - ry, vic - to - ry, Through Je - sus Christ our Lord!
Through Je - sus Christ, Through Christ our Lord!

8 God, Our Father, Hear Us Pray

Annie Malin

Arr. from Louis Gottschalk

Worshipfully ♩ = 72

mp

1. God, our Fa - ther, hear us pray; Send thy grace this ho - ly day;
2. Grant us, Fa - ther, grace di - vine; May thy smile up - on us shine;
3. As we drink the wa - ter clear, Let thy Spir - it lin - ger near;

As we take of em - blems blest, On our Sav - ior's love we rest.
As we eat the bro - ken bread, Thine ap - prov - al on us shed.
Par - don faults, O Lord, we pray; Bless our ef - forts day by day.

9 In Hymns of Praise

Ada Blenkhorn

A. Beirly

Allegro ♩=100

1. In hymns of praise your voic-es raise To him who reigns on high;
2. Be-neath his hand, at his com-mand, The shin-ing plan-ets move;
3. The lit-tle flow'r that lasts an hour, The spar-row in its fall,
4. Then sing a-gain in loft-y strain To him who dwells on high;

Whose coun-sels keep the might-y deep, Who rul-eth earth and sky.
To all be-low they dai-ly show His wis-dom and his love.
They, too, shall share his ten-der care; He made and loves them all.
To prayers you raise, and songs of praise, He sweet-ly will re-ply.

Ex-alt his name in loud ac-claim, His might-y pow'r a-dore!

And hum-bly bow be-fore him now, Our King for-ev-er-more.

Christ the Lord Is Risen Today

Charles Wesley

Henry Carey

With exultation ♩ = 104

1. Christ the Lord is ris'n to - day,
2. Love's re - deem - ing work is done, Al - le - lu - ia!
3. Lives a - gain our glo - rious King;

Sons of men and an - gels say,
Fought the fight, the vic - tory won. Al - le - lu - ia!
Where, O death, is now thy sting?

Raise your joys and tri - umphs high;
Je - sus' ag - o - ny is o'er. Al - le - lu - ia!
Once he died our souls to save;

Sing, ye heav'ns, and earth re - ply,
Dark - ness veils the earth no more. Al - le - lu - ia!
Where thy vic - to - ry, O grave?

Come All Ye Saints and Sing His Praise

Lorin F. Wheelwright

Simply ♩= 76

1. Come all ye Saints and sing his praise Who formed the worlds on high, Who taught the plan - ets where to trace Their or - bits through the sky.
2. O sing the fer - vor of his love, The won - ders of his grace, Who sent the Sav - ior from a - bove To save a dy - ing race.
3. In songs de - clare the works and ways Of our E - ter - nal God, Whose king - dom in these lat - ter days Is spread -ing far a - broad.

4. In Zion let his name be praised
Who has a feast prepared,
The glorious gospel standard raised,
The ancient faith restored.

5. Swift heralds, the glad news to bear,
O'er land and ocean fly;
And to the wond'ring world declare
The message from on high.

6. Ye nations of the earth, attend!
Let kings and princes hear,
And all the powers of darkness bend,
Messiah's reign is near.

7. The Savior comes! Ye Saints, be pure,
And fix your hearts on high;
Lift up your heads, rejoice, for your
Redemption draweth nigh.

12 Come, All Ye Saints Who Dwell on Earth

William W. Phelps

Old Tune

With simplicity ♩= 44

1. Come, all ye Saints who dwell on earth, Your cheer-ful voic-es raise;
2. His love is great; he died for us; Shall we un-grate-ful be,
3. The straight and nar-row way we've found! Then let us trav-el on,
4. And there we'll join the heaven-ly choir And sing his praise a-bove,

Our great Re-deem-er's love to sing, And cel-e-brate his praise.
Since he has marked a road to bliss, And said,"Come, fol-low me"?
Till we, in the cel-es-tial world, Shall meet where Christ is gone.
While end-less a-ges roll a-round, Per-fect-ed by his love.

Our great Re-deem-er's love to sing, And cel-e-brate his praise.
Since he has marked a road to bliss, And said,"Come, fol-low me"?
Till we, in the cel-es-tial world, Shall meet where Christ is gone.
While end-less a-ges roll a-round, Per-fect-ed by his love.

12-A Sweet Is the Hour When Thus We Meet

Evan Stephens

1 Sweet is the hour when thus we meet
  Around the sacred board,
And each the other kindly greet
  While worshipping the Lord,
And each the other kindly greet
  While worshipping the Lord.

2 Sweet are the songs we gladly sing
  In harmony and love,
The echo of diviner things
  Heard in the courts above,
The echo of diviner things
  Heard in the courts above.

3 Lord, may we have Thy Spirit pure
  To hallow every deed,
That when we part we may be sure
  We have been blest indeed,
That when we part we may be sure
  We have been blest indeed.

13 Come, Come, Ye Saints

William Clayton

Old English Tune

Resolutely ♩=66

1. Come, come, ye Saints, no toil nor la-bor fear; But with joy
2. Why should we mourn or think our lot is hard? 'Tis not so;
3. We'll find the place which God for us pre-pared, Far a-way
4. And should we die be-fore our jour-ney's through, Hap-py day!

wend your way. Though hard to you this jour-ney may ap-pear,
all is right. Why should we think to earn a great re-ward,
in the West, Where none shall come to hurt or make a-fraid;
all is well! We then are free from toil and sor-row, too;

Grace shall be as your day. 'Tis bet-ter far for
If we now shun the fight? Gird up your loins; fresh
There the Saints will be blessed. We'll make the air with
With the just we shall dwell! But if our lives are

us to strive Our use-less cares from us to drive; Do
cour-age take; Our God will nev-er us for-sake; And
mu-sic ring, Shout prais-es to our God and King; A-
spared a-gain To see the Saints their rest ob-tain, O

Come, Come, Ye Saints

this, and joy your hearts will swell— All is well! all is well!
soon we'll have this tale to tell— All is well! all is well!
bove the rest these words we'll tell— All is well! all is well!
how we'll make this cho-rus swell— All is well! all is well!

14

Come, Follow Me

John Nicholson

S. McBurney

Suppliantly ♩ = 69

1. "Come, fol-low me," the Sav-ior said, Then let us
2. "Come, fol-low me," a sim-ple phrase, Yet truth's su-
3. Is it e-nough a-lone to know That we must
4. Not on-ly shall we em-u-late His course while

in his foot-steps tread, For thus a-lone can
blime, ef-ful-gent rays Are in these sim-ple
fol-low him be-low, While trav-'ling thro' this
in this earth-ly state, But when we're freed from

we be one With God's own loved, be-got-ten Son.
words com-bined To urge, in-spire the hu-man mind.
vale of tears? No, this ex-tends to ho-lier spheres.
pres-ent cares, If, with our Lord we would be heirs.

5 We must the onward path pursue
As wider fields expand to view,
And follow Him unceasingly
Whate'er our lot or sphere may be.

6 For thrones, dominions, kingdoms, powers,
And glory great and bliss are ours
If we, throughout eternity,
Obey his words, "Come, follow me."

15 Come, Go With Me, Beyond the Sea

Cyrus H. Wheelock

Arr. by Thomas C. Griggs

Slowly ♩ = 56

1. Come, go with me, be-yond the sea, Where hap-pi-ness is true,
2. Up-on those ev-er-last-ing hills, And in the val-leys fair,
3. There Is-rael's sons, so long op-pressed, Are free and hap-py, too;
4. There, too, are proph-ets, priests, and seers Who have the priest-hood's pow'rs,

Where Jo-seph's land, blest by God's hand, In-vit-ing waits for you.
Be-side the murmur-ing moun-tain rills, We'll bow in hum-ble prayer,
And daught-ers in true vir-tue dressed, A-wait to wel-come you,
To guide our souls through end-less years And light our dark-est hours;

With joy-ful hearts you'll un-der-stand The bless-ings that a-wait you there.
And praise our God in joy-ful strains, That we are safe-ly gath-ered there.
To greet you with a kin-dred hand, And with you ev-'ry bless-ing share.
Yea, truth, which light-ed E-noch's band, Is free-ly giv-en to them there.

I know it is the prom-ised land, My home, my home is there.

16   Come, Hail the Cause of Zion's Youth

Bertha A. Kleinman

Energetically ♩ = 80

1. Come, hail the cause of Zi - on's youth, M. I. A., our M. I. A.
2. Be - neath her en - sign brave and free, M. I. A., our M. I. A.
3. 'Mid hills and plains ten thou - sand strong, M. I. A., our M. I. A.

Come, hail her code of ev - 'ry truth, M. I. A., our M. I. A.
A loy - al band is proud to be, M. I. A., our M. I. A.
Come, push the might - y work a - long, M. I. A., our M. I. A.

God's bless - ings on each ward and stake; Let praise re-sound, let song a-wake
As on and on and ev - er on, Where ser-vice calls us, we be-long;
O Thou Su-preme o'er world's a - far, 'Tis thou who guides our top-most star,

In ev - 'ry heart that helps to make M. I. A., our M. I. A.
While God's ap - prov - al smiles up - on M. I. A., our M. I. A.
O praise be thine for all we are, M. I. A., our M. I. A.

17   Come, Let Us Anew

Charles Wesley   *me*   **James Lucas**

Resolutely ♩= 72

1. Come, let us a-new our jour-ney pur-sue; Roll round with the year; And nev-er stand still till the Mas-ter ap-pear. His a-dor-a-ble will let us glad-ly ful-fil, And our tal-ents im-prove By the pa-tience of hope and the la-bor of love.

2. Our life as a dream, our time as a stream Glide swift-ly a-way, And the fu-gi-tive mo-ment re-fus-es to stay. The ar-row is flown; the mo-ments are gone; The mil-len-ni-al year Press-es on to our view; and e-ter-ni-ty's near.

3. O that each in the day of his com-ing may say, "I have fought my way through. I have fin-ished the work thou didst give me to do." O that each from his Lord may re-ceive the glad word: "Well and faith-ful-ly done; En-ter in-to my joy and sit down on my throne."

Come, Let Us Anew

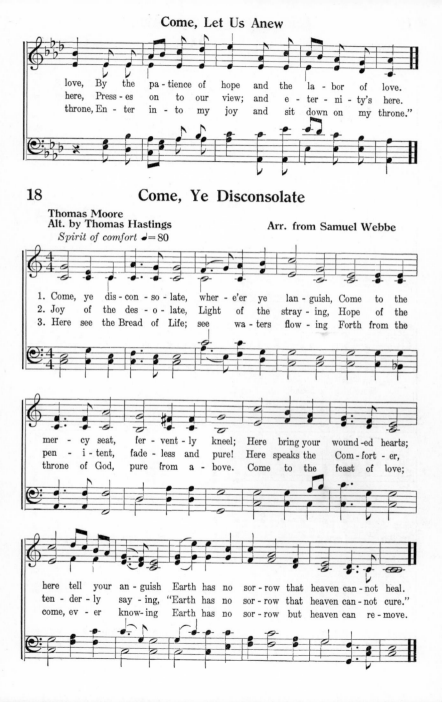

love, By the pa - tience of hope and the la - bor of love.
here, Press - es on to our view; and e - ter - ni - ty's here.
throne, En - ter in - to my joy and sit down on my throne."

18   Come, Ye Disconsolate

Thomas Moore
Alt. by Thomas Hastings

Arr. from Samuel Webbe

Spirit of comfort ♩=80

1. Come, ye dis - con - so - late, wher - e'er ye lan - guish, Come to the
2. Joy of the des - o - late, Light of the stray - ing, Hope of the
3. Here see the Bread of Life; see wa - ters flow - ing Forth from the

mer - cy seat, fer - vent - ly kneel; Here bring your wound - ed hearts;
pen - i - tent, fade - less and pure! Here speaks the Com - fort - er,
throne of God, pure from a - bove. Come to the feast of love;

here tell your an - guish Earth has no sor - row that heaven can - not heal.
ten - der - ly say - ing, "Earth has no sor - row that heaven can - not cure."
come, ev - er know - ing Earth has no sor - row but heaven can re - move.

19 Come Along, Come Along

William Willes

A. C. Smyth

Marching style ♩=100

1. Come a-long, come a-long, is the call that will win, To lead us to
2. Come to me, come to me, sweet-ly falls on the ear, The word of the
3. Let us gov-ern by kind-ness and nev-er by force, All cheer-ing and

vir - tue, and keep us from sin; Most men can be led, but
Lord full of com - fort and cheer, To bind up the bro - ken, the
bright, like the sun in its course; O - be - dience will spring from each

few can be driv'n, In shun-ning per - di - tion, and striv-ing for heav'n.
cap - tive set free, In the good time that's com - ing, we hope soon to see.
heart with a bound, And broth - er - hood flour - ish the wide world a-round.

Come a-long, come a - long, is the call that will win, In lead-ing to

vir - tue, and keep-ing from sin; Come a - long, come a - long, is the

21 Think not, When You Gather to Zion

Eliza R. Snow

John Tullidge

Thoughtfully ♩ = 84

1. Think not when you gath - er to Zi - on, Your trou - bles and tri - als are through, That noth - ing but com - fort and pleas - ure Are wait - ing in Zi - on for you: No, no, 'tis de - signed as a fur - nace, All sub - stance, all tex - tures to try, To

2. Think not when you gath - er to Zi - on, That all will be ho - ly and pure; That fraud and de - cep - tion are ban - ished, And con - fi - dence whol - ly se - cure: No, no, for the Lord our Re - deem - er Has said that the tares with the wheat Must

3. Think not when you gath - er to Zi - on, The Saints here have noth - ing to do But to look to your per - son - al wel - fare, And al - ways be com - fort - ing you. No; those who are faith - ful are do - ing What they find to do with their might; To

4. Think not when you gath - er to Zi - on, The prize and the vic - to - ry won. Think not that the war - fare is end - ed, The work of sal - va - tion is done. No, no; for the great prince of dark - ness A ten - fold ex - er - tion will make, When

Think not, When You Gather to Zion

burn all the "wood, hay, and stub - ble," The gold from the dross pur - i - fy.
grow till the great day of burn - ing Shall ren - der the har-vest com-plete.
gath - er the scat - tered of Is - rael They la - bor by day and by night.
he sees you go to the foun - tain, Where free - ly the truth you may take.

22   Come Unto Jesus

O. P. Huish   O. P. Huish

Entreatingly ♩=56

1. Come un - to Je - sus; Ye heav - y la - den, Care - worn and
2. Come un - to Je - sus; He'll ev - er heed you, Though in the
3. Come un - to Je - sus; He'll sure - ly hear you If you in
4. Come un - to Je - sus from ev - 'ry na - tion, From ev - 'ry

faint - ing, by sin op - pressed; He'll safe - ly guide you
dark - ness you've gone a - stray; His love will find you,
meek - ness plead for his love; Oh, know you not that
land and isle of the sea; Un - to the high and

rit.

un - to that ha - ven Where all who trust him may rest, may rest.
and gent - ly lead you From dark - est night in - to day, to day.
an - gels are near you From the bright man - sions a - bove, a - bove?
low - ly in sta - tion, Ev - er he calls, "Come to me, to me".

23 Come, Ye Children of the Lord

James H. Wallis

Spanish Melody

Joyously ♩=108

1. Come, ye chil-dren of the Lord, Let us sing with one ac-cord,
2. O how joy-ful it will be, When our Sav-ior we shall see!
3. All ar-rayed in spot-less white, We will dwell 'mid truth and light;

Let us raise a joy-ful strain, To our Lord who soon will reign
When in splen-dor he'll de-scend, Then all wick-ed-ness will end.
We will sing the songs of praise; We will shout in joy-ous lays.

On this earth, when it shall be Cleansed from all in-iq-ui-ty;
O what songs we then will sing To our Sav-ior, Lord and King!
Earth shall then be cleansed from sin. Ev-'ry liv-ing thing there-in

When all men from sin will cease, And will live in love and peace.
O what love will then bear sway, When our fears shall flee a-way!
Shall in love and beau-ty dwell; Then with joy each heart will swell.

24   Behold Thy Sons and Daughters, Lord

Parley P. Pratt   Alexander Schreiner

With devotion ♩=72

1. Be - hold thy sons and daugh-ters, Lord, On whom we lay our hands;
2. Oh, now send down the heav'n-ly dove, And o - ver-whelm their souls
3. Seal them by thine own Spir - it's pow'r, Which pur - i - fies from sin;
4. In - crease their faith; con - firm their hope; And guide them in the way;

They have ful - filled the gos - pel word, And bowed at thy com-mands.
With peace and joy and per - fect love, As lambs with-in thy fold.
And may they find, from this good hour, They are a - dopt - ed in.
With com - fort bear their spir - its up, Un - til the per - fect day.

25   Come, We That Love the Lord

Isaac Watts   Aaron Williams

Flowing ♩=88

1. Come, we that love the Lord, And let our joys be known; Join
2. Let those re - fuse to sing Who nev - er knew our God, But
3. The God who rules on high, And all the earth sur - veys— Who
4. This might - y God is ours, Our Fa - ther and our Love; He

in a song with sweet ac - cord, And wor - ship at his throne.
ser - vants of the heav'n - ly King May speak their joys a - broad.
rides up - on the storm - y sky And calms the roar - ing seas—
will send down his heav'n - ly pow'rs To car - ry us a - bove.

Dear to the Heart of the Shepherd

Mary B. Wingate

William J. Kirkpatrick

Duet

Calmly ♩.=48

1. Dear to the heart of the Shep - herd, Dear are the sheep of his fold; Dear is the love that he gives them, Dear - er than sil - ver or gold. Dear to the heart of the Shep - herd, Dear are his "oth - er" lost sheep;

2. Dear to the heart of the Shep - herd, Dear are the lambs of his fold; Some from the pas - tures are stray - ing, Hun - gry and help - less and cold. See, the good Shep- herd is seek - ing, Seek - ing the lambs that are lost;

3. Dear to the heart of the Shep - herd, Dear are the "nine - ty and nine;" Dear are the sheep that have wan - dered Out in the des - ert to pine. Hark! he is ear - nest - ly call - ing, Ten - der - ly plead - ing to - day:

4. Green are the pas - tures in - vit - ing; Sweet are the wa - ters and still; Lord, we will an - swer thee glad - ly, "Yes, bless - ed Mas - ter, we will! Make us thy true un - der - shep - herds; Give us a love that is deep;

Dear to the Heart of the Shepherd

O - ver the moun - tains he fol - lows, O - ver the
Bring - ing them in with re - joic - ing, Saved at such
"Will you not seek for my lost ones, Off from my
Send us out in - to the des] - ert, Seek - ing thy

Chorus

wa - ters so deep.
in - fi - nite cost. Out in the des - ert they wan - der,
shel - ter a - stray?"
wan - der - ing sheep."

poco rit.   *a tempo*

Hun - gry and help - less and cold; Off to the

res - cue { he has - tens, Bring - ing them back to the fold.
(*4th verse*) { we'll has - ten,

27 Do What Is Right

E. Kaillmark

With marked accent ♩=100

1. Do what is right; the day-dawn is break-ing, Hail- ing a
2. Do what is right; the shack-les are fall - ing; Chains of the
3. Do what is right; be faith - ful and fear - less; On - ward, press

fu - ture of free - dom and light; An - gels a - bove us are
bonds-men no long - er are bright; Light-ened by hope soon they'll
on - ward, the goal is in sight; Eyes that are wet now, ere

si - lent notes tak - ing Of ev - 'ry ac - tion; do what is right!
cease to be gall - ing; Truth go - eth on - ward; do what is right!
long will be tear - less; Bless-ings a - wait you in do - ing what's right!

Do what is right; let the con - se-quence fol - low; Bat - tle for

free - dom in spir - it and might; And with stout hearts look ye

Do What Is Right

forth till to-mor-row; God will pro-tect you; then do what is right!

28
The Lord Be With Us

Anon.

Tracy Y. Cannon

Stately ♩= 92

1. The Lord be with us as we walk A-long our home-ward road.
2. The Lord be with us till the night En-fold our day of rest;
3. The Lord be with us through the hours Of slum-ber calm and deep,

In si-lent thought or friend-ly talk Our hearts be near to God.
Be he of ev-'ry heart the light, Of ev-'ry home the guest.
Pro-tect our homes, re-new our powers, And guard his peo-ple's sleep.

In si-lent thought or friend-ly talk Our hearts be near to God.
Be he of ev-'ry heart the light, Of ev-'ry home the guest.
Pro-tect our homes, re-new our powers, And guard his peo-ple's sleep.

Come, Ye Thankful People

Henry Alford

George J. Elvey

With gladness ♩ = 104

1. Come, ye thank-ful peo-ple, come, Raise the song of har-vest home;
2. All the world is God's own field, Fruit un-to his praise to yield;

All is safe-ly gath-ered in, Ere the win-ter storms be-gin;
Wheat and tares to-geth-er sown, Un-to joy or sor-row grown;

God, our Mak-er, doth pro-vide For our wants to be sup-plied;
First the blade, and then the ear, Then the full corn shall ap-pear;

Come to God's own tem-ple, come, Raise the song of har-vest home.
Lord of har-vest, grant that we Whole-some grain and pure may be.

30 Earth, With Her Ten Thousand Flowers

William W. Phelps

Thomas C. Griggs

Calmly ♩ = 80

1. Earth, with her ten thou - sand flow'rs, Air, with all its beams and show'rs, Heav - en's in - fi - nite ex - panse, Sea's re - splen - dent coun - te - nance, All a - round and all a - bove, Bear this rec - ord, God is love.

2. Sounds a - mong the vales and hills, In the woods and by the rills, Of the breeze and of the bird, By the gen - tle mur - mur stirred, Sa - cred songs, be - neath, a - bove, Have one cho - rus, God is love.

3. All the hopes that sweet - ly start From the foun - tain of the heart, All the bliss that ev - er comes To our earth - ly hu - man homes, All the voic - es from a - bove, Sweet - ly whis - per, God is love.

31 Ere You Left Your Room This Morning

Mrs. M. A. Kidder

W. O. Perkins

Sincerely ♩= 72

1. Ere you left your room this morn - ing, Did you think to pray?
2. When your heart was filled with an - ger, Did you think to pray?
3. When sore tri - als came up - on you, Did you think to pray?

In the name of Christ, our Sav - ior, Did you sue for lov - ing
Did you plead for grace, my broth - er, That you might for - give an -
When your soul was full of sor - row, Balm of Gil - ead did you

fav - or As a shield to - day?
oth - er Who had crossed your way? O how pray - ing rests the
bor - row At the gates of day?

wea - ry! Prayer will change the night to day;

So when life gets dark and drear - y, Don't for - get to pray.

Come, Sing to the Lord

Gerrit de Jong, Jr.

Gerrit de Jong, Jr.

Joyfully ♩ = 126

1. Come, sing to the Lord, His name to praise. He in these lat - ter days did raise A proph - et to his name, The bless - ed gos - pel to re - store; Come, sing to the Lord, His name a - dore!

2. The proph - ets of old be - held this day, Its glo - ry told in won - drous lay; They saw our proph - et dear, Who times of ful - ness ush - ered in; Come, sing to the Lord, His prais - es ring!

3. The keys of the priest - hood of our Lord To us in ful - ness are re - stored Their bless - ings to be - stow, And pow'rs di - vine are man - i - fest; Come, sing to the Lord, His name be blessed!

tooFar, Far Away on Judea's Plains

J. MacFarlane 39 **J. MacFarlane**

Joyously ♩ = 100

1. Far, far a-way on Ju-de-a's plains,
2. Sweet are these strains of re-deem-ing love,
3. Lord, with the an-gels we too would re-joice;
4. Has-ten the time when, from ev-'ry clime,

Shep-herds of old heard the joy-ous strains:
Mes-sage of mer-cy from heav'n a-bove:
Help us to sing with the heart and voice:
Men shall u-nite in the strains sub-lime:

Glo-ry to God, Glo-ry to God,
Glo-ry to God in the
Glo-ry to God in the high - est,

Glo-ry to God in the high - est; Peace on earth, good-
high - est,

will to men, Peace on earth, Good-will to men!

Father in Heaven

Agnus S. Hibbard   **Friedrich F. Flemming**

Prayerfully ♩= 100

1. Fa - ther in heav - en, in thy love a - bound - ing,
2. Filled be our hearts with peace be - yond com - par - ing,
3. God of our Fa - thers, strength - en ev - 'ry na - tion

Hear these thy chil - dren through the world re -
Peace in thy world, joy to all hearts des -
In thy great peace where on - ly is sal -

sound - ing, Loud in thy prais - es. Thanks for peace a -
pair - ing, Firm is our trust in thee for peace en -
va - tion; So may the world its fu - ture spread be -

bid - ing, Ev - er a - bid - ing.
dur - ing, Ev - er en - dur - ing.
fore thee, Thus to a - dore thee.

Farewell, All Earthly Honors

Mary W. Bone

William B. Bradbury

Solemnly ♩=80

1. Fare - well, all earth - ly hon - ors; I bid you all a - dieu;
2. I want my name en - grav - en With all the right - eous ones,
3. I'm will - ing to be chas - tened And bear my dai - ly cross;

Fare - well, all sin - ful pleas - ures; I want no more of you.
Who wor - ship God the Fa - ther, Up - on ce - les - tial thrones.
I'm will - ing to be part - ed From ev - 'ry kind of dross.

I want my hab - i - ta - tion In that e - ter - nal home,
For such e - ter - nal rich - es, I'm will - ing to pass through
En - dure the fier - y fur - nace, Till free from guilt - y stains,

Be - yond the pow'rs of Sa - tan, Where sin can nev - er come.
All need - ful trib - u - la - tions, And count them my just due.
Till all al - loy is melt - ed And naught but gold re - mains.

There is sweet rest in heav'n, There is sweet rest in heav'n,

Farewell, All Earthly Honors

There is sweet rest, There is sweet rest, There is sweet rest in heav'n.

4. All earthly tribulations
   Are but a moment here;
   And then if we prove faithful,
   A righteous crown we'll wear.
   We shall be counted worthy·
   To mingle with the good,
   And minister in glory
   Before the throne of God.

5. There Christ himself has promised
   A mansion to prepare,
   And all who love and serve him
   The victor's wreath shall wear.
   Bright crowns shall then be given
   To all the ransomed throng,
   And glory! glory! glory!
   Shall be the conqu'ror's song.

36   God of Power, God of Right

Wallace F. Bennett

Tracy Y. Cannon

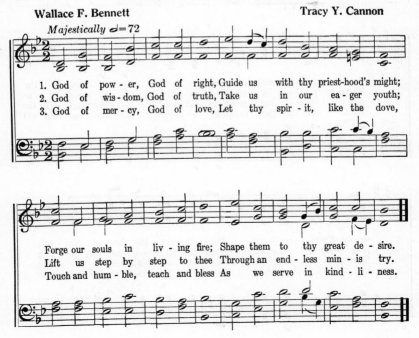

Majestically ♩=72

1. God of pow - er, God of right, Guide us with thy priest-hood's might;
2. God of wis - dom, God of truth, Take us in our ea - ger youth;
3. God of mer - cy, God of love, Let thy spir - it, like the dove,

Forge our souls in liv - ing fire; Shape them to thy great de - sire.
Lift us step by step to thee Through an end - less min - is try.
Touch and hum - ble, teach and bless As we serve in kind - li - ness.

37   Up, Awake, Ye Defenders of Zion

Charles W. Penrose   Melody "Red White and Blue"

Martial ♩=104

1. Up, a-wake, ye de-fend-ers of Zi - on! The foe's at the
2. By the moun-tains our Zi-on's sur-round-ed; Her war - riors are
3. Shall we bear with op-pres-sion for - ev - er? Shall we tame-ly sub-
4. Though as-sist-ed by le-gions in-fer-nal, The plun-der-ing

door of your homes; Let each heart be the heart of a li - on,
no - ble and brave; And their faith on Je-ho-vah is found-ed,
mit to the foe, While the ties of our kin-dred they sev - er
wretch-es ad - vance, With a host from the re - gions e - ter-nal,

Un - yield-ing and proud as he roams. Re - mem - ber the
Whose pow - er is might-y to save. Op - posed by a
And the blood of our proph-ets shall flow? No! the thought sets the
We'll scat - ter their troops at a glance. Soon "the King-dom" will

wrongs of Mis - sou - ri; For - get not the fate of Nau - voo.
proud boast-ing na - tion, Their num-bers, com-pared, may be few;
heart wild-ly beat-ing; Our vows at each pulse we re - new:
be in - de - pen-dent; In won-der the na-tions will view

Up, Awake, Ye Defenders of Zion

When the God - hat - ing foe is be - fore you, Stand firm and be
But their un - ion is known through cre - a - tion, And they've al - ways been
Ne'er to rest till our foes are re - treat ing, And to be ev - er
The de-spised ones in glo - ry re - splen-dent; Then let us be

faith - ful and true, Stand firm and be faith - ful and true,
faith - ful and true, And they've al - ways been faith - ful and true,
faith - ful and true, And to be ev - er faith - ful and true,
faith - ful and true, Then let us be faith - ful and true,

Stand firm and be faith - ful and true; When the God - hat - ing
And they've al - ways been faith - ful and true, But their u - nion is
And to be ev - er faith - ful and true; Ne'er to rest till our
Then let us be faith - ful and true! The de-spised ones in

foe is be - fore you, Stand firm and be faith - ful and true.
known through cre - a - tion, And they've al - ways been faith - ful and true.
foes are re - treat - ing, And to be ev - er faith - ful and true.
glo - ry re - splen-dent; Then let us be faith - ful and true!

38   Each Cooing Dove

Robert Morris   H. R. Palmer

Quietly ♩ = 66

1. Each coo- ing dove   and sigh- ing bough   That makes the
2. Each flow-'ry glen   and moss- y dell   Where hap-py
3. And when I read   the thrill-ing lore   Of Him who

eve   so blest to me   Has something far   di - vin - er
birds in song a - gree   Thro' sun-ny morn   the prais - es
walked up - on the sea   I long, oh, how   I long once

now   It bears me back   to Gal - i - lee.
tell   Of sights and sounds in Gal - i - lee.
more   To fol - low Him   in Gal - i - lee.

O Gal - i - lee! sweet Gal - i - lee! Where Je - sus loved so much to be; O

Gal - i - lee! blue Gal - i - lee! Come, sing thy song a - gain to me.

The First Noel

39

last 30

Jubilantly ♩=84

1. The first No - el the an - gel did say Was to
2. They look - ed up and saw a star Shin - ing

cer - tain poor shep-herds in fields as they lay, In
in the East be - yond them far, And

fields where they lay keep-ing their sheep On a cold win-ter's
to the earth it gave great light, And so it con-

night that was so deep. No - el, No - el, No-
tin - ued both day and night.

el, No - el, Born is the King of Is - ra - el!

40   From Greenland's Icy Mountains

Reginald Heber   Lowell Mason

With motion ♩ = 60

1. From Green-land's i - cy moun - tains, From In - dia's cor - al
2. What though the spi - cy breez - es Blow soft o'er Cey - lon's
3. Shall we, whose souls are light - ed With wis - dom from on
4. Waft, waft, ye winds, his sto - ry, And you, ye wa - ters,

strand; Where Af - ric's sun - ny foun - tains Roll
isle; Though ev - 'ry pros - pect pleas - es, And
high, Shall we, to men be - night - ed, The
roll, Till, like a sea of glo - ry, It

down their gold - en sand; From many an an - cient riv - er, From
on - ly man is vile? In vain with lav - ish kind - ness The
lamp of life de - ny? Sal - va - tion! O sal - va - tion! The
spreads from pole to pole; Till o'er our ran - somed na - ture, The

many a palm - y plain, They call us to de -
gifts of God are strewn; The hea - then in his
joy - ful sound pro - claim, Till earth's re - mot - est
Lamb for sin - ners slain, Re - deem - er, King, Cre -

From Greenland's Icy Mountains

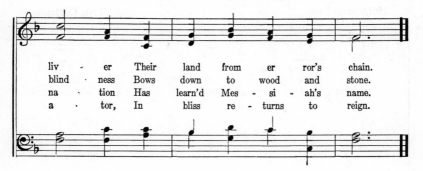

liv	er	Their	land	from	er	ror's	chain.
blind	ness	Bows	down	to	wood	and	stone.
na	tion	Has	learn'd	Mes	si	ah's	name.
a	tor,	In	bliss	re	turns	to	reign.

41   Father in Heaven, We Do Believe

Parley P. Pratt   Jane Romney Crawford

Devotionally ♩=80

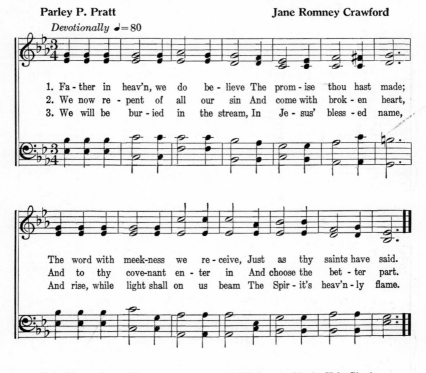

1. Fa - ther in heav'n, we do be - lieve The prom - ise thou hast made;
2. We now re - pent of all our sin And come with brok - en heart,
3. We will be bur - ied in the stream, In Je - sus' bless - ed name,

The word with meek-ness we re - ceive, Just as thy saints have said.
And to thy cove-nant en - ter in And choose the bet - ter part.
And rise, while light shall on us beam The Spir - it's heav'n - ly flame.

4. O Lord, accept us while we pray,
   And all our sins forgive;
   New life impart to us this day.
   And bid the sinners live.

5. Baptize us with the Holy Ghost
   And seal us as thine own
   That we may join the ransomed host,
   And with the saints be one.

42   Firm as the Mountains Around Us

Ruth May Fox   Alfred M. Durham

Jubilantly ♩=104

1. Firm as the moun-tains a-round us,
2. We'll build on the rock they plant-ed A

Stal-wart and brave we stand On the rock our fa-thers
pal-ace to the King. In - to its shin-ing

plant - ed For us in this good - ly land. The
cor - ri - dors, Our songs of praise we'll bring, For the

Firm as the Mountains Around Us

Firm as the Mountains Around Us

hear the des - ert sing - ing, Car - ry on, car - ry on,

car - ry on! Hills and vales and moun - tains

ring - ing, Car - ry on, car - ry on, car - ry on!

Firm as the Mountains Around Us

Hold - ing a - loft our col - ors, We march in the glo - rious dawn. O youth of the no - ble birth - right, Car - ry on, car - ry on, car - ry on!

43   Father, Thy Children to Thee Now Raise

Evan Stephens

Evan Stephens

Joyfully ♩=100

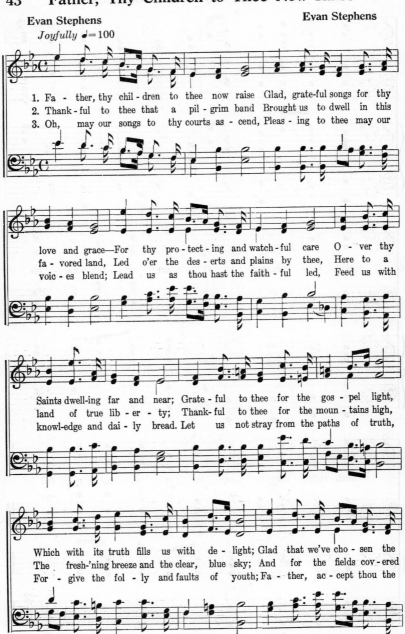

1. Fa - ther, thy chil - dren to thee now raise Glad, grate-ful songs for thy
2. Thank - ful to thee that a pil - grim band Brought us to dwell in this
3. Oh, may our songs to thy courts as - cend, Pleas - ing to thee may our

love and grace—For thy pro - tect - ing and watch - ful care O - ver thy
fa - vored land, Led o'er the des - erts and plains by thee, Here to a
voic - es blend; Lead us as thou hast the faith - ful led, Feed us with

Saints dwell-ing far and near; Grate - ful to thee for the gos - pel light,
land of true lib - er - ty; Thank - ful to thee for the moun - tains high,
knowl-edge and dai - ly bread. Let us not stray from the paths of truth,

Which with its truth fills us with de - light; Glad that we've cho - sen the
The fresh-'ning breeze and the clear, blue sky; And for the fields cov - ered
For - give the fol - ly and faults of youth; Fa - ther, ac - cept thou the

Father, Thy Children to Thee Now Raise

bet - ter part, Songs of de - light fill each grate - ful heart.
o'er with corn, Which now our loved moun - tain vales a - dorn.
songs of praise Which from our hearts un - to thee we raise.

44   Glory to God on High

James Allen

Praisingly ♩=92

Felice Giardini

1. Glo - ry to God on high! Let heav'n and earth re - ply;
2. Je - sus, our Lord and God, Bore sin's tre - men - dous load;
3. Let all the hosts a - bove Join in one song of love,

Praise ye his name. His love and grace a - dore, Who all our
Praise ye his name! Tell what his arm has done, What spoils from
Prais - ing his name; To him as - crib - ed be Hon - or and

sor - rows bore; Sing a - loud ev - er - more, Wor - thy the Lamb!
death he won; Sing his great name a - lone, Wor - thy the Lamb!
maj - es - ty Through all e - ter - ni - ty: Wor - thy the Lamb!

45 The Glorious Gospel Light Has Shone

Joel H. Johnson   Leroy J. Robertson

With dignity ♩=52

1. The glo - rious gos - pel light has shone In this the lat - ter day With such in - tel - li - gence that none From truth need turn a - way.

2. The pre - cious things which had been sealed And from the world kept hid, The Lord has to his Saints re - vealed As an - cient - ly he did.

3. And through the priest - hood now re - stored A - gain pre - pared the way Through which the dead may hear his word And all his laws o - bey.

4. As Christ to spir - its went to preach Who were to pris - on led, So man - y Saints have gone to teach The gos - pel to the dead.

5. And we for them can be baptized,
   Yes, for our friends most dear,
   That they can with the just be raised
   When Gabriel's trump they hear;

6. That they may come with Christ again
   When he to earth descends,
   A thousand years with him to reign,
   And with their earthly friends.

7. Now, O ye Saints, rejoice today
   That you can saviors be
   Of all your dead who will obey
   The gospel and be free.

8. Then let us rise without restraint
   And act for those we love,
   For they are giving their consent
   And wait for us to move.

Come, Listen to a Prophet's Voice

Joseph J. Daynes

Joyously ♩=72

1. Come, lis-ten to a proph-et's voice, And hear the word of God,
2. The gloom of sul-len dark-ness spread Through earth's ex-tend-ed space
3. 'Tis not in man they put their trust Nor on his arm re-ly;

And in the way of truth re-joice, And sing for joy a-loud.
Is ban-ished by our liv-ing Head, And God has shown his face.
Full well as-sured, all are ac-cursed, Who Je-sus Christ de-ny.

We've found the way the pro-phets went Who lived in days of yore;
Through err-ing schemes in days now past, The world has gone a-stray;
The Sav-ior to his peo-ple saith, "Let all my words o-bey,

An-oth-er proph-et now is sent This knowledge to re-store.
Yet Saints of God have found at last The straight and nar-row way.
And signs shall fol-low liv-ing faith, Down to the lat-est day."

47 God be with You

J. E. Rankin

W. G. Tomer

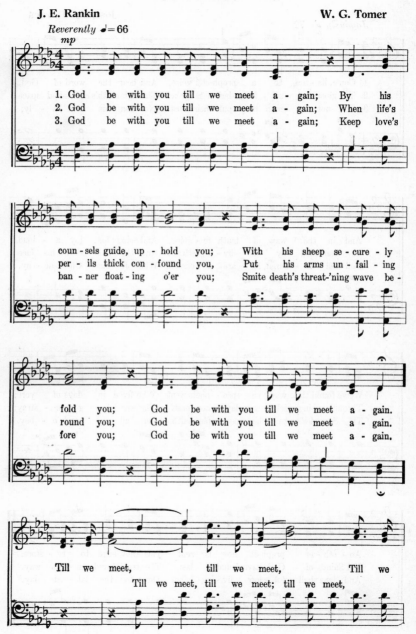

Reverently ♩ = 66
mp

1. God be with you till we meet a - gain; By his
2. God be with you till we meet a - gain; When life's
3. God be with you till we meet a - gain; Keep love's

coun - sels guide, up - hold you; With his sheep se - cure - ly
per - ils thick con - found you, Put his arms un - fail - ing
ban - ner float - ing o'er you; Smite death's threat-'ning wave be -

fold you; God be with you till we meet a - gain.
round you; God be with you till we meet a - gain.
fore you; God be with you till we meet a - gain.

Till we meet, till we meet, Till we
Till we meet, till we meet; till we meet,

God be with You

meet at Je - sus' feet. Till we meet, till we meet; Till we meet,
till we meet, meet, till we meet, God be with you till we meet a - gain.

48   God Moves in a Mysterious Way

William Cowper   William B. Bradbury

In a chanting style ♩= 54

1. God moves in a mys - ter - ious way   His won - ders to per - form;
2. Deep in un - fath - om - a - ble mines   Of nev - er fail - ing skill,
3. Ye fear - ful Saints, fresh cour - age take;   The clouds ye so much dread
4. Judge not the Lord by fee - ble sense,   But trust him for his grace;

He plants his foot-steps in the sea   And rides up - on the storm.
He treas-ures up his bright de - signs   And works his sov - 'reign will.
Are big with mer - cy and shall break   In bless-ings on your head.
Be - hind a frown - ing prov - i - dence   He hides a smil - ing face.

5. His purposes will ripen fast,
    Unfolding every hour;
The bud may have a bitter taste,
    But sweet will be the flower.

6. Blind unbelief is sure to err
    And scan his works in vain;
God is his own interpreter,
    And he will make it plain.

49 In Humility, Our Savior

Mabel Jones Gabbott   Rowland H. Prichard

Simply ♩=80

1. In hu - mil - i - ty, our Sav - ior, Grant thy Spir - it here, we pray;
2. Fill our hearts with sweet for - giv - ing; Teach us tol - er - ance and love;

As we bless the bread and wa - ter In thy name, this ho - ly day.
Let our prayers find ac - cess to thee In thy ho - ly courts a - bove.

Let me not for - get, O Sav - ior, Thou didst bleed and die for me
Then, when we have prov - en wor - thy Of thy sac - ri - fice di - vine,

When thy heart was stilled and bro - ken On the cross at Cal - va - ry.
Lord, let us re - gain thy pres - ence; Let thy glo - ry round us shine.

50 God of Our Fathers, We Come Unto Thee

Charles W. Penrose

Ebenezer Beesley

Unhurried ♩=88

1. God of our fa - thers, we come un - to thee, Chil - dren of
2. Grate - ful for all that thy boun - ty im - parts, Prais - es we
3. Blessed with the gifts of the gos - pel of peace, Dwell- ing in
4. Strengthened by thee for the con - flict with sin, On - ward we'll

those whom thy truth has made free; Grant us the joy of thy pres-ence to -
of - fer with voi - ces and hearts; Life of our be - ing, and sun of our
Zi - on, whose light shall in - crease, Led by the priest-hood a- long the bright
press till life's bat - tle we'll win; Then in thy glo - ry for - ev - er we'll

day, Nev - er from thee let us stray!
day, Nev - er from thee let us stray! Nev - er! nev - er! Nev - er from
way, Nev - er from thee should we stray!
stay— Nev - er from thee should we stray!

thee let us stray! Ev - er! ev - er! Ev - er to thee will we pray!

Abide With Me!

51

Henry F. Lyte

William Henry Monk

Reverently ♩ = 80

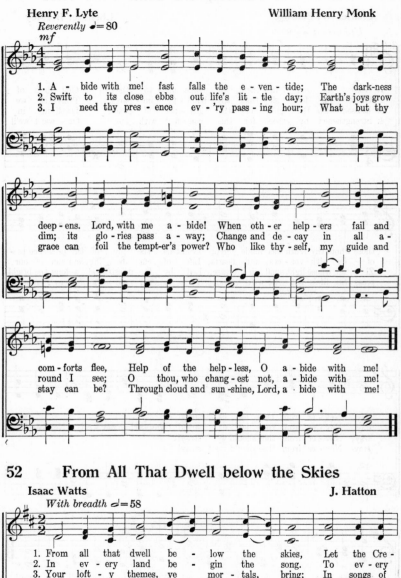

1. A - bide with me! fast falls the e - ven - tide; The dark-ness
2. Swift to its close ebbs out life's lit - tle day; Earth's joys grow
3. I need thy pres - ence ev - 'ry pass - ing hour; What but thy

deep - ens. Lord, with me a - bide! When oth - er help - ers fail and
dim; its glo - ries pass a - way; Change and de - cay in all a -
grace can foil the tempt - er's power? Who like thy - self, my guide and

com - forts flee, Help of the help - less, O a - bide with me!
round I see; O thou, who chang - est not, a - bide with me!
stay can be? Through cloud and sun - shine, Lord, a - bide with me!

From All That Dwell below the Skies

52

Isaac Watts

J. Hatton

With breadth ♩ = 58

1. From all that dwell be - low the skies, Let the Cre -
2. In ev - ery land be - gin the song. To ev - ery
3. Your loft - y themes, ye mor - tals, bring; In songs of
4. E - ter - nal are thy mer - cies, Lord; E - ter - nal

From All That Dwell Below the Skies

a - tor's praise a - rise; Let the Re - deem - er's
land the strains be - long; In cheer - ful sounds all
praise di - vine - ly sing. The great sal - va - tion
truth at - tends thy word: Thy praise shall sound from

name be sung, Through ev - er - y land, by ev - er - y tongue.
voic - es raise And fill the world with loud - est praise.
loud pro - claim, And shout for joy the Sav - ior's name.
shore to shore, Till suns shall rise and set no more.

53 Great King of Heaven, Our Hearts We Raise

Carrie S. Thomas   LeRoy J. Robertson

With praise ♩ = 76

1. Great King of heav'n, our hearts we raise To thee in
2. O Is - rael's God! Thine arm is strong; To thee all

pray'r, to thee in praise. The vales ex - ult; the hills ac -
earth and skies be - long, And with one voice in one glad

claim; And all thy works re - vere thy name.
chord, With myr - iad ech - oes, praise the Lord.

54 God of Our Fathers, Whose Almighty Hand

Daniel C. Roberts

G. W. Warren

1. God of our fa - thers, Whose al-might - y
2. Thy love di - vine hath led us in the
3. From war's a - larms, from dead - ly pes - ti-

hand   Leads forth in beau - ty all the star - ry band
past;   In this free land by thee our lot is cast;
lence,   Be thy strong arm our ev - er sure de - fense;

Of   shin - ing worlds in splen - dor through the skies,
Be   thou our Rul - er, Guar - dian, Guide, and Stay,
Thy   true re - li - gion in our hearts in - crease,

Our   grate - ful songs be - fore thy throne a - rise.
Thy   word our law, thy paths our cho - sen way.
Thy   boun - teous good - ness nour - ish us in peace.

55 Down by the River's Verdant Side

Somberly ♩ = 54

1. Down by the riv-er's ver-dant side, Low by the sol-i-
ta-ry tide, There, while the peace-ful wa-ters slept, We
pen-sive-ly sat down and wept, And on the bend-ing
wil-lows hung Our si-lent harps through grief un-strung.

2. For they who wast-ed Zi-on's bowers And laid in dust her
ruin-ed towers In scorn their wea-ry slaves de-sire To
strike the chords of Is-rael's lyre, And in their im-pious
ears to sing The sa-cred songs to Zi-on's King.

3. How shall we tune those loft-y strains On Ba-by-lon's pol-
lut-ed plains, When low in ru-in on the earth Remains the place that gave us birth, And stern de-struc-tion's
i-ron hand Still sways our des-o-lat-ed land.

4. O nev-er shall our harps a-wake, Laid in the dust for
Zi-on's sake. For-ev-er on the wil-lows hung, Their
mu-sic hushed; their chords un-strung; Lost Zi-on! ci-ty
of our God, While groan-ing 'neath the ty-rant's rod.

5 Still mould'ring lie thy leveled walls
And ruin stalks along thy halls.
And brooding o'er thy ruined towers
Such desolation sternly lowers,
That when we muse upon thy woe,
The gushing tears of sorrow flow!

6 And while we toil through wretched life
And drink the bitter cup of strife,
Until we yield our weary breath,
And sleep released from woe in death,
Will Zion in our memory stand—
Our lost, our ruined native land.

56 Guide Us, O Thou Great Jehovah

Robert Robinson

Majestically ♩=84

John Hughes

388

1. Guide us, O thou great Je-ho-vah, Guide us to the prom-ised land.
2. O - pen, Je - sus, Zi - on's foun-tains; Let her rich-est bless-ings come;
3. When the earth be - gins to trem-ble, Bid our fear-ful thoughts be still;

We are weak, but thou art a - ble; Hold us with thy pow'r-ful hand.
Let the fie - ry, cloud-y pil - lar Guard us to this ho - ly home.
When thy judg-ments spread de-struc - tion, Keep us safe on Zi - on's hill,

Ho - ly Spir - it, Ho - ly Spir - it, Feed us till the Sav - ior
Great Re-deem - er, Great Re - deem'- er, Bring, O bring the wel - come
Sing - ing prais - es, Sing - ing prais - es, Songs of glo - ry un - to

comes, Sav - ior comes, Feed us till the Sav - ior comes.
day! wel - come day! Bring, O bring the wel - come day!
thee; un - to thee; Songs of glo - ry un - to thee.

57 Guide Us, O Thou Great Jehovah

Robert Robinson

(Familiar Tune)

Annie F. Harrison
(Adapted)

Imploringly ♩=96

1. Guide us, O Thou great Je-ho-vah, Guide us to the prom-ised land,
2. O - pen, Je - sus, Zi - on's foun-tains, Let her rich - est bless-ings come,
3. When the earth be - gins to trem - ble, Bid our fear - ful thoughts be still;

We are weak but Thou art a - ble— Hold us with Thy pow'r - ful hand.
Let the fie - ry, cloud - y pil - lar Guard us to this ho - ly home.
When Thy judg-ments spread de-struc - tion, Keep us safe on Zi - on's hill,

Ho - ly Spir - it, Ho - ly Spir - it, Feed us till the Sav-ior comes.
Great Re-deem - er, Great Re-deem - er, Bring, O bring the wel-come day!
Sing - ing prais - es, Sing - ing prais - es, Songs of glo - ry un - to Thee;

Ho - ly Spir - it, Ho - ly Spir - it, Feed us till the Sav - ior comes.
Great Re-deem - er, Great Re -deem - er, Bring, O bring the wel - come day!
Sing - ing prais - es, Sing - ing prais - es, Songs of glo - ry un - to Thee.

58 Have I Done Any Good?

Will L. Thompson   Will L. Thompson

Brightly ♩. = 54

1. Have I done an - y good in the world to - day? Have I helped an - y
2. There are chanc -es for work all a - round just now, Op - por - tu - ni -ties

one in need? Have I cheered up the sad, and made some-one feel glad? If
right in our way; Do not let them pass by, say-ing,"Some-time I'll try," But

not, I have failed in - deed. Has an - y one's bur-den been light - er to - day,
go and do some-thing to-day. 'Tis no - ble of man to work and to give,

Rit.

Be - cause I was will - ing to share? Have the sick and the wea - ry been
Love's la - bor has mer - it a - lone; On - ly he who does some-thing is

a tem.

helped on their way? When they needed my help was I there? ⎫ Then wake up, and
wor - thy to live, The world has no use for the drone. ⎭ Then wake, wake up and

Have I Done Any Good?

do something more Than dream of your man-sion a-bove: Do-ing
your man-sion a-bove;

good is a pleas-ure, a joy be-yond meas-ure, A bless-ing of du-ty and love.

59 Great God, to Thee My Evening Star

M. M. Steel

Edward P. Kimball

With devotion ♩=96

1. Great God, to thee my even-ing song With hum-ble
2. My days, un-cloud-ed as they pass, And eve-ry
3. With hope in thee mine eye-lids close, With sleep re-

grat-i-tude I raise; O let thy mer-cy
on-ward roll-ing hour Are mon-u-ments of
fresh my fee-ble frame. Safe in thy care may

tune my tongue And fill my heart with live-ly praise.
won-drous grace, And wit-ness to thy love and power.
I re-pose And wake with prais-es to thy name.

60 Hark! The Herald Angels Sing

Charles Wesley

Felix Mendelssohn

Vigorously ♩=96

1. Hark! the her-ald an-gels sing Glo-ry to the new-born King!
2. Hail! the heaven-born Prince of Peace! Hail! the Son of right-eous-ness!

Peace on earth and mer-cy mild, God and sin-ners re-con-ciled!
Light and life to all he brings, Risen with heal-ing in his wings.

Joy-ful, all ye na-tions, rise; Join the tri-umph of the skies;
Mild he lays his glo-ry by, Born that man no more may die:

With th'an-gel-ic host pro-claim Christ is born in Beth-le-hem!
Born to raise the sons of earth, Born to give them sec-ond birth.

Hark! the her-ald an-gels sing Glo-ry to the new-born King!

61 He Is Risen

Cecil Alexander **Joachim Neander**

Stately ♩ = 92

1. He is ris - en; he is ris - en!
Tell it out with joy - ful voice: He has burst his
three days' pris - on; Let the whole wide earth re - joice:
Death is con-quered, man is free. Christ has won the vic - to - ry.

2. Come with high and ho - ly hymn - ing
Chant our Lord's tri - um - phant lay; Not one dark - some
cloud is dim - ming Yon - der glo - rious morn - ing ray,
Break-ing o'er the pur - ple east, Sym - bol of our East - er feast.

3. He is ris - en; he is ris - en!
He hath o - pened heav - en's gate: We are free from
sin's dark pris - on, Ris - en to a ho - lier state;
And a bright - er East - er beam On our long - ing eyes shall stream.

62 High on the Mountain Top

Joel H. Johnson

Ebenezer Beesley

Not too fast ♩=60

1. High on the moun-tain top A ban-ner is un-furled;
2. For God re-mem-bers still His prom-ise made of old
3. His house shall there be reared His glo-ry to dis-play;
4. For there we shall be taught The law that will go forth,

Ye na-tions, now look up; It waves to all the world;
That he on Zi-on's hill Truth's stan-dard would un-fold!
And peo-ple shall be heard In dis-tant lands to say,
With truth and wis-dom fraught, To gov-ern all the earth;

In Des-er-et's sweet, peace-ful land—
Her light should there at-tract the gaze
We'll now go up and serve the Lord,
For-ev-er there his ways we'll tread,

On Zi-on's mount be-hold it stand!
Of all the world in lat-ter days.
O-bey his truth and learn his word.
And save our-selves with all our dead.

5 Then hail to Deseret!
   A refuge for the good,
And safety for the great,
   If they but understood
That God with plagues will shake the world
Till all its thrones shall down be hurled.

6 In Deseret doth truth
   Rear up its royal head;
Though nations may oppose,
   Still wider it shall spread;
Yes, truth and justice, love and grace,
In Deseret find ample place.

Holy Temples on Mount Zion

Archibald F. Bennett   Alexander Schreiner

Stately ♩ = 108

1. Ho - ly tem - ples on Mount Zi - on   In   a loft - y splen - dor shine,
2. Mer - ci - ful and gra - cious Fa - ther, Pur - i - fy our hearts, we pray;
3. Sing a - loud, ye heaven - ly cho - rus, An - thems of e - ter - nal praise

Av - en - ues to ex - al - ta - tion, Sym - bols of   a   love di - vine.
Bless our mis - sion of re - demp - tion In   thy hal - lowed house each day;
To   the glo - rious King Im - man - uel! Sing with Saints of lat - ter - days!

And   their kind - ly por - tals beck - on To ser - en - i - ty and prayer,
Till   at length our faith - ful kin - dred, Sealed with us   e - ter - nal - ly
Let   the moun - tains shout for glad - ness, And   the val - leys joy - ful be,

Val - iant chil - dren of   the prom - ise, Pledged to sa - cred serv - ice there.
In   ce - les - tial bonds of   un - ion, Sing   ho - san - nas un - to thee.
While the stars ac - claim in rap - ture, For   the pris - oners shall go free.

64 Hope of Israel

Joseph L. Townsend   **William Clayson**

In march style ♩ = 120

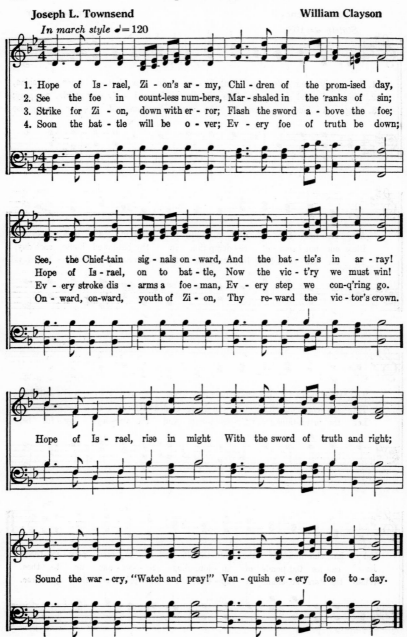

1. Hope of Is - rael, Zi - on's ar - my, Chil - dren of the prom - ised day,
2. See the foe in count-less num-bers, Mar - shaled in the 'ranks of sin;
3. Strike for Zi - on, down with er - ror; Flash the sword a - bove the foe;
4. Soon the bat - tle will be o - ver; Ev - ery foe of truth be down;

See, the Chief-tain sig - nals on - ward, And the bat - tle's in ar - ray!
Hope of Is - rael, on to bat - tle, Now the vic - t'ry we must win!
Ev - ery stroke dis - arms a foe - man, Ev - ery step we con-q'ring go.
On - ward, on-ward, youth of Zi - on, Thy re - ward the vic - tor's crown.

Hope of Is - rael, rise in might With the sword of truth and right;

Sound the war - cry, "Watch and pray!" Van - quish ev - ery foe to - day.

65 How Beautiful Thy Temples, Lord

Frank I. Kooyman   Tracy Y. Cannon

Flowing ♩= 66

1. How beau-ti-ful thy tem-ples, Lord! Each one a sa-cred shrine,
2. How beau-ti-ful thy mes-sage, Lord, The gos-pel, pure and true,
3. How beau-ti-ful our out-look, Lord, That we may grow in truth,

Where faith-ful Saints, with one ac-cord, En-gage in work di-vine.
In these our days to earth re-stored And taught to men a-new.
And live, ex-alt-ed by thy word, In end-less, glo-rious youth.

How beau-ti-ful some aid to give To dear ones we call dead,
How beau-ti-ful its faith and hope, All man-kind it would save,
With loved ones sealed in ho-li-ness By sa-cred tem-ple rites;

But who in-deed as spir-its live: They've on-ly gone a-head.
In-clud-ing in its aim and scope The souls be-yond the grave.
Worlds with-out end we may pro-gress From heights to great-er heights.

How Firm a Foundation

How Firm a Foundation

4. When through the deep waters I call thee to go,
   The rivers of sorrow shall not thee o'erflow,
   For I will be with thee, thy troubles to bless,
   And sanctify to thee thy deepest distress.

5. When through fiery trials thy pathway shall lie,
   My grace, all sufficient, shall be thy supply.
   The flame shall not hurt thee; I only design
   Thy dross to consume and thy gold to refine.

6. E'en down to old age, all my people shall prove
   My sovereign, eternal, unchangeable love;
   And then, when gray hair shall their temples adorn,
   Like lambs shall they still in my bosom be borne.

7. The soul that on Jesus hath leaned for repose
   I will not, I cannot, desert to his foes;
   That soul, though all hell should endeavor to shake,
   I'll never, no never, no never forsake!

67 How Gentle God's Commands

Philip Doddridge

H. G. Naegeli

Gently ♩=76

mf

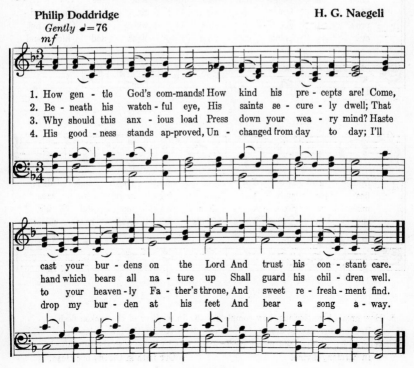

1. How gen - tle God's com-mands! How kind his pre - cepts are! Come,
2. Be - neath his watch - ful eye, His saints se - cure - ly dwell; That
3. Why should this anx - ious load Press down your wea - ry mind? Haste
4. His good - ness stands ap-proved, Un - changed from day to day; I'll

cast your bur - dens on the Lord And trust his con - stant care.
hand which bears all na - ture up Shall guard his chil - dren well.
to your heaven - ly Fa - ther's throne, And sweet re - fresh - ment find.
drop my bur - den at his feet And bear a song a - way.

68 How Great the Wisdom and the Love

Eliza R. Snow   Thomas McIntyre

Calmly ♩=66

1. How great the wis-dom and the love That filled the courts on high And sent the Sav-ior from a-bove To suf-fer, bleed, and die!

2. His pre-cious blood he free-ly spilt; His life he free-ly gave, A sin-less sac-ri-fice for guilt, A dy-ing world to save.

3. By strict o-be-dience Je-sus won The prize with glo-ry rife: "Thy will, O God, not mine be done," A-dorned his mor-tal life.

4. He marked the path and led the way, And ev-ery point de-fines To light and life and end-less day Where God's full pres-ence shines.

5. How great, how glorious, how complete,
   Redemption's grand design,
   Where justice, love, and mercy meet
   In harmony divine!

6. In memory of the broken flesh
   We eat the broken bread;
   And witness with the cup, afresh,
   Our faith in Christ, our Head.

69 How Long, O Lord, Most Holy and True

John A. Widtsoe

B. Cecil Gates

Sincerely ♩ = 88

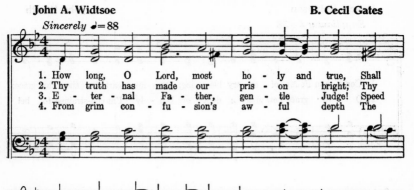

1. How long, O Lord, most ho - ly and true, Shall
2. Thy truth has made our pris - on bright; Thy
3. E - ter - nal Fa - ther, gen - tle Judge! Speed
4. From grim con - fu - sion's aw - ful depth The

shad - owed hope our joy de - lay? Our
light has dimmed the dy - ing past; We
on the day re - demp - tion's hour; Set
wail of hosts, faith's ur - gent plea: Re -

hearts con - fess, our souls be - lieve Thy
bend be - neath thy lov - ing will And
up thy king - dom; from thy house Un -
lease our an - guished, wea - ry souls; Swing

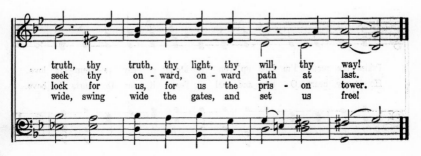

truth, thy truth, thy light, thy will, thy way!
seek thy on - ward, on - ward path at last.
lock for us, for us the pris - on tower.
wide, swing wide the gates, and set us free!

70 Come, Thou Fount of Every Blessing

Robert Robinson   **John Wyeth**

Suppliantly ♩=58

1. Come, thou Fount of ev-ery bless-ing; Tune my heart to sing thy grace;
2. O to grace how great a debt-or Dai-ly I'm con-strained to be!

Streams of mer-cy, nev-er ceas-ing, Call for songs of loud-est praise.
Let thy good-ness, as a fet-ter, Bind my wan-dering heart to thee.

Teach me some me-lo-dious son-net, Sung by flam-ing tongues a-bove;
Prone to wan-der, Lord, I feel it, Prone to leave the God I love;

Praise the mount; I'm fixed up-on it: Mount of thy re-deem-ing love.
Here's my heart, O take and seal it; Seal it for thy courts a-bove.

71 I Have Work Enough to Do

Josephine Pollard

William J. Kirkpatrick

With motion ♩=72

1. I have work e-nough to do, Ere the sun goes down,
2. I must speak the lov-ing word, Ere the sun goes down;
3. As I jour-ney on my way, Ere the sun goes down,

Ere the sun, ere the sun goes down.

For my-self and kin-dred too, Ere the sun goes down;
I must let my voice be heard, Ere the sun goes down;
God's com-mands I must o-bey, Ere the sun goes down;

Ere the sun, ere the sun goes down;

Ev-ery i-dle whis-per still-ing With a pur-pose firm and will-ing,
Ev-ery cry of pit-y heed-ing, For the in-jured in-ter-ced-ing,
There are sins that need con-fess-ing; There are wrongs that need re-dress-ing,

All my dai-ly tasks ful-fill-ing, Ere the sun goes down.
To the light the lost ones lead-ing, Ere the sun goes down.
If I would ob-tain the bless-ing, Ere the sun goes down.

72 There Is a Land Whose Sunny Vales

O. P. Huish

O. P. Huish

March time ♩=112

1. There is a land whose sun-ny vales Are fair as dreams of
2. How rich and fer-tile is thy soil! How vast the wealth thy
3. Then sing her prais-es loud and long, Ye sons and daught-ers

par - a - dise, Where white-robed vir-tue e'er pre-vails, And
moun-tains hold! When sought with dil - i - gence and toil, Yield
of her soil, Stand for the right, op - pose the wrong, And

hon - est man-hood has no price; Where moun-tains capped with vir-gin
of their treas-ures man-i-fold; In all the range of man's de-
'neath op-pres-sion ne'er re-coil; For truth and hon-or let your

snow, Pure as the babe on moth-er's breast, The land I
sire, Thou art a land di - vine-ly blest; None know thee,
mien Be loft - y as the moun-tain crest; Keep U - tah

sing of would you know? 'Tis U - tah, star of all the west;
on - ly to ad - mire, Fair U - tah, star of all the west;
what she's ev - er been, The bright-est star of all the west;

Used by permission.

There Is a Land Whose Sunny Vale

Poco rit.

The land I sing of, would you know? 'Tis star of all the west.
None know thee, on - ly to ad - mire, Fair star of all the west.
Keep U - tah what she's ev - er been, The star of all the west.

U - tah, U - tah, beau - ti - ful, beau - ti - ful land,
beau - ti - ful land,

and grand.....

Fair are thy val - leys, thy moun - tains tall, and tall and grand.

Ev - er my praise shall be, U - tah, for thine and thee,

Land of the brave and free; U - tah the star of the west.

Improve the Shining Moments

R. B. Baird   R. B. Baird

Lightly ♩ = 60

1. Im - prove the shin - ing mo - ments; Don't let them pass you by;
2. Time flies on wings of light - ning; We can - not call it back;
3. As win - ter - time doth fol - low The pleas - ant sum - mer days,
4. Im - prove each shin - ing mo - ment; In this you are se - cure,

Work while the sun is ra - diant; Work, for the night draws nigh.
It comes, then pass - es for - ward A - long its on - ward track;
So may our joys all van - ish And pass far from our gaze.
For prompt - ness bring - eth safe - ty And bless - ings rich and pure.

We can - not bid the sun - beams To length - en out their stay,
And if we are not mind - ful, The chance will fade a - way;
Then should we not en - deav - or Each day some point to gain,
Let pru - dence guide your ac - tions; Be hon - est in your heart;

Nor can we ask the shad - ow To ev - er stay a - way.
For life is quick in pass - ing. 'Tis as a sin - gle day.
That we may here be use - ful, And ev - ery wrong dis - dain?
And God will love and bless you And help to you im - part.

74 In a World Where Sorrow

Lanta Wilson Smith
E. O. Excell

Joyously ♩.=84

1. In a world where sor-row Ev - er will be known, Where are found the need - y, And the sad and lone; How much joy and com - fort You can all be - stow, If you scat - ter sun-shine Ev - ery-where you go.

2. Slight-est ac - tions oft - en Meet the sor - est needs, For the world wants dai - ly Lit - tle kind - ly deeds; Oh, what care and sor - row You may help re - move, With your songs and cour - age, Sym - pa-thy and love.

3. When the days are gloom - y, Sing some hap - py song; Meet the world re - pin - ing With a cour - age strong; Go with faith un - daunt - ed Thro' the ills of life, Scat - ter smiles and sun-shine O'er its toil and strife.

Scat - ter sun-shine all a - long your way Cheer and bless and bright - en Ev - ery pass - ing day; Ev - ery pass - ing day.

Scatter the smiles and sunshine all a - long over your way, Ev - ery pass - ing, pass - ing day;

1. **2.**

75 It May Not Be on the Mountain Height

Mary Brown   **Carrie E. Rounsefell**

Sincerely ♩. = 52

1. It may not be on the moun-tain height Or o-ver the storm-y sea; It may not be at the bat-tle's front My Lord will have need of me; But if, by a still, small voice he calls To paths that I

2. Per-haps to-day there are lov-ing words Which Je-sus would have me speak; There may be now in the paths of sin Some wan-d'rer whom I should seek; O Sav-ior, if thou wilt be my guide, Though dark and

3. There's sure-ly some-where a low-ly place In earth's har-vest fields so wide, Where I may la-bor through life's short day For Je-sus, the Cru-ci-fied; So trust-ing my all to thy ten-der care, And know-ing thou

It May Not Be on the Mountain Height

do not know, I'll an-swer, dear Lord, with my
rug - ged the way, My voice shall ech - o the
lov · est me, I'll do thy will with a

poco   rit.

hand in thine: I'll go where you want me to go.
mes - sage sweet; I'll say what you want me to say.
heart sin - cere; I'll be what you want me to be.

I'll go where you want me to go, dear Lord, O - ver

moun - tain, or plain, or sea; I'll say what you want me to

poco   rit.

say, dear Lord; I'll be what you want me to be.

God of Our Fathers, Known of Old

Rudyard Kipling   (FAMILIAR TUNE)   Issac B. Woodbury

1. God of our fathers known of old, Lord of our
2. The tu-mult and the shout-ing dies, The cap-tains
3. Far-called, our na-vies melt a-way, On dune and

far-flung bat-tle-line, Be-neath whose aw-ful hand we
and the kings de-part; Still stands thine an-cient sac-ri-
head-land sinks the fire; Lo, all our pomp of yes-ter-

hold Do-min-ion o-ver palm and pine, Lord God of
fice, An hum-ble and a con-trite heart, Lord God of
day Is one with Nin-e-veh and Tyre! Judge of the

Hosts, be with us yet, Lest we for-get, lest we for-get!
Hosts, be with us yet, Lest we for-get, lest we for-get!
na-tions, spare us yet, Lest we for-get, lest we for-get!

God of Our Fathers, Known of Old

Rudyard Kipling

LeRoy J. Robertson

With dignity ♩=63

1. God of our fathers, known of old, Lord of our far-flung battle line, Beneath whose awful hand we hold Dominion over palm and pine; Lord God of hosts, be with us yet, Lest we forget, lest we forget.

2. The tumult and the shouting dies; The captains and the kings depart; Still stands thine ancient sacrifice, An humble and a contrite heart; Lord God of hosts, be with us yet, Lest we forget, lest we forget.

3. Far-called, our navies melt away; On dune and headland sinks the fire; Lo, all our pomp of yesterday Is one with Nineveh and Tyre! Judge of the nations, spare us yet, Lest we forget, lest we forget.

Beautiful Zion, Built Above

Lightly ♩ = 112

J. G. Fones

1. Beau - ti - ful Zi - on, built a - bove; Beau - ti - ful cit - y
2. Beau - ti - ful heaven, where all is light; Beau - ti - ful an - gels,
3. Beau - ti - ful crowns on ev - ery brow; Beau - ti - ful palms the

that I love; Beau - ti - ful gates of pearl - y white; Beau - ti - ful
clothed in white; Beau - ti - ful strains that nev - er tire; Beau - ti - ful
con - q'rors show; Beau - ti - ful robes the ran - somed wear; Beau - ti - ful

tem - ple—God its light; He who was slain on Cal - va - ry,
harps thro' all the choir; There shall I join the cho - rus sweet,
all who en - ter there; Thith - er I press with ea - ger feet—

O - pens those pear - ly gates to me. Zi - on, Zi - on, love - ly
Wor - ship - ing at the Sav - ior's feet.
There shall my rest be long and sweet.

Zi - on, Beau - ti - ful Zi - on, Zi - on, cit - y of our God!

79 I Need Thee Every Hour

Annie S. Hawkes   **Robert Lowry**

Tenderly ♩ = 60

1. I need thee ev-ery hour, Most gra - cious Lord;
2. I need thee ev-ery hour, Stay thou near - by;
3. I need thee ev-ery hour, In joy or pain;
4. I need thee ev-ery hour, Most ho - ly One;

No ten - der voice like thine Can peace af - ford.
Temp - ta - tions lose their power When thou art nigh.
Come quick - ly and a - bide, Or life is vain.
O make me thine in - deed, Thou bless - ed Son!

I need thee; O I need thee; Ev - ery hour I need thee!

O bless me now, my Sav - ior; I come to thee!

I Stand All Amazed

Charles H. Gabriel

Charles H. Gabriel

Thoughtfully ♩ = 66
mf

1. I stand all a - mazed at the love Je - sus
2. I mar - vel that he would de - scend from his
3. I think of his hands pierced and bleed - ing to

of - fers me, Con - fused at the grace that so
throne di - vine To res - cue a soul so re -
pay the debt! Such mer - cy, such love, and de -

ful - ly he prof - fers me; I trem - ble to
bel - lious and proud as mine; That he should ex -
vo - tion can I for - get? No, no, I will

know that for me he was cru - ci - fied, That
tend his great love un - to such as I, Suf -
praise and a - dore at the mer - cy seat, Un -

I Stand All Amazed

for me, a sin - ner, he suf - fered, he bled and died.
fi - cient to own, to re - deem, and to jus - ti - fy.
till at the glo - ri - fied throne I kneel at his feet.

Oh, it is won - der - ful that he should
Oh, it is won - der - ful that he should
Oh, it is won - der - ful that he should

care for me, E - nough to die for me!
care for me, E - nough to die for me!
care for me, E - nough to die for me!

won - der - ful!   won - der - ful!

Oh, it is won - der - ful, won - der - ful to me!
Oh, it is won - der - ful, won - der - ful to me!
Oh, it is won - der - ful, won - der - ful to me!

Israel, Israel, God Is Calling

Richard Smyth

Charles C. Converse

Suppliantly ♩=72

1. Is - rael, Is - rael, God is call - ing, Call - ing thee from lands of woe:
2. Is - rael, Is - rael, God is speak - ing; Hear your great De - liv-erer's voice!
3. Is - rael, an - gels are de - scend - ing From ce - les - tial worlds on high,
4. Is - rael! Is - rael! canst thou lin - ger Still in er - ror's gloom-y ways?

Bab - y - lon the great is fall - ing. God shall all her towers o'er-throw.
Now a glo - rious morn is break - ing For the peo - ple of his choice.
And to man their power ex - tend - ing, That the Saints may home-ward fly.
Mark how judg-ment's point-ing fin - ger Jus - ti - fies no vain de - lays.

Come to Zi - on, come to Zi - on Ere his floods of an - ger flow.
Come to Zi - on, come to Zi - on, And with - in her walls re - joice.
Come to Zi - on, come to Zi - on, For your com - ing Lord is nigh.
Come to Zi - on, come to Zi - on! Zi - on's walls shall ring with praise.

Come to Zi - on, come to Zi - on Ere his floods of an - ger flow.
Come to Zi - on, come to Zi - on, And with - in her walls re - joice.
Come to Zi - on, come to Zi - on, For your com - ing Lord is nigh.
Come to Zi - on, come to Zi - on! Zi - on's walls shall ring with praise.

82 It Came Upon the Midnight Clear

Edwin H. Sears

Richard S. Willis

1. It came up-on the mid-night clear, That glo-rious song of old,
2. Still through the clo-ven skies they come, With peace-ful wings un-furled;
3. For lo! the days are has-tening on, By prophets seen of old,

From an-gels bend-ing near the earth, To touch their harps of gold:
And still their heaven-ly mu-sic floats O'er all the wea-ry world,
When with the ev-er-cir-cling years Shall come the time fore-told,

"Peace on the earth, good will to men From heaven's all gra-cious King."
A-bove its sad and low-ly plains, They bend on hov-ering wing,
When the new heaven and earth shall own The Prince of Peace their King,

The world in sol-emn still-ness lay To hear the an-gels sing.
And ev-er o'er its Ba-bel sounds The bless-ed an-gels sing.
And the whole world send back the song Which now the an-gels sing.

Jehovah, Lord of Heaven and Earth

Oliver Holden

Boldly ♩=88

1. Je - ho - vah, Lord of heav'n and earth, Thy word of
2. We long to see thy Church in - crease, Thy own new
3. Roll on thy work in all its power! The dis - tant
4. One gen - eral cho - rus then shall rise From men of

truth pro - claim! O may it spread from pole to pole,
king - dom grow, That all the earth may live in peace,
na - tions bring! In thy new king - dom may they stand,
ev - ery tongue, And songs of joy sal - ute the skies,

Till all shall know thy name; O may it spread from
And heav'n be seen be - low; That all the earth may
And own thee, God and King; In thy new king - dom
By ev - ery na - tion sung; And songs of joy sal -

pole to pole, Till all shall know thy name.
live in peace, And heav'n be seen be - low.
may they stand, And own thee, God and King.
ute the skies, By ev - ery na - tion sung.

84 Jesus, Lover of My Soul

Charles Wesley

Simeon B. Marsh

With devotion ♩=108

1. Je - sus, lov - er of my soul, Let me to thy bos - om fly
2. Oth - er ref - uge have I none; Hangs my help - less soul on thee;

While the near - er wa - ters roll, While the tem - pest still is high;
Leave, oh, leave me not a - lone; Still sup - port and com - fort me.

Hide me, O my Sav - ior, hide, Till the storm of life is past;
All my trust on thee is stayed; All my help from thee I bring;

Safe in - to the ha - ven guide; Oh, re - ceive my soul at last.
Cov - er my de - fense - less head With the shad - ow of thy wing.

Jesus, My Savior True

O. P. Huish   **O. P. Huish**

Fervently ♪ = 104

1. Je - sus, my Sav - ior true, Guide me to thee;
2. Through this dark world of strife, Guide me to thee;
3. When strife and sin a - rise, Guide me to thee;
4. When si - lent death draws near, Guide me to thee;

Help me thy will to do; Guide me to thee;
Teach me a bet - ter life; Guide me to thee;
When tears be - dim my eyes, Guide me to thee;
Calm thou my trem - bling fear; Guide me to thee;

E'en in the dark - est night, As in the morn - ing bright,
Let thy re - deem - ing power Be with me ev - ery hour;
When hopes are crushed and dead, When earth - ly joys are fled,
Let me thy mer - cy prove; Let thy en - dur - ing love,

Be thou my bea - con light; Guide me to thee.
Be thou my safe - ty tower; Guide me to thee.
Thy glo - ry round me shed; Guide me to thee.
Guide me to heaven a - bove; Guide me to thee.

86   Jesus of Nazareth, Savior and King

Hugh W. Dougall   Hugh W. Dougall

Simply ♩ = 84

1. Je - sus of Naz - a - reth, Sav - ior and King!
2. While of this bro - ken bread, Hum - bly we eat,
3. As to our lips, the cup Gent - ly we press,

Tri - um - phant o - ver death, Life thou didst bring.
Our thoughts to thee are led In rev - 'rence sweet.
Our hearts are lift - ed up, Thy name we bless!

Leav - ing thy Fa - ther's throne, On earth to live,
Bruised, bro - ken, torn for us, On Cal - vary's hill,
Guide us wher - e'er we go, Till in the end,

Thy work to do a - lone, Thy life to give.
Thy suf - f'ring borne for us, Lives with us still.
Life ev - er - more we'll know, Through thee, our Friend.

87 Oh What Songs of the Heart

Joseph L. Townsend   **William Clayson**

Sincerely ♩=88

1. Oh what songs of the heart We shall sing all the day,
2. Though our rap - ture and bliss There's no song can ex - press;
3. Oh the vi - sions we'll see In that home of the blest,
4. Oh what songs we'll em - ploy! Oh what wel - come we'll hear!

When a - gain we as - sem - ble at home: When we meet ne'er to part,
We will shout, we will sing o'er and o'er, As we greet with a kiss,
There's no word, there's no thought can im - part, But our rap - ture will be
While our trans- ports of love are com- plete; As the heart swells with joy

With the blest o'er the way, There no more from our
And with joy we ca - ress All our loved ones that
All the soul can at - test In the heav - en - ly
In em - brac - es most dear When our heav - en - ly

loved ones to roam! When we meet ne'er to part, O what
passed on be - fore; As we greet with a kiss, In our
songs of the heart; But our rap - ture will be In the
par - ents we meet! As the heart swells with joy O what

Oh What Songs of the Heart

songs of the heart We shall sing in our beau - ti - ful home.
rap - ture and bliss, All our loved ones that passed on be - fore.
vi - sion we'll see Best ex - pressed in the songs of the heart.
songs we'll em - ploy, When our heav - en - ly Par - ents we meet.

88 Jesus, Once of Humble Birth

Parley P. Pratt

From "English Chorister"

138

Solemnly ♩ = 69

1. Je - sus, once of hum - ble birth, Now in glo - ry
2. Once a meek and low - ly Lamb, Now the Lord, the
3. Once he groaned in blood and tears; Now in glo - ry
4. Once for - sak - en, left a - lone, Now ex - alt - ed

comes to earth. Once he suf - fered grief and pain; Now he
great I Am; Once up - on the cross he bowed, Now his
he ap - pears; Once re - ject - ed by his own, Now their
to a throne; Once all things he meek - ly bore, But he

comes on earth to reign; Now he comes on earth to reign.
char - iot is the cloud; Now his char - iot is the cloud.
King he shall be known; Now their King he shall be known.
now will bear no more; But he now will bear no more.

Joy to the World

Issac Watts

George Frederick Handel

90   Know This, That Every Soul Is Free

William C. Clegg

Evan Stephens

Maestoso ♩ = 60

1. Know this, that ev-ery soul is free To choose his
2. He'll call, per-suade, di-rect a-right, And bless with
3. Free-dom and rea-son make us men; Take these a-

life and what he'll be, For this e-ter-nal
wis-dom, love, and light, In name-less ways be
way, what are we then? Mere an-i-mals, and

truth is given That God will force no man to heav'n.
good and kind, But nev-er force the hu-man mind.
just as well The beasts may think of heav'n or hell.

4. May we no more our powers abuse,
But ways of truth and goodness choose;
Our God is pleased when we improve
His grace and seek his perfect love.

5. It is my free will to believe;
'Tis God's free will me to receive;
To stubborn willers this I'll tell,
'Tis all free grace and all free will.

6. Those who despise grow harder still:
If they adhere, he turns their will;
And thus despisers sink to hell,
While those who heed in glory dwell.

7. But if we take the downward road,
And make in hell our last abode,
Our God is clear; and we shall know
We plunged ourselves in endless woe.

91 Let Each Man Learn to Know Himself

SOLO OR DUET

Simply ♩=84

1. Let each man learn to know himself; To gain that knowl-edge let him la - bor, Im - prove those fail - ings in him - self Which he con- demns so in his neigh-bor. How le - nient our own faults we view, And con - science's voice a - dept - ly smoth - er,

2. And if you meet an err - ing one Whose deeds are blam - a - ble and thought-less, Con - sid - er, ere you cast the stone, If you your - self are pure and fault-less. Oh, list to that small voice with - in, Whose whis - perings oft make men con - found - ed,

3. And in self judg - ment if you find Your deeds to oth - ers' are su - per - ior, To you has Prov - i - dence been kind, As you should be to those in - fe - rior. Ex - am - ple sheds a ge - nial ray Of light which men are apt to bor - row,

Let Each Man Learn to Know Himself

Yet, oh, how harsh - ly we re - view The self - same fail - ings
And trump - et not an - oth - er's sin; You'd blush deep if your
So first im - prove your - self to - day And then im - prove your

in an - oth - er! Let each man learn to know him - self; To
own were sound - ed.
friends to - mor - row.

gain that know-ledge let him la - bor, Im - prove those fail - ings

in him - self, Which he con - demns so in his neigh - bor.

92 Gently Raise the Sacred Strain

William W. Phelps

Thomas C. Griggs

1. Gent - ly raise the sa - cred strain, For the Sab - bath's
2. Ho - ly day, de - void of strife; Let us seek e -
3. Sweet - ly swells the sol - emn sound While we bring our

come a - gain That man may rest, That man may rest,
ter - nal life That great re - ward, That great re - ward,
gifts a - round Of bro - ken hearts, Of bro - ken hearts,

And re - turn his thanks to God, For his bless - ings
And par - take the sac - ra - ment In re - mem - brance
As a will - ing sac - ri - fice, Show-ing what his

to the blest, For his bless - ings to the blest.
of our Lord, In re - mem - brance of our Lord.
grace im - parts, Show - ing what his grace im - parts.

Gently Raise the Sacred Strain

4. Happy type of things to come,
   When the Saints are gathered home
   To praise the Lord
   In eternity of bliss,
   All as one with sweet accord.

5. Holy, holy is the Lord;
   Precious, precious is his word;
   Repent and live;
   Though your sins be crimson red,
   Oh, repent, and he'll forgive.

6. Softly sing the joyful lay,
   For the Saints to fast and pray!
   As God ordains,
   For his goodness and his love,
   While the Sabbath day remains.

93 Let Earth's Inhabitants Rejoice

William Clegg

Leroy J. Robertson

With dignity ♩=63

1. Let earth's in-hab-i-tants re-joice And glad-ly hail the glo-rious hour; A-gain is heard a proph-et's voice; And all may feel the gos-pel's power.

2. The bliss-ful time will soon ar-rive, The day by ho-ly men fore-told, When man no more with man will strive, And all in each a friend be-hold.

3. Op-pres-sion will no more be found Nor ty-rant hold re-lent-less sway; But love to God and man a-bound Through-out the long mil-len-nial day.

94 Let Us Oft Speak Kind Words

Joseph L. Townsend   **Ebenezer Beesley**

Fluently ♩=63

1. Let us oft speak kind words to each oth - er, At
2. Like the sun - beams of morn on the moun - tains, The

home or wher-e'er we may be; Like the war - blings of
soul they a-wake to good cheer; Like the mur - mur of

birds on the heath - er, The tones will be wel-come and free.
cool, pleas-ant foun - tains, They fall in sweet ca - denc - es near.

They'll glad - den the heart that's re - pin - ing, Give
Let's oft, then, in kind - ly toned voic - es, Our

Let Us Oft Speak Kind Words

cour - age and hope from a - bove, And where the dark clouds hide the
mu - tu - al friend-ship re - new, Till heart meets with heart and re -

shin - ing, Let in the bright sun - light of love.
joic - es In friend - ship that ev - er is true,

O the kind words we give shall in mem - o - ry live And sun-shine for-ev - er im-part;

Let us oft speak kind words to each oth - er; Kind words are sweet tones of the heart.

95   I Know That My Redeemer Lives

Samuel Medley   Lewis D. Edwards

Unison With devotion ♩=60

1. I know that my Re - deem - er lives; What com - fort this sweet sen-tence gives!
2. He lives to grant me rich sup - ply, He lives to guide me with his eye.
3. He lives, my kind, wise, heav'nly friend. He lives and loves me to the end.
4. He lives, all glo - ry to his name! He lives, my Sav - ior, still the same;

Accomp.

He lives, he lives, who once was dead. He lives, my ev - er - liv - ing head.
He lives to com-fort me when faint. He lives to hear my soul's com-plaint.
He lives, and while he lives, I'll sing, He lives, my Proph-et, Priest and King.
O sweet the joy this sen-tence gives: "I know that my Re-deem-er lives!"

Sop. Alto

He lives to bless me with his love. He lives to plead for me a - bove.
He lives to si - lence all my fears. He lives to wipe a - way my tears.
He lives and grants me dai - ly breath. He lives, and I shall con-quer death.
He lives, all glo - ry to his name! He lives, my Sav-ior, still the same;

Tenor Bass

He lives my hun-gry soul to feed. He lives to bless in time of need.
He lives to calm my trou-bled heart. He lives, all bless-ings to im-part.
He lives my man-sion to pre-pare. He lives to bring me safe-ly there.
O sweet the joy this sen-tence gives: "I know that my Re-deem-er lives!"

96 Hear Thou Our Hymn, O Lord

Frank W. Asper

Frank W. Asper

Fervently ♩=88

1. Hear thou our hymn, O Lord, With thank-ful hearts we pray.
2. Keep thou our hearts a - glow With thy e - ter - nal word.

Help us thy will to fol-low now, And walk the nar-row way.
Give us thy spir-it ev-ery hour. We ask thee, gra-cious Lord.

97 Lo! On the Water's Brink We Stand

Leroy J. Robertson

With fervor ♩=52

1. Lo! on the wa-ter's brink we stand, To do the
2. Lord, we have sinned, but we re - pent And put our
3. Thou wilt ac - cept our hum-ble prayer, And all our

Fa-ther's will, To be bap-tized by his com-mand, And
sins a - way; With joy re-ceive the mes-sage sent In
sins for - give; For Je-sus' sake the sin - ner spare, He

thus the word ful - fil, And thus the word ful - fil.
this, the lat-ter day, In this, the lat - ter day.
died that we might live, He died that we might live.

Let Us All Press On

Evan Stephens

Evan Stephens

With marked accent ♩= 104

1. Let us all press on in the work of the Lord, That when
2. We will not re - treat, though our num - bers may be few, When com -
3. If we do what's right we have no need to fear, For the

life is o'er we may gain a re - ward; In the fight for
pared with the op - po - site host in view; But an un - seen
Lord, our help - er, will ev - er be near; In the days of

right let us wield a sword, The might - y sword of truth.
pow - er will aid me and you In the glo - rious cause of truth.
tri - al his Saints he will cheer, And pros - per the cause of truth.

Fear not, though the en - e - my de - ride, Cour - age, for the
Fear not, cour-age, though the en - e - my de - ride, We must be vic-to-rious, for the

Lord is on our side; We will heed not what the wick - ed may say,
Lord is on our side; We'll not fear the wick-ed or give heed to what they say,

Let Us All Press On

But the Lord a - lone we will o - bey.
But the Lord, our heaven-ly Fa - ther, him a - lone we will o - bey.

99   In Memory of the Crucified

Frank I. Kooyman   Alexander Schreiner

Prayerfully ♩ = 64

1. In   mem - ory   of   the   Cru - ci - fied,   Our
2. Our   Sav - ior,   in   Geth - sem - an - e,   Shrank
3. We   rev - erence   with   the   bro - ken   bread,   To -
4. Our   Fa - ther!   May   this   sac - ra - ment   To

Fa - ther,   we   have   met   this   hour.   May   thy   sweet   Spir - it
not   to   drink   the   bit - ter   cup;   And   then,   for   us,   on
geth - er   with   the   cup   we   take,   The   bod - y   bruised,   the
ev - ery   soul   be   sanc - ti - fied,   Who   eats   and   drinks   with

here   a - bide,   That   all   may   feel   its   glow - ing   power.
Cal - va - ry,   Up - on   the   cross   was   lift - ed   up.
life - blood   shed,   A   sin - less   ran - som   for   our   sake.
pure   in - tent,   That   in   our   Sav - ior   he'll   a - bide.

100 Lord, Accept Into Thy Kingdom

Mabel Jones Gabbott

Alexander Schreiner

With exultation ♩ = 72

1. Lord, ac - cept in - to thy king-dom Each re - pent - ant, hum - bled one,
2. Know ye not that he was ho - ly, Yet he wit-nessed un - to men
3. Like the sound of rush-ing wa - ters In this day his word is said;

Born of wa - ter and the spir - it In thy name; be - lov - ed Son,
That the way is straight and nar-row Lead - ing un - to God a - gain.
"Ho - ly or - di - nance of mer - cy For the liv - ing and the dead!"

Let the Ho - ly Ghost, de - scend-ing, Com - fort, guide the path of youth.
Hark, glad tid - ings of sal - va - tion, Hear his word, "Come, fol - low me
Let your hearts re - joice in glad-ness! Let the earth break forth and sing!

Chan - nel of all light and glo - ry, Key to vi - sion, know-ledge, truth.
Un - to glo - ry in my king-dom, Un - to life e - ter - nal - ly."
Let the dead speak prais-ing an-thems To our God, e - ter - nal King!

101 Lord, Accept Our True Devotion

R. Alldridge

Joseph J. Daynes

Worshipfully ♩=72

200

1. Lord, ac-cept our true de-vo-tion; Let thy Spir-it whis-per peace;
2. Aid us all to do thy bid-ding, And our dai-ly wants sup-ply;
3. May we with the fu-ture dawn-ing, Day by day from sin be free;

Swell our hearts with fond e-mo-tion; And our joy in thee in-crease.
Give thy Ho-ly Spir-it's guid-ing Till we reach the goal on high.
That on res-ur-rec-tion morn-ing We may rise at peace with thee;

Nev-er leave us, nev-er leave us, Help us, Lord, to win the race;
Ev-er guard us, ev-er guard us, Till we gain the vic-to-ry;
Ev-er prais-ing, ev-er prais-ing, Through-out all e-ter-ni-ty;

Nev-er leave us, nev-er leave us,

Nev-er leave us, nev-er leave us, Help us, Lord, to win the race
Ev-er guard us, ev-er guard us, Till we gain the vic-to-ry.
Ev-er prais-ing, ev-er prais-ing, Through-out all e-ter-ni-ty.

Nev-er leave us, nev-er leave us,

102 Though in the Outward Church Below

W. A. Mozart

Somberly ♩=76

1. Though in the out - ward Church be - low Both wheat and
2. Will it re - lieve the hor - ror there To rec - ol -
3. No; this will ag - gra - vate their case; They per - ish

tares to - geth - er grow, Ere long will Je - sus
lect their sta - tions here? How much they heard, how
un - der means of grace; To them the word of

weed the crop And pluck the tares in an - ger up.
much they knew? How much a - mong the wheat they grew?
life and faith Be - came an in - stru - ment of death.

Brightly ♩=84

For soon the reap - ing time will come. And an - gels

Though in the Outward Church Below

shout the har - vest home. And an-gels shout the har-vest home.

For soon the reap-ing time will come. And an - gels

shout the har - vest home. And an- gels shout the har -vest home.

4. We seem alike when here we meet;
Strangers may think we are all wheat;
But to the Lord's all-searching eyes,
Each heart appears without disguise.

5. The tares are spared for various ends,
Some for the sake of praying friends,
Others the Lord against their will,
Employs, his counsels to fulfil.

6. But though they grow so tall and strong,
His plan will not require them long;
In harvest, when he saves his own,
The tares shall into hell be thrown.

7. O! awful thought, and is it so?
Must all mankind the harvest know?
Is every man a wheat or tare?
Me for the harvest, Lord, prepare.

103 The Lord Is My Light

James Nicholson

John R. Sweney

Resolutely ♩=80

1. The Lord is my light; then why should I fear? By
2. The Lord is my light; though clouds may a-rise, Faith,
3. The Lord is my light; the Lord is my strength. I
4. The Lord is my light, my all and in all. There

day and by night his pres-ence is near. He is my sal-
strong-er than sight, looks up through the skies Where Je-sus for-
know in his might I'll con-quer at length. My weak-ness in
is in his sight no dark-ness at all. He is my Re-

va-tion from sor-row and sin; This bless-ed as-sur-
ev-er in glo-ry doth reign. Then how can I ev-
mer-cy he cov-ers with power, And, walk-ing by faith,
deem-er, my Sav-ior, and King. With Saints and with an-

ance the Spir-it doth bring. The Lord is my
er in dark-ness re-main?
I am blest ev-ery hour.
gels his prais-es I'll sing. The Lord is my light, the

The Lord Is My Light

light;
Lord   is   my   light;

He is my joy
He   is   my   joy

and my song.
and   my   song;

By   day   and   by
By   day   and   by   night,   by

night   he leads, he leads me a - long.
day   and   by   night   he   leads,   he   leads   me   a - long.

5. The Lord is my light; his way is straight and clear;
   It leads to life eternal; I know the Lord is near.
   He will not forsake me, if I will show my love
   And walk along the narrow road that leads to heaven above.

6. The Lord is my light; and though my spirit fail
   Because of sin and sorrow, God's plan will yet prevail.
   I know he will hear me and answer every plea
   For guidance to my heavenly home where joy will ever be.

7. The Lord is my light; his Spirit seeks no rest;
   His love is ever with me; it fills my troubled breast.
   He gives me direction no matter where I roam;
   His beacon of eternal love will guide me safely home.

8. The Lord is my light, and when I kneel to pray
   I feel his presence near me, my fear all fades away.
   I'll sing loud his praises; I'll honor his great name,
   He is my God, my Savior, King, eternally the same.

Stanzas 5, 6, 7, 8, added by compilers

104 The Lord Is My Shepherd

23rd Psalm
Thomas Koschat

Worshipfully ♩=60

1. The Lord is my Shep-herd; no want shall I know. I feed in green pas-tures, safe fold-ed I rest. He lead-eth my soul where the still wa-ters flow, Re-stores me when wan-dering, re-deems when op-pressed; Re-stores me when wan-dering, re-deems when op-pressed.

2. Through the val-ley and shad-ow of death though I stray, Since thou art my Guard-ian, no e-vil I fear. Thy rod shall de-fend me; thy staff be my stay; No harm can be-fall, with my Com-fort-er near; No harm can be-fall, with my Com-fort-er near.

3. In the midst of af-flic-tion my ta-ble is spread, With bless-ings un-meas-ured my cup run-neth o'er. With per-fume and oil thou a-noint-est my head. Oh, what shall I ask of thy prov-i-dence more? Oh, what shall I ask of thy prov-i-dence more?

105 Lord, Dismiss Us With Thy Blessing

John Fawcett

Jean Jacques Rousseau

Cheerfully ♩=69

1. Lord, dis-miss us with thy bless-ing; Fill our hearts with joy and peace;
2. Thanks we give, and ad - o - ra - tion, For the gos - pel's joy - ful sound;

Let us each, thy love pos - sess - ing, Tri - umph in re - deem-ing grace.
May the fruits of thy sal - va - tion In our hearts and lives a - bound.

O re - fresh us, O re - fresh us, Trav-eling through this wil - der - ness,
Ev - er faith - ful, Ev - er faith-ful To the truth may we be found.

O re - fresh us, O re - fresh us, Trav-eling through this wil - der - ness.
Ev - er faith - ful, Ev - er faith-ful To the truth may we be found.

106 Master, The Tempest Is Raging

M. A. Baker   H. R. Palmer

Imploringly ♩.=58

1. Mas - ter, the tem - pest is rag - ing! The bil - lows are toss - ing high!
2. Mas - ter, with an - guish of spir - it I bow in my grief to - day.
3. Mas - ter, the ter - ror is o - ver. The el - e - ments sweet - ly rest.

The sky is o'er-shad-owed with black-ness. No shel - ter or help is nigh.
The depths of my sad heart are trou-bled. Oh, wak - en and save, I pray!
Earth's sun in the calm lake is mir-rored, And heav-en's with - in my breast.

Car - est thou not that we per - ish? How canst thou lie a - sleep
Tor-rents of sin and of an - guish Sweep o'er my sink - ing soul,
Lin - ger, Oh, bless - ed Re - deem - er! Leave me a - lone no more,

When each mo-ment so mad-ly is threat-ening A grave in the an - gry deep?
And I per - ish! I per - ish! dear Mas - ter. Oh, has-ten and take con - trol!
And with joy I shall make the blest har - bor And rest on the bliss - ful shore.

mp   p

The winds and the waves shall o - bey my will; Peace, be
Peace, be still,

Master, the Tempest Is Raging

107 For Our Devotions, Father

Henry W. Naisbitt

J. G. Fones

Reverently ♩ = 92

1. For our de-vo-tions, Fa-ther, we In-voke Thy Spir-it
2. In Sab-bath hours, what peace, what rest, What food, what life, dost
3. Pass to each one the bro-ken bread, Give each the cup,— a
4. And when the word comes clothed in power, Truth gives its sure, un-

us to aid; From world-ly thoughts, oh set us free, To trust the
Thou im-part! One day in seven,—of days the best,— This or-der
to-ken true; Dis-ci-ples by the Priest-hood led In the true
err-ing sound; Comes there a more re-fresh-ing shower In all of

prom-ise Je-sus made, To trust the prom-ise Je-sus made:
shows how wise Thou art, This or-der shows how wise Thou art.
gos-pel, old, yet new, In the true gos-pel, old, yet new.
du-ty's sa-cred round? In all of du-ty's sa-cred round?

"When in my name, but two or three Shall meet, I there will
O pre-cious boon, when Saints can meet As one a-round the
What strength in cov-enants so re-newed, And with the Spir-it's
From ben-e-dic-tion Saints re-tire, And hearts are warmed by

For Our Devotions, Father

sure - ly be! Shall meet, I there will sure - ly be."
mer - cy seat! As one a - round the mer - cy seat!
life im - bued! And with the Spir - it's life im - bued!
new de - sire! And hearts are warmed by new de - sire!

108 Jesus, Mighty King In Zion

Fellows   Tracy Y. Cannon

Stately ♩ = 108

1. Je - sus, might - y King in Zi - on,
2. As an em - blem of thy pas - sion,
3. Fear - less of the world's des - pis - ing,

Thou a - lone our guide shalt be; Thy com - mis - sion
And thy vic - tory o'er the grave, We, who know thy
We the an - cient path pur - sue, Bur - ied with the

we re - ly on, We will fol - low none but thee.
great sal - va - tion, Are bap - tized be - neath the wave.
Lord, and ris - ing To a life di - vine - ly new.

109 Precious Savior, Dear Redeemer

H. R. Palmer

H. R. Palmer

Reverently ♩=72

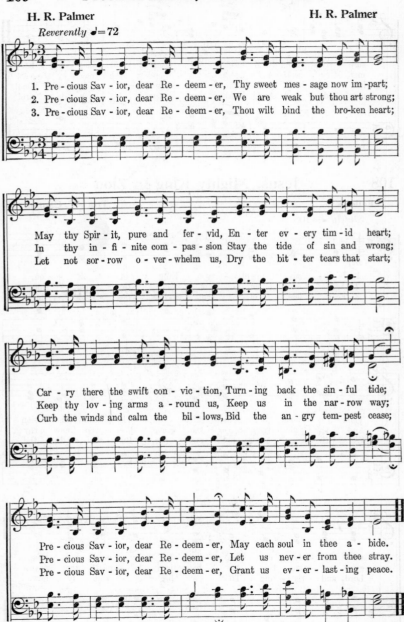

1. Pre - cious Sav - ior, dear Re - deem - er, Thy sweet mes - sage now im - part;
2. Pre - cious Sav - ior, dear Re - deem - er, We are weak but thou art strong;
3. Pre - cious Sav - ior, dear Re - deem - er, Thou wilt bind the bro-ken heart;

May thy Spir - it, pure and fer - vid, En - ter ev - ery tim - id heart;
In thy in - fi - nite com - pas - sion Stay the tide of sin and wrong;
Let not sor - row o - ver - whelm us, Dry the bit - ter tears that start;

Car - ry there the swift con - vic - tion, Turn - ing back the sin - ful tide;
Keep thy lov - ing arms a - round us, Keep us in the nar - row way;
Curb the winds and calm the bil - lows, Bid the an - gry tem - pest cease;

Pre - cious Sav - ior, dear Re - deem - er, May each soul in thee a - bide.
Pre - cious Sav - ior, dear Re - deem - er, Let us nev - er from thee stray.
Pre - cious Sav - ior, dear Re - deem - er, Grant us ev - er - last - ing peace.

110 Choose the Right

James Townsend

Henry A. Tuckett

Earnestly ♩ = 96

1. Choose the right, when a choice is placed be - fore you; In the
2. Choose the right! let no spir - it of di - gres - sion O - ver -
3. Choose the right! there is peace in right - eous do - ing; Choose the

right the Ho - ly Spir - it guides; And its light is for -
come you in the e - vil hour; There's the right and the
right! there's safe - ty for the soul; Choose the right in all

ev - er shin - ing o'er you, When in the right your heart con - fides.
wrong to ev - ery ques - tion, Be safe through in - spir - a - tion's power.
la - bors you're pur - su - ing; Let God and heav - en be your goal.

Choose the right! Choose the right! Let wis - dom mark the way be - fore;

In its light, Choose the right! And God will bless you ev - er - more.

111 M. I. A., We Hail Thee

Ruth May Fox

W. O. Robinson

Tenderly ♩ = 72

1. M. I. A., we hail thee! Loud thy praise we sing;
2. Flow-er of the des-ert. Fra-grant is thy bloom,

For thy lov-ing guid-ance We our hom-age bring;
Blest with God's own sun-shine, Ra-diant as the moon.

Found-ed by a proph-et On the rock of truth,
'Neath thy heaven-wrought ban-ner, March the brave and free.

May thy light and glo-ry Di-a-dem our youth.
For thy right-eous stan-dards, Hail, all hail, to thee!

M. I. A., We Hail Thee

112 Lead, Kindly Light

John Henry Newman
John B. Dykes

Prayerfully ♩=52

1. Lead, kind-ly Light, a-mid th'en-cir-cling gloom; Lead thou me on!
2. I was not ev-er thus, nor prayed that thou Shouldst lead me on;
3. So long thy power hath blest me, sure it still Will lead me on

The night is dark, and I am far from home; Lead thou me on!
I loved to choose and see my path; but now Lead thou me on!
O'er moor and fen, o'er crag and tor-rent, till The night is gone,

Keep thou my feet; I do not ask to see
I loved the gar-ish day, and, spite of fears,
And with the morn those an-gel fac-es smile,

The dis-tant scene— one step e-nough for me.
Pride ruled my will. Re-mem-ber not past years.
Which I have loved long since, and lost a-while!

113   The Lord My Pasture Will Prepare

Joseph Addison   Dimitri Bortniansky

With simplicity ♩=84

1. The Lord my pas-ture will pre-pare And feed me
2. When in the sul-try glebe I faint Or on the

with a shep-herd's care; His pres-ence will my wants sup-ply,
thirst-y moun-tain pant, To fer-tile vales and dew-y meads

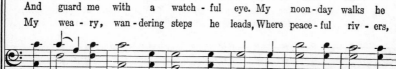

And guard me with a watch-ful eye. My noon-day walks he
My wea-ry, wan-dering steps he leads, Where peace-ful riv-ers,

will at-tend, And all my si-lent mid-night hours de-fend.
soft and slow, A-mid the cool-ing ver-dant land-scape flow.

114 More Holiness Give Me

Philip Paul Bliss

Philip Paul Bliss

Prayerfully ♩.=50

1. More ho - li - ness give me, More striv - ings with - in;
2. More grat - i - tude give me, More trust in the Lord;
3. More pur - i - ty give me, More strength to o'er - come;

More pa - tience in suf - fering, More sor - row for sin;
More pride in his glo - ry, More hope in his word;
More free - dom from earth - stains, More long - ing for home;

More faith in my Sav - ior, More sense of his care;
More tears for his sor - rows, More pain at his grief;
More fit for the king - dom, More used would I be;

rit.

More joy in his serv - ice, More pur - pose in prayer.
More meek - ness in tri - al, More praise for re - lief.
More bless - ed and ho - ly, More, Sav - ior, like thee.

115   My Country, 'Tis of Thee

Samuel F. Smith   Henry Carey

With emphasis ♩=76

1. My coun-try! 'tis of thee, Sweet land of lib-er-ty,
Of thee I sing; Land where my fa-thers died, Land of the
pil-grim's pride, From ev-ery moun-tain side, Let free-dom ring!

2. My na-tive coun-try, thee, Land of the no-ble, free,
Thy name I love; I love thy rocks and rills, Thy woods and
tem-pled hills. My heart with rap-ture thrills Like that a-bove.

3. Let mu-sic swell the breeze And ring from all the trees
Sweet free-dom's song; Let mor-tal tongues a-wake; Let all that
breathe par-take; Let rocks their si-lence break, The sound pro-long.

4. Our fa-thers' God to thee, Auth-or of lib-er-ty,
To thee we sing. Long may our land be bright With free-dom's
ho-ly light. Pro-tect us by thy might, Great God, our King!

115-A   God Save the King

(Attributed to John Bull 1652)

1. God save our gracious King,
Long live our noble King,
God save the King;
Send him victorious,
Happy and glorious,
Long to reign over us;
God save the King.

2. The choicest gifts in store,
On him be pleased to pour;
Long may he reign;
May he defend our laws,
And ever give us cause
To sing with heart and voice,
God save the King.

Nay, Speak No Ill

With contemplation ♩=76

1. Nay, speak no ill; a kind-ly word Can nev-er leave a
2. Give me the heart that fain would hide, Would fain an-oth-er's
3. Then speak no ill, but len-ient be To oth-er's fail-ings

sting be-hind; And, oh, to breathe each tale we've heard Is far be-
faults ef-face. How can it please the hu-man pride To prove hu-
as your own. If you're the first a fault to see, Be not the

neath a no-ble mind. Full oft a bet-ter seed is sown
man-i-ty but base? No, let us reach a high-er mood,
first to make it known, For life is but a pass-ing day;

By choos-ing thus the kind-er plan, For, if but lit-tle
A no-bler es-ti-mate of man; Be ear-nest in the
No lip may tell how brief its span; Then, O the lit-tle

good is known, Still let us speak the best we can.
search for good And speak of all the best we can.
time we stay, Let's speak of all the best we can.

117 Nearer, Dear Savior, to Thee

Joseph L. Townsend

William Clayson

Gently ♩.=66

1. Near - er, dear Sav - ior, to thee, Near - er, near - er to thee,
2. Near - er, dear Sav - ior, to thee, Near - er, near - er to thee,
3. Near - er, dear Sav - ior, to thee, Near - er, near - er to thee,
4. Near - er, dear Sav - ior, to thee, Near - er, near - er to thee,

Ev - er I'm striv - ing to be Near - er, yet near - er to thee!
Proved by my tri - als I'll be Near - er, yet near - er to thee!
Ev - er my an - them will be Near - er, yet near - er to thee!
Let me by ho - li - ness be Near - er, yet near - er to thee!

Trust - ing, in thee I con - fide; Hop - ing, in thee I a - bide.
Hum - bly I come to thee now; Ear - nest, I prayer - ful - ly bow.
Lov - ing thee, ev - er I pray, Aid me thy will to o - bey.
When all my tri - als are done, When my re - ward I have won,

Take, O take, and cher - ish me: Near - er, dear Sav - ior, to thee.

118   Now Let Us Rejoice

William W. Phelps

Cheerfully ♩ = 104

1. Now let us re - joice in the day of sal - va - tion. No long - er as
2. We'll love one an - oth - er and nev - er dis - sem - ble, But cease to do
3. In faith we'll re - ly on the arm of Je - ho - vah To guide through these

stran - gers on earth need we roam. Good ti - dings are sound - ing to
e - vil and ev - er be one. And when the un - god - ly are
last days of trou - ble and gloom; And af - ter the scourg - es and

us and each na - tion, And short - ly the hour of re - demp - tion will come,
fear - ing and trem - ble, We'll watch for the day when the Sav - ior will come,
har - vest are o - ver, We'll rise with the just when the Sav - ior doth come.

When all that was prom - ised, the Saints will be giv - en, And none will mo -
When all that was prom - ised, the Saints will be giv - en, And none will mo -
Then all that was prom - ised, the Saints will be giv - en, And they will be

Now Let Us Rejoice

lest them from morn un - til ev'n, And earth will ap - pear as the
lest them from morn un - til ev'n, And earth will ap - pear as the
crowned with the an - gels of heav'n, And earth will ap - pear as the

gar - den of E - den, And Je - sus will say to all Is-rael, "Come home."
gar - den of E - den, And Je - sus will say to all Is-rael, "Come home."
gar - den of E - den, And Christ and his peo - ple will ev - er be one.

119 Lord, We Ask Thee, Ere We Part

George Manwaring   Ebenezer Beesley

Simply ♩ = 66

1. Lord, we ask thee, ere we part, Bless the teach - ings of this day;
2. In the in - no - cence of youth, We would all thy laws ful - fil;
3. Fa - ther, mer - ci - ful and kind, While we la - bor for the right,
4. All our fol - lies, Lord, for - give; Keep us from temp - ta - tions free;

Plant them deep in ev - ery heart, That with us they'll ev - er stay.
Lead us in the way of truth; Give us strength to do thy will.
May we in thy serv - ice find Sweet - est pleas - ure, pure de - light.
Help us ev - er - more to live Lives of ho - li - ness to thee.

Now Thank We All Our God

Martin Rinkart **Johann Cruger**

With deep feeling ♩=66

1. Now thank we all our God With heart and hands and voic-
2. O may our boun-teous God Through all our life be near

es, Who won-drous things hath done, In whom his earth re-joic-
us With ev-er joy-ful hearts And bless-ed peace to cheer

es, Who from our moth-ers' arms Hath blessed us on our way
us, And keep us in his love, And guide us day and night,

With count-less gifts of love, And still is ours to-day.
And free us from all ills, Pro-tect us by his might.

121   Jesus, Savior, Pilot Me

Edward Hopper   **J. E. Gould**

Suppliantly ♩=58

1. Je - sus, Sav - ior, pi - lot me O - ver
2. As a moth - er stills her child, Thou canst
3. When, at last, I near the shore, And the

life's tem - pes - tuous sea; Un - known waves be - fore me
hush the o - cean wild; Bois - terous waves o - bey thy
fear - ful break - ers roar 'Twixt me and the peace - ful

roll, Hid - ing rock and treach-erous shoal; Chart and
will When thou say'st to them, "Be still!" Won - drous
rest, Then, while lean - ing on thy breast, May I

com - pass came from thee: Je - sus, Sav - ior, pi - lot me.
Sov - ereign of the sea. Je - sus, Sav - ior, pi - lot me.
hear thee say to me, "Fear not: I will pi - lot thee."

122

Now the Day Is Over

Sabine Baring-Gould

Joseph Barnby

Solemnly ♩=54

mp

1. Now the day is o - ver; Night is draw - ing nigh;
2. Je - sus, give the wea - ry Calm and sweet re - pose:

Shad - ows of the eve - ning Steal a - cross the sky.
With thy ten - derest bless - ing May our eye - lids close.

123

O God, Our Help In Ages Past

Isaac Watts

William Croft

Resolutely ♩=69

1. O God, our help in a - ges past, Our hope for years to come,
2. With - in the shad - ow of thy throne, Still may we dwell se - cure.
3. Be - fore the hills in or - der stood, Or earth re-ceived her frame,

Our shel - ter from the storm - y blast, And our e - ter - nal home.
Suf - fi - cient is thine arm a - lone, And our de - fence is sure.
From ev - er - last - ing thou art God, To end - less years the same.

4. A thousand ages in thy sight
Are like an evening gone;
Short as the watch that ends the night
Before the rising sun.

5. O God, our help in ages past,
Our hope for years to come,
Be thou our guide while life shall last
And our eternal home.

Nearer, My God, to Thee

Sarah F. Adams

Lowell Mason

Suppliantly ♩ = 60

1. Near - er, my God, to thee, Near - er to thee!
2. Though like the wan - der - er, The sun gone down,
3. There let the way ap - pear, Steps un - to heaven.

E'en though it be a cross That rais - eth me.
Dark - ness be o - ver me, My rest a stone,
All that thou send - est me, In mer - cy given;

Still all my song shall be Near - er, my God, to thee,
Yet in my dreams I'd be Near - er, my God, to thee,
An - gels to beck - on me Near - er, my God, to thee,

Near - er, my God, to thee, Near - er to thee!
Near - er, my God, to thee, Near - er to thee!
Near - er, my God, to thee, Near - er to thee!

4. Then with my waking thoughts
Bright with thy praise,
Out of my stony griefs
Bethel I'll raise;
So by my woes to be
Nearer, my God, to thee,
Nearer, my God, to thee,
Nearer to thee!

5. Or if, on joyful wing
Cleaving the sky,
Sun, moon, and stars forgot,
Upward I fly,
Still all my song shall be,
Nearer, my God, to thee,
Nearer, my God, to thee,
Nearer to thee!

125   O God, The Eternal Father

William W. Phelps   Felix Mendelssohn

With simplicity ♩ = 69

1. O God, th'E-ter-nal Fa-ther, Who dwells a-mid the sky,
2. That sa-cred ho-ly of-fering By man least un-der-stood,
3. When Je-sus, the A-noint-ed, De-scend-ed from a-bove,
4. How in-fi-nite that wis-dom, The plan of ho-li-ness,

In Je-sus' name we ask thee, To bless and sanc-ti-fy,
To have our sins re-mit-ted, And take his flesh and blood;
And gave him-self a ran-som To win our souls with love,
That made sal-va-tion per-fect And veiled the Lord in flesh.

If we are pure be-fore thee, This bread and cup of wine,
That we may ev-er wit-ness, The suf-fering of thy Son.
With no ap-par-ent beau-ty, That man should him de-sire,
To walk up-on his foot-stool, And be like man, al-most,

That we may all re-mem-ber That of-fer-ing di-vine.
And al-ways have his Spir-it, To make our hearts as one.
He was the prom-ised Sav-ior, To pur-i-fy with fire.
In his ex-alt-ed sta-tion, And die or all was lost.

126   Oh Beautiful for Spacious Skies

Katherine Lee Bates   Samuel A. Ward

Without dragging ♩=84

1. Oh beau - ti - ful for spa - cious skies, For am - ber waves of grain,
2. Oh beau - ti - ful for pil - grim feet, Whose stern im - pas-sioned stress
3. Oh beau - ti - ful for he - roes proved In lib - er - at - ing strife,
4. Oh beau - ti - ful for pa - triot dream That sees be - yond the years.

For pur - ple moun-tain maj - es - ties A - bove the fruit - ed plain!
A thor - ough-fare of free - dom beat A - cross the wil - der - ness!
Who more than self their coun - try loved, And mer - cy more than life!
Thine al - a - bas - ter cit - ies gleam Un-dimmed by hu - man tears.

A - mer - i - ca! A - mer - i - ca! God shed his grace on thee
A - mer - i - ca! A - mer - i - ca! God mend thine ev - ery flaw,
A - mer - i - ca! A - mer - i - ca! May God thy gold re - fine
A - mer - i - ca! A - mer - i - ca! God shed his grace on thee

And crown thy good with broth - er-hood From sea to shin - ing sea.
Con - firm thy soul in self - con-trol, Thy lib - er - ty in law.
Till all suc - cess be no - ble-ness, And ev - ery gain di - vine.
And crown thy good with broth - er-hood From sea to shin - ing sea.

127 O'er the Gloomy Hills of Darkness

Williams

H. H. Petersen

Steadily ♩=72

1. O'er the gloom-y hills of dark-ness, Look, my soul, be
2. Let the In - dian and the Ne - gro, Let the rude bar -
3. King-doms wide that sit in dark-ness, Grant them, Lord, the
4. Fly a - broad, thou might - y gos - pel; Win and con - quer,

still and gaze; All the prom - is - es do trav - ail
bar - ian see That di - vine and glo - rious con - quest
glo - rious light; And from east - ern coast to west - ern,
nev - er cease; So Im - man - uel's fair do - min - ions

With the glo - rious day of grace; Bless - ed ju - bilee,
Once ob - tained on Cal - va - ry. Let the gos - pel,
May the morn - ing chase the night— Chase the dark - ness,
Shall ex - tend and still in - crease, Till the king-doms,

Bless - ed ju - bilee, Let thy glo - rious morn - ing dawn!
Let the gos - pel, Soon re - sound from pole to pole.
Chase the dark - ness From their long be - night - ed eyes.
Till the king-doms Of the world are all his own.

128 Onward, Christian Soldiers

Sabine Baring-Gould

Arthur S. Sullivan

Martial ♩ = 104

1. On-ward, Chris-tian sol - diers! March-ing as to war, With the cross of
2. At the sign of tri - umph, Sa - tan's host doth flee; On, then, Chris-tian
3. Like a might-y ar - my Moves the Church of God. Broth-ers, we are
4. On-ward, then, ye peo - ple, Join our hap-py throng; Blend with ours your

Je - sus Go - ing on be - fore. Christ, the roy - al Mas - ter,
sol - diers, On to vic - to - ry. Hell's foun-da-tions quiv - er
tread - ing Where the Saints have trod. We are not di - vid - ed,
voic - es In the tri - umph - song; Glo - ry, laud and hon - or,

Leads a-gainst the foe; For-ward in - to bat - tle, See his ban-ners go!
At the shout of praise; Broth-ers, lift your voic - es, Loud your an-thems raise.
All one bod - y we, One in hope and doc - trine, One in char - i - ty.
Un - to Christ, the King; This through count-less a - ges Men and an-gels sing.

On-ward, Chris-tian sol - diers, March-ing as to war,
war, With the

With the cross of Je - sus Go - ing on be - fore.
cross of Je - sus

129   Oh Come, All Ye Faithful

With great dignity ♩=92

1. Oh come, all ye faith-ful, Joy-ful and tri-um-phant,
2. ✕ Sing, choirs of an-gels, Sing in ex-ul-ta-tion,
3. ✕ Yea, Lord, we greet thee, Born this hap-py morn-ing,

Oh come ye, Oh come ye to Beth-le-hem; Come and be-hold him
✕ Sing, all ye cit-i-zens of heaven a-bove; Glo-ry to God,
✕ Je-sus, to thee be all glo-ry given; Son of the Fa-ther,

Born the King of an-gels; Oh come, let us a-dore him, Oh
Glo-ry in the high-est; Oh come, let us a-dore him, Oh
Now in flesh ap-pear-ing; Oh come, let us a-dore him, Oh

come, let us a-dore him, Oh come, let us a-dore him, Christ, the Lord.
come, let us a-dore him, Oh come, let us a-dore him, Christ, the Lord.
come, let us a-dore him, Oh come, let us a-dore him, Christ, the Lord.

130 O Thou Rock of Our Salvation

Joseph L. Townsend

William Clayson

Steadily ♩=84

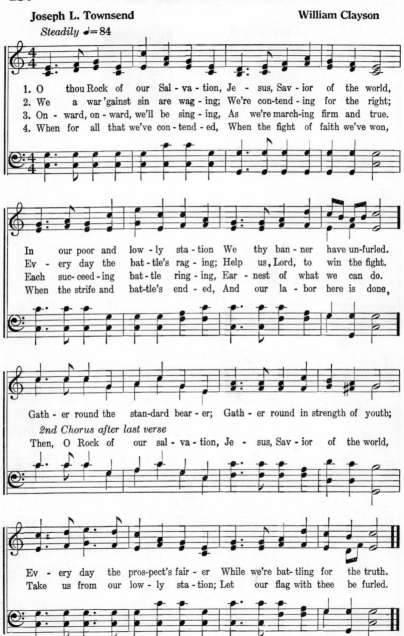

1. O thou Rock of our Sal-va-tion, Je-sus, Sav-ior of the world,
2. We a war 'gainst sin are wag-ing; We're con-tend-ing for the right;
3. On-ward, on-ward, we'll be sing-ing, As we're march-ing firm and true.
4. When for all that we've con-tend-ed, When the fight of faith we've won,

In our poor and low-ly sta-tion We thy ban-ner have un-furled.
Ev-ery day the bat-tle's rag-ing; Help us, Lord, to win the fight.
Each suc-ceed-ing bat-tle ring-ing, Ear-nest of what we can do.
When the strife and bat-tle's end-ed, And our la-bor here is done,

Gath-er round the stan-dard bear-er; Gath-er round in strength of youth;

2nd Chorus after last verse

Then, O Rock of our sal-va-tion, Je-sus, Sav-ior of the world,

Ev-ery day the pros-pect's fair-er While we're bat-tling for the truth.
Take us from our low-ly sta-tion; Let our flag with thee be furled.

Oh Say, Can You See

Francis Scott Key

John Stafford Smith

With spirit ♩= 104

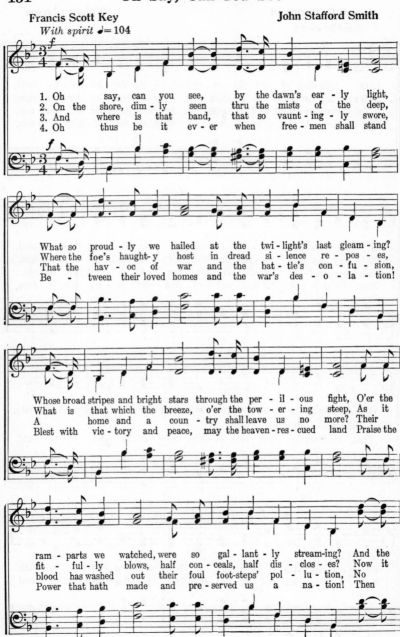

1. Oh say, can you see, by the dawn's ear - ly light,
2. On the shore, dim - ly seen thru the mists of the deep,
3. And where is that band, that so vaunt - ing - ly swore,
4. Oh thus be it ev - er when free - men shall stand

What so proud - ly we hailed at the twi - light's last gleam - ing?
Where the foe's haught - y host in dread si - lence re - pos - es,
That the hav - oc of war and the bat - tle's con - fu - sion,
Be - tween their loved homes and the war's des - o - la - tion!

Whose broad stripes and bright stars through the per - il - ous fight, O'er the
What is that which the breeze, o'er the tow - er - ing steep, As it
A home and a coun - try shall leave us no more? Their
Blest with vic - tory and peace, may the heaven - res - cued land Praise the

ram - parts we watched, were so gal - lant - ly stream - ing? And the
fit - ful - ly blows, half con - ceals, half dis - clos - es? Now it
blood has washed out their foul foot-steps' pol - lu - tion, No
Power that hath made and pre - served us a na - tion! Then

Oh Say, Can You See

132 Now We'll Sing with One Accord

William W. Phelps

Joseph J. Daynes

Boldly ♩ = 68

1. Now we'll sing with one ac-cord, For a proph-et of the Lord,
2. And an an-gel, sure-ly then, For a bless-ing un-to men,
3. And the Book of Mor-mon, true, With its cov-enant ev-er new,
4. Pre-cious are the years to come, While the right-eous gath-er home

Bring-ing forth his pre-cious word, Cheers the Saints as an-cient-ly.
Brought the priest-hood back a-gain In its an-cient pur-i-ty.
For the Gen-tile and the Jew, He trans-lat-ed sa-cred-ly.
For the great mil-len-ni-um, When they'll rest in bless-ed-ness.

When the world in dark-ness lay, Lo! he sought the bet-ter way,
E-ven Jos-eph he in-spired, Yea, his heart he tru-ly fired
God's com-mand-ments to man-kind, For be-liev-ing Saints de-signed,
Pru-dent in this world of woes, They will tri-umph o'er their foes,

rit.

And he heard the Sav-ior say, "Go and prune my vine-yard, son!"
With the light that he de-sired For the work of right-eous-ness.
And to bless the seek-ing mind, Came to him from Je-sus Christ.
While the realm of Zi-on grows Pur-er for e-ter-ni-ty.

133   O Happy Home! O Blest Abode

Mary Ann Morton

Leroy J. Robertson

Joyously ♩= 80

1. O hap - py home! O blest a - bode! Where Saints com-mun - ion
2. In Ba - by - lon I loathe to stay; Dire are the e - vils
3. Come, sa - cred power, ex - ert thy sway, To guide in the ce -
4. Let friends or kin - dred, near and dear, Ex - ert their power, nor

hold with God With - out a doubt or fear, When shall I
day by day With - in her pre - cincts dark. Truth's bright - er
les - tial way, Tra - di - tion to for - sake, My Sav - ior's
ser - vile fear Shall e'er my spir - it bind; Though now af -

reach thy fer - tile plains, As - cend the mount where vir - tue gains
rays ex - pose the night; Each hon - est mind re - ceives the light
foot - steps to pur - sue, Each sel - fish prin - ci - ple sub - due,
fec - tions warm - er rise In souls en - light - ened from the skies

A more ex - alt - ed sphere? A more ex - alt - ed sphere?
And press - es to the mark, And press - es to the mark.
To right - eous-ness a - wake, To right - eous-ness a - wake.
And blest with Je - sus' mind, And blest with Je - sus' mind.

134 Oh Hark! A Glorious Sound Is Heard

W. O. Robinson

Frank W. Asper

With vigor ♩=120

1. Oh hark! a glo-rious sound is heard, In tri-umph of the right
2. And down the a-ges, on and on, In-creas-ing ev-ery hour,
3. A-rise and sing, ye sons of men; All praise and hon-or give;

As Zi-on's youth, in league with truth, Go forth in won-drous might.
In loy-al-ty and faith we go, In man-hood, grace, and power.
A-rise and sing to his great name, Who died that we might live.

We raise our voice in loy-al shout, A great ex-ul-tant cry:
The Light of Light, God's torch of truth, As bea-con points the way.
On Zi-on's hill in strength and might, Send forth a joy-ous strain.

"Je-ho-vah reigns! Lord God of hosts, All hail thee, King most high."
To end-less glo-ry, king-doms great, In realms of per-fect day.
In tri-umph o-ver sin and strife, With him in glo-ry reign.

135   O Holy Words of Truth and Love

Joseph L. Townsend

Edwin F. Parry

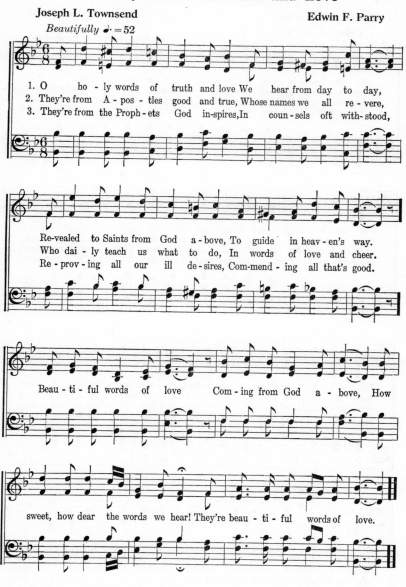

1. O ho - ly words of truth and love We hear from day to day,
2. They're from A - pos - tles good and true, Whose names we all re - vere,
3. They're from the Proph - ets God in-spires, In coun - sels oft with-stood,

Re-vealed to Saints from God a - bove, To guide in heav - en's way.
Who dai - ly teach us what to do, In words of love and cheer.
Re - prov - ing all our ill de - sires, Com-mend - ing all that's good.

Beau - ti - ful words of love Com - ing from God a - bove, How

sweet, how dear the words we hear! They're beau - ti - ful words of love.

4. And from each chosen one that speaks
   By aid the Spirit gives,
For every sphere of life it seeks,
   For every one that lives.

5. As gems of wisdom, pure and bright,
   That glow with lustrous ray,
We'll seek to gain these words of light,
   Their counsels to obey.

136   Oh, How Lovely Was the Morning

George Manwaring   A. C. Smyth

Cheerfully ♩ = 84

1. Oh, how love-ly was the morn-ing! Ra-diant beamed the sun a-bove.
2. Hum-bly kneel-ing, sweet ap-peal-ing—'Twas the boy's first ut-tered prayer—
3. Sud-den-ly a light de-scend-ed, Bright-er far than noon-day sun,
4. "Jo-seph, this is my be-lov-ed; Hear him!" Oh, how sweet the word!

Bees were hum-ming, sweet birds sing-ing, Mu-sic ring-ing through the grove,
When the powers of sin as-sail-ing Filled his soul with deep de-spair;
And a shin-ing glo-rious pil-lar O'er him fell, a-round him shone,
Jo-seph's hum-ble prayer was an-swered, And he list-ened to the Lord.

When with-in the shad-y wood-land Jos-eph sought the God of love;
But un-daunt-ed still, he trust-ed In his heaven-ly Fa-ther's care;
While ap-peared two heaven-ly be-ings, God the Fa-ther and the Son;
Oh, what rap-ture filled his bos-om, For he saw the liv-ing God;

When with-in the shad-y wood-land, Jos-eph sought the God of love.
But un-daunt-ed, still he trust-ed In his heaven-ly Fa-ther's care.
While ap-peared two heaven-ly be-ings, God the Fa-ther and the Son.
Oh, what rap-ture filled his bos-om, For he saw the liv-ing God.

137 Oh Give Me Back My Prophet Dear

John Taylor

George Careless

Pleadingly ♩ = 72

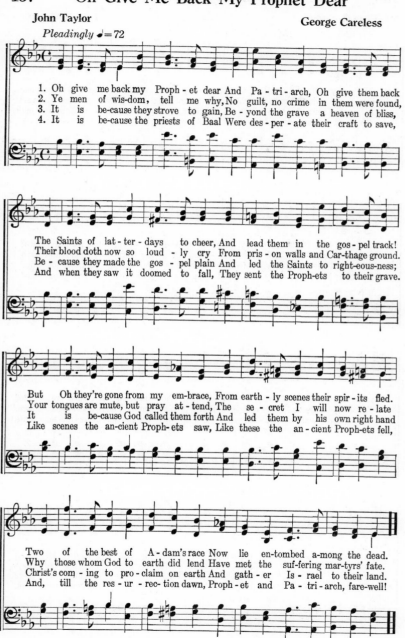

1. Oh give me back my Proph - et dear And Pa - tri - arch, Oh give them back
2. Ye men of wis-dom, tell me why, No guilt, no crime in them were found,
3. It is be-cause they strove to gain, Be - yond the grave a heaven of bliss,
4. It is be-cause the priests of Baal Were des - per - ate their craft to save,

The Saints of lat - ter - days to cheer, And lead them in the gos - pel track!
Their blood doth now so loud - ly cry From pris - on walls and Car-thage ground.
Be - cause they made the gos - pel plain And led the Saints to right-eous-ness;
And when they saw it doomed to fall, They sent the Proph-ets to their grave.

But Oh they're gone from my em - brace, From earth - ly scenes their spir - its fled.
Your tongues are mute, but pray at - tend, The se - cret I will now re - late
It is be-cause God called them forth And led them by his own right hand
Like scenes the an-cient Proph-ets saw, Like these the an - cient Proph-ets fell,

Two of the best of A - dam's race Now lie en-tombed a-mong the dead.
Why those whom God to earth did lend Have met the suf-fering mar-tyrs' fate.
Christ's com - ing to pro - claim on earth And gath - er Is - rael to their land.
And, till the res - ur - rec - tion dawn, Proph-et and Pa - tri - arch, fare-well!

138 O My Father

Eliza R. Snow **Lowell Mason**

With contemplation ♩ = 58

1. O my Fa - ther, thou that dwell - est In the high and glo - rious place,
2. For a wise and glo - rious pur - pose Thou hast placed me here on earth,
3. I had learned to call thee Fa - ther, Through thy Spir - it from on high,
4. When I leave this frail ex - ist - ence, When I lay this mor - tal by,

When shall I re - gain thy pres - ence, And a - gain be - hold thy face?
And with - held the rec - ol - lec - tion Of my form - er friends and birth.
But un - til the key of know - ledge Was re - stored, I knew not why.
Fa - ther, Moth - er, may I meet you In your roy - al courts on high?

In thy ho - ly hab - i - ta - tion, Did my spir - it once re - side?
Yet oft - times a se - cret some - thing Whis - pered, "You're a stran - ger here;"
In the heavens are par - ents sin - gle? No; the thought makes rea - son stare!
Then, at length, when I've com - plet - ed All you sent me forth to do,

In my first prim - e - val child - hood, Was I nur - tured near thy side?
And I felt that I had wan - dered From a more ex - alt - ed sphere.
Truth is rea - son, truth e - ter - nal Tells me I've a moth - er there.
With your mu - tual ap - pro - ba - tion Let me come and dwell with you.

139

O My Father
(Familiar Tune)

Eliza R. Snow

James McGranahan

With contemplation ♩.= 42

1. O my Fa - ther, thou that dwell-est In the high and glo-rious place,
2. For a wise and glo-rious pur-pose Thou hast placed me here on earth,
3. I had learned to call thee Fa-ther, Through thy Spir-it from on high;
4. When I leave this frail ex - ist-ence, When I lay this mor-tal by,

When shall I re - gain thy pres-ence, And a - gain be - hold thy face?
And with-held the rec - ol - lec - tion Of my form - er friends and birth,
But un - til the key of knowl-edge Was re - stored, I knew not why.
Fa - ther, Moth-er, may I meet you In your roy - al courts on high?

In thy ho - ly hab - i - ta - tion, Did my spir - it once re - side?
Yet oft - times a se - cret some-thing Whis-pered,"You're a stran-ger here;"
In the heavens are par-ents sin - gle? No; the thought makes rea-son stare!
Then, at length, when I've com-plet - ed All you sent me forth to do,

In thy ho-ly hab - i - ta - tion, Did my spir-it once re - side?

In my first pri - me-val child-hood, Was I nur - tured near thy side?
And I felt that I had wan-dered From a more ex - alt - ed sphere.
Truth is rea - son, truth e - ter - nal Tells me I've a moth - er there.
With your mu - tual ap-pro - ba - tion Let me come and dwell with you.

In my first pri-me-val child-hood, Was I nur-tured near thy side?

Land of the Mountains High

Evan Stephens

Patriotically ♩ = 72

1. Land of the moun-tains high, U - tah, we love thee!
2. Co - lum-bia's new - est star,* U - tah, we love thee!
3. Land of the pi - o - neers, U - tah, we love thee!

Land of the sun - ny sky, U - tah, we love thee!
Thy lus - tre shines a - far; U - tah, we love thee!
Grow with the com - ing years, U - tah, we love thee!

Far in the glo - rious west, Throned on the moun-tains' crest,
Bright in our ban - ner's blue, A - mong her sis - ters true,
With wealth and peace in store, To fame and glo - ry soar,

In robes of state - hood dressed, U - tah, we love thee!
She proud - ly comes to view; U - tah, we love thee!
God - guard - ed ev - er - more, U - tah, we love thee!

* This hymn was specially written to commemorate Utah's statehood when she became the "newest" star.

141   Lead Me Into Life Eternal

John A. Widtsoe

Alexander Schreiner

Stately ♩=108

1. Lead me in - to life e - ter - nal By the gos - pel's ho - ly call;
2. Fa - ther, all my heart I give thee; All my ser - vice shall be thine;
3. Hear me as I pray in meek-ness; Let my strength be as thy day;

Let thy prom-ise rest up - on me; Grant me read - y strength for all.
Guide me as I search in weak-ness. Let thy lov - ing light be mine.
Give me faith, the great - er know-ledge; Fa - ther, bless me as I pray.

142   Lord, We Come Before Thee Now

Wm. Hammond

Harry A. Dean

Prayerfully ♩=66

1. Lord, we come be - fore thee now; At thy feet we hum - bly bow;
2. In thine own ap - point-ed way, Now we seek thee; here we stay;
3. Send some mes-sage from thy word That may joy and peace af - ford;
4. Grant we all may seek and find Thee, our gra-cious God and kind;

Do not thou our suit dis - dain; Shall we seek thee, Lord, in vain?
Lord, from hence we would not go, Till a bless - ing thou be - stow.
Com - fort those who weep and mourn; Let "the time of love" re - turn.
Heal the sick, the cap - tive free, Let us all re - joice in thee.

Words of this hymn may be sung to music of hymn No. 162.

143 Oh Say, What Is Truth?

John Jaques   Ellen Knowles Melling

Sturdily ♩=76

1. Oh say, what is truth? 'Tis the fair-est gem That the rich-es of worlds can pro-duce, And price-less the val-ue of truth will be when The proud mon-arch's cost-li-est di-a-dem Is count-ed but dross and ref-use.

2. Yes, say, what is truth? 'Tis the bright-est prize To which mor-tals or Gods can as-pire; Go search in the depths where it glit-ter-ing lies Or as-cend in pur-suit to the loft-iest skies. 'Tis an aim for the no-blest de-sire.

3. The scep-tre may fall from the des-pot's grasp When with winds of stern jus-tice he copes, But the pil-lar of truth will en-dure to the last, And its firm root-ed bul-warks out-stand the rude blast, And the wreck of the fell ty-rant's hopes.

4. Then say, what is truth? 'Tis the last and the first, For the lim-its of time it steps o'er. Though the heav-ens de-part and the earth's foun-tains burst, Truth, the sum of ex-ist-ence, will weath-er the worst, E-ter-nal, un-changed, ev-er-more.

144 Our Mountain Home So Dear

Emmeline B. Wells

Evan Stephens

With simplicity ♩=88

1. Our moun-tain home so dear, Where crys-tal wa-ters clear
2. We'll roam the ver-dant hills, And by the spark-ling rills
3. In syl-van depth and shade, In for-est and in glade,
4. The stream-let, flower, and sod Be-speak the works of God;

Flow ev-er free, Flow ev-er free: While through the val-leys wide
Pluck the wild flowers, Pluck the wild flowers; The fra-grance on the air,
Wher-e'er we pass, Wher-e'er we pass, The hand of God we see,
And all com-bine, And all com-bine, With most trans-port-ing grace,

The flowers on ev-ery side, Bloom-ing in state-ly pride, Are fair to see.
The land-scape bright and fair, And sun-shine ev-ery-where, Make pleas-ant hours.
In leaf and bud and tree, Or bird or hum-ming bee, Or blade of grass.
His hand-i-work to trace, Through na-ture's smil-ing face, In art di-vine.

144-A Our God, We Raise to Thee

Alternate words by B. Snow

1. Our God, we raise to thee
Thanks for thy blessings free
We here enjoy,
We here enjoy.
In this far western land,
A true and chosen band,
Led hither by thy hand,
We sing for joy.

2. Bless thou our prophet dear;
May health and comfort cheer
His noble heart,
His noble heart;
His words with fire impress
On souls that thou wilt bless
To choose in righteousness,
The better part.

3. So shall thy Kingdom spread
As by thy prophets said,
From sea to sea,
From sea to sea;
As one united whole
Truth burns in every soul,
While hastening to the goal
We long to see.

4. Oh, may thy Saints be one,
Like Father and the Son,
Nor disagree,
Nor disagree.
United heart and hand,
So may they ever stand,
A firm and valiant band,
Eternally.

145 O Ye Mountains High

Charles W. Penrose

Brightly ♩ = 69

1. O ye moun-tains high, where the clear blue sky Arch-es
2. Though the great and the wise all thy beau-ties de-spise, To the
3. In thy moun-tain re-treat, God will strength-en thy feet; With-out
4. Here our voic-es we'll raise, and we'll sing to thy praise, Sa-cred

o-ver the vales of the free, Where the pure breez-es blow and the
hum-ble and pure thou art dear; Though the haugh-ty may smile and the
fear of thy foes thou shalt tread; And their sil-ver and gold, as the
home of the proph-ets of God; Thy de-liv-erance is nigh; thy op-

clear stream-lets flow, How I've longed to your bos-om to flee!
wick-ed re-vile, Yet we love thy glad ti-dings to hear.
Proph-ets have told, Shall be brought to a-dorn thy fair head.
press-ors shall die; And thy land shall be free-dom's a-bode.

O Zi-on! dear Zi-on! land of the free, Now my own moun-tain
O Zi-on! dear Zi-on! home of the free, Though thou wert forced to
O Zi-on! dear Zi-on! home of the free, Soon thy tow-ers shall
O Zi-on! dear Zi-on! land of the free, In thy tem-ples we'll

O Ye Mountains High

home, un-to thee I have come, All my fond hopes are cen-tered in thee.
fly to thy cham-bers on high, Yet we'll share joy and sor-row with thee.
shine with a splen-dor di-vine, And e-ter-nal thy glo-ry shall be.
bend, all thy rights we'll de-fend; And our home shall be ev-er with thee.

146 How Wondrous and Great

Henry U. Onderdonk

J. Michael Haydn

With dignity ♩ = 76

1. How won-drous and great Thy works, God of praise! How
2. To na-tions long dark Thy light shall be shown; Their

just, King of Saints, And true are thy ways! O
wor-ship and vows Shall come to thy throne; Thy

who shall not fear thee, And hon-or thy name? Thou
truth and thy judg-ments Shall spread all a-broad, Till

on-ly art ho-ly, Thou on-ly su-preme.
earth's ev-ery peo-ple Con-fess thee their God.

147 Praise to the Man

William W. Phelps

Brightly ♩ = 76

1. Praise to the man who com-muned with Je-ho-vah! Je-sus a-
2. Praise to his mem-ory, he died as a mar-tyr; Hon-ored and
3. Great is his glo-ry and end-less his priest-hood. Ev-er and
4. Sac-ri-fice brings forth the bless-ings of heav-en; Earth must a-

noint-ed that Proph-et and Seer. Bless-ed to o-pen the
blest be his ev-er great name! Long shall his blood, which was
ev-er the keys he will hold. Faith-ful and true, he will
tone for the blood of that man. Wake up the world for the

last dis-pen-sa-tion, Kings shall ex-tol him, and na-tions re-vere.
shed by as-sas-sins, Plead un-to heaven while the earth lauds his fame.
en-ter his king-dom, Crowned in the midst of the proph-ets of old.
con-flict of jus-tice. Mil-lions shall know "broth-er Jos-eph" a-gain.

Hail to the Proph-et, as-cend-ed to heav-en! Trait-ors and

Praise to the Man

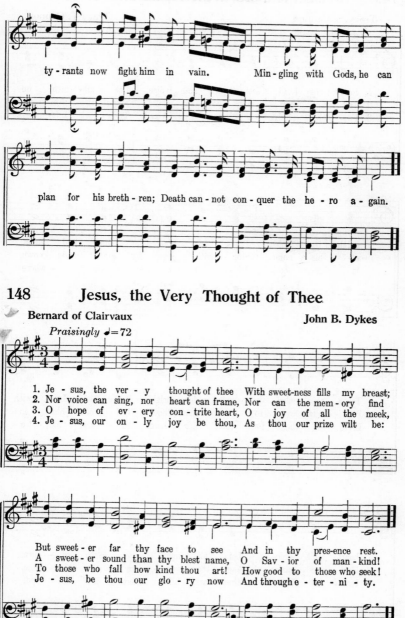

ty - rants now fight him in vain. Min - gling with Gods, he can

plan for his breth - ren; Death can - not con - quer the he - ro a - gain.

148   Jesus, the Very Thought of Thee

Bernard of Clairvaux

John B. Dykes

Praisingly ♩=72

1. Je - sus, the ver - y thought of thee With sweet-ness fills my breast;
2. Nor voice can sing, nor heart can frame, Nor can the mem - ory find
3. O hope of ev - ery con - trite heart, O joy of all the meek,
4. Je - sus, our on - ly joy be thou, As thou our prize wilt be:

But sweet - er far thy face to see And in thy pres-ence rest.
A sweet - er sound than thy blest name, O Sav - ior of man - kind!
To those who fall how kind thou art! How good to those who seek!
Je - sus, be thou our glo - ry now And through e - ter - ni - ty.

149 Praise the Lord With Heart and Voice

Tracy Y. Cannon

Tracy Y. Cannon

Joyfully ♩ = 96

1. Praise the Lord with heart and voice. Let all men on earth re - joice. Praise to him for life and light, Truth re - vealed in splen - dor bright! Praise the Lord with heart and voice. Let all men on earth re - joice.

2. Tell of him in loud ac - claim. Sing the won - ders of his name. Sing with joy for grace made known, Won - drous love to all men shown. Tell of him in loud ac - claim. Sing the won - ders of his name.

3. Fa - ther, God, e - ter - nal Friend, Thou art Life; there is no end. All cre - a - tion ev - ery - where Lives in thee, for thou art there. Fa - ther, God, e - ter - nal Friend, thou art Life; there is no end.

150 Praise to the Lord

Joachim Neander

Joyfully with dignity ♩=100

1. Praise to the Lord, the Al-might-y, the King of cre-a-tion; O my soul, praise him, for he is thy health and sal-va-tion; Join the great throng, Psal-ter-y, or-gan, and song, Sound-ing in glad ad-o-ra-tion.

2. Praise to the Lord! o-ver all things he glo-rious-ly reign-eth. Borne as on ea-gle wings, safe-ly his Saints he sus-tain-eth. Hast thou not seen How all thou need-est hath been Grant-ed in what he or-dain-eth?

3. Praise to the Lord, who doth pros-per thy way and de-fend thee. Sure-ly his good-ness and mer-cy shall ev-er at-tend thee. Pon-der a-new What the Al-might-y can do, Who with his love doth be-friend thee.

4. Praise to the Lord! O let all that is in me a-dore him! All that hath breath join with A-bra-ham's seed to a-dore him! Let the "A-men" Sum all our prais-es a-gain Now as we wor-ship be-fore him.

151 Rejoice, the Lord Is King

Charles Wesley   **Horatio Parker**

With vigor ♩=100

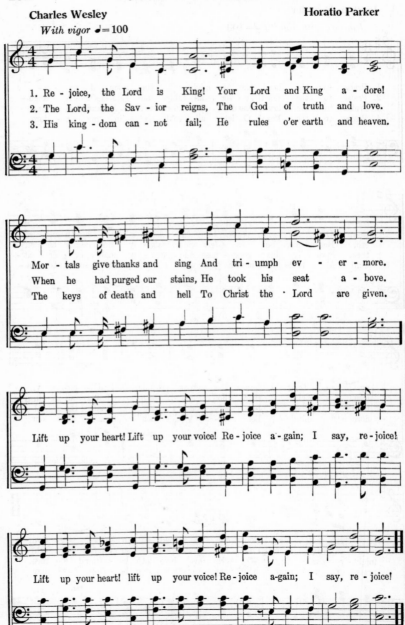

1. Re - joice, the Lord is King! Your Lord and King a - dore!
2. The Lord, the Sav - ior reigns, The God of truth and love.
3. His king - dom can - not fail; He rules o'er earth and heaven.

Mor - tals give thanks and sing And tri - umph ev - er - more.
When he had purged our stains, He took his seat a - bove.
The keys of death and hell To Christ the Lord are given.

Lift up your heart! Lift up your voice! Re - joice a - gain; I say, re - joice!

Lift up your heart! lift up your voice! Re - joice a - gain; I say, re - joice!

O Sons of Zion

Ed M. Rowe

Robert P. Manookin

With elation ♩=100

1. O sons of Zi - on, hear the voice Of him from courts on high.
2. En - treat the Lord in hum-ble prayer That all the sons of men
3. Be - hold, the glo - ry of the Lord Sets Zi - on's mount a - glow,

Pre - pare the path - way of the Lord; His reign on earth is nigh.
His right - eous king - dom will re - ceive And shout the glad "A - men".
For Zi - on is an en - sign pure; All na - tions to her flow.

Pre - pare the sup - per of the Lamb; In - vite the world to dine;
The sa - cred keys you now pos - sess; De - clare the gos - pel plan;
O sons of Zi - on, tread the paths Your faith-ful fa - thers trod;

Be - hold the might - y Bride-groom comes In maj - es - ty di - vine.
Make known the won - drous words of truth Re - vealed a - gain to man.
Lift up your hearts in grat - i - tude And serve the liv - ing God!

153   A Poor Wayfaring Man of Grief

Montgomery

Peacefully ♪=96

1. A poor way-far-ing Man of grief Hath of-ten crossed me on my way, Who sued so hum-bly for re-lief That I could nev-er an-swer, Nay. I had not power to ask his name, Where-to he went, or whence he came; Yet there was

2. Once, when my scant-y meal was spread, He en-tered, not a word he spake; Just per-ish-ing for want of bread, I gave him all; he blessed it, brake, And ate, but gave me part a-gain; Mine was an an-gel's por-tion then, For while I

3. I spied him where a foun-tain burst Clear from the rock; his strength was gone; The heed-less wa-ter mocked his thirst; He heard it, saw it, hurry-ing on. I ran and raised the suf-fer-er up; Thrice from the stream he drained my cup, Dipped and re-

A Poor Wayfaring Man of Grief

some-thing in his eye That won my love; I knew not why.
fed with ea - ger haste, The crust was man - na to my taste.
turned it run - ning o'er; I drank and nev - er thirst-ed more.

4. 'Twas night; the floods were out; it blew
   A winter hurricane aloof;
   I heard his voice abroad and flew
   To bid him welcome to my roof.
   I warmed and clothed and cheered my guest,
   And laid him on my couch to rest,
   Then made the earth my bed, and seemed
   In Eden's garden while I dreamed.

5. Stript, wounded, beaten nigh to death,
   I found him by the highway side;
   I roused his pulse, brought back his breath,
   Revived his spirit, and supplied
   Wine, oil, refreshment—he was healed;
   I had myself a wound concealed,
   But from that hour forgot the smart,
   And peace bound up my broken heart.

6. In prison I saw him next, condemned
   To meet a traitor's doom at morn;
   The tide of lying tongues I stemmed,
   And honored him 'mid shame and scorn.
   My friendship's utmost zeal to try,
   He asked if I for him would die;
   The flesh was weak; my blood ran chill;
   But the free spirit cried, "I will!"

7. Then in a moment to my view
   The stranger started from disguise;
   The tokens in his hands I knew;
   The Savior stood before mine eyes.
   He spake, and my poor name he named,
   "Of me thou hast not been ashamed;
   These deeds shall thy memorial be,
   Fear not, thou didst them unto me."

154   Raise Your Voices to the Lord

Evan Stephens   Evan Stephens

With dignity ♩=69

1. Raise your voic - es to the Lord, Ye who here have heard his word;
2. Shout thanks-giv - ing! let our song Still our joy and praise pro - long,

As we part his praise pro-claim, Shout thanks-giv - ing to his name.
Un - til here we meet a - gain To re - new the glad re - frain.

155 Savior, Redeemer of My Soul

Orson F. Whitney

Harry A. Dean

With devotion ♩=96

1. Sav - ior, Re - deem - er of my soul, Whose might-y hand hath
2. Nev - er can I re - pay thee, Lord; But I can love thee.
3. O'er - rule mine acts to serve thine ends; Change frown-ing foes to

made me whole, Whose won -drous power hath raised me up
Thy pure word, Hath it not been my one de - light,
smil - ing friends; Chas - ten my soul till I shall be

And filled with sweet my bit - ter cup! What tongue my grat - i -
My joy by day, my dream by night? Then let my lips pro -
In per - fect har - mo - ny with thee. Make me more wor - thy

tude can tell, O gra - cious God of Is - ra - el.
claim it still, And all my life re - flect thy will.
of thy love, And fit me for the life a - bove.

Shall We Meet

Horace L. Hastings

Elihu S. Rice

Happily ♩=69

1. Shall we meet be-yond the riv - er, Where the surg - es cease to roll,
2. Shall we meet in that blest har - bor, When our storm - y voyage is o'er?
3. Shall we meet in yon - der cit - y, Where the towers of crys - tal shine,
4. Shall we meet with Christ our Sav - ior, When he comes to claim his own?

Where in all the bright for - ev - er, Sor - row ne'er shall press the soul?
Shall we meet and cast the an - chor By the fair ce - les - tial shore?
Where the walls are all of jas - per, Built by work - man-ship di - vine?
Shall we know his bless - ed fa - vor, And sit down up - on his throne?

We shall meet, we shall meet, We shall meet be-yond the riv - er;

We shall meet be-yond the riv - er Where the surg - es cease to roll.

157   Shall the Youth of Zion Falter?

Evan Stephens   Evan Stephens

Firm march time ♩=100

1. Shall the youth of Zi - on fal - ter In de-fend-ing truth and right?
2. While we know the powers of dark-ness Seek to thwart the work of God,
3. We will work out our sal - va - tion; We will cleave un - to the truth;
4. We will strive to be found wor-thy Of the king-dom of our Lord,

While the en - e - my as - sail - eth, Shall we shrink or shun the fight? No!
Shall the chil-dren of the prom - ise Cease to grasp the "i - ron rod"? No!
We will watch and pray and la - bor With the fer - vent zeal of youth. Yes!
With the faith-ful ones re - deem - ed, Who have loved and kept his word. Yes!

True to the faith that our par - ents have cher - ished, True to the

Organ accomp.

Pedal obbligato

Shall the Youth of Zion Falter?

truth   for which mar-tyrs   have per-ished, To God's com-mand,

Soul, heart, and   hand,   Faith-ful and true   we will   ev-   er   stand.

158

Sing Praise to Him

From the Bohemian Brethren's
Song Book

Johann J. Schultz

With dignity ♩=60

1. Sing praise to him who reigns a-bove, The Lord of all cre-
2. What his al-might-y power hath made, His gra-cious mer-cy
3. The Lord is nev-er far a-way, But through all grief dis-
4. Thus, all my toil-some way a-long, I sing a-loud thy

a - tion, The source of power, the fount of love, The
keep - eth. By morn-ing glow or ev-ening shade His
tress - ing, An ev-er-pres-ent help and stay, Our
prais - es, That men may hear the grate-ful song My

rock of our sal - va-tion. With heal-ing balm my soul he fills,
watch-ful eye ne'er sleep-eth. With-in the king-dom of his might,
peace and joy and bless-ing. As with a moth-er's ten-der hand,
voice un-wea-ried rais-es. Be joy-ful in the Lord, my heart!

And ev-ery faith-less mur-mur stills. To him all praise and glo-ry!
Lo! all is just and all is right. To him all praise and glo-ry!
He leads his own, his cho-sen band. To him all praise and glo-ry!
Both soul and bod-y bear your part. To him all praise and glo-ry!

159 Should You Feel Inclined to Censure

Philip Paul Bliss

With great feeling ♩= 66

1. Should you feel in-clined to cen-sure Faults you may in
2. Do not, then, in i-dle pleas-ure, Tri-fle with a

oth-ers view, Ask your own heart, ere you ven-ture, If that
broth-er's fame; Guard it as a val-ued treas-ure, Sa-cred

has not fail-ings, too. Let not friend-ly vows be
as your own good name. Do not form o-pin-ions

bro-ken; Rath-er strive a friend to gain; Many a
blind-ly. Has-ti-ness to trou-ble tends; Those of

word in an-ger spo-ken Finds its pas-sage home a-gain.
whom we thought un-kind-ly, Oft be-come our warm-est friends.

160

Silent Night

Joseph Mohr

Franz Gruber

Quietly ♪ = 112
mp

1. Si - lent night! Ho - ly night! All is calm; all is bright
2. Si - lent night! Ho - ly night! Shep - herds quake at the sight!
3. Si - lent night! Ho - ly night! Son of God, love's pure light

Round yon vir - gin moth - er and Child, Ho - ly In - fant, so ten - der and
Glo - ries stream from heav - en a - far; Heaven-ly hosts sing Al - le - lu -
Ra - diant beams from thy ho - ly face, With the dawn of re - deem - ing

mild. Sleep in heav - en - ly peace; Sleep in heav - en - ly peace;
ia; Christ, the Sav - ior, is born! Christ, the Sav - ior, is born!
grace, Je - sus, Lord, at thy birth, Je - sus, Lord, at thy birth.

161

Sing We Now at Parting

George Manwaring

Ebenezer Beesley

Reverently ♩ = 72

1. Sing we now at part - ing One more strain of praise. To our heaven-ly
2. Praise him for his mer - cy; Praise him for his love; For un - num-bered
3. Je - sus, our Re - deem - er, Now our prais - es hear; While we bow be -

Sing We Now at Parting

Fa - ther Sweet-est songs we'll raise. For his lov - ing kind - ness,
bless-ings Praise the Lord a - bove. Let our hap - py voic - es
fore thee, Lend a list - ening ear. Save us, Lord, from er - ror;

For his ten - der care, Let our songs of glad - ness Rend this Sab-bath air.
Still the notes pro - long; One a - lone is wor - thy Of our sweet-est song.
Watch us day by day; Help us now to serve thee In a pleas-ing way.

162   Softly Now the Light of Day

George W. Doane

C. M. von Weber

Reverently ♩ = 58
mp

Soft - ly now the light of day Fades up - on my sight a - way.

Free from care, from la - bor free, Lord, I would com-mune with thee.

Words of this hymn may be sung to music of hymn No. 142.

163 Sons of Michael, He Approaches

Edward L. T. Harrison

Charles J. Thomas

Triumphantly ♩ = 92

1. Sons of Mi-chael, he ap-proach-es! Rise, the an-cient Fa-ther
2. Sons of Mi-chael, 'tis his char-iot Rolls its burn-ing wheels a-
3. Moth-er of our gen-er-a-tions, Glo-rious by great Mi-chael's
4. Raise a cho-rus, sons of Mi-chael, Like old O-cean's roar-ing

greet; Bow, ye thou-sands, low be-fore him; Min-is-ter be-
long! Raise a-loft your voic-es mil-lion In a tor-rent
side, Take thy chil-dren's ad-o-ra-tion; End-less with thy
swell, Till the might-y ac-cla-ma-tion Through re-bound-ing

fore his feet; Hail, hail the Pa-tri-arch's glad reign, Hail,
power of song: Hail, hail our Head with mu-sic soft! Hail,
Lord pre-side; Lo, lo, to greet thee now ad-vance, Lo,
space doth tell That, that the An-cient One doth reign, That,

hail the Pa-tri-arch's glad reign, Spread-ing o-ver sea and main.
hail our Head with mu-sic soft! Raise sweet mel-o-dies a-loft!
lo, to greet thee now ad-vance Thou-sands in the glo-rious dance!
that the An-cient One may reign In his Par-a-dise a-gain!

164 Stars of Morning, Shout for Joy

Thomas Durham

1. Stars of morn - ing, shout for joy; Sing re - demp - tion's
2. E - thi - o - pia, stretch thy hand! Come, ye tribes of
3. Bend thy bow, and come, good Lord; Send thy Spir - it
4. My be - liev - ing spir - it fill; Faith de - mands, it

mys - te - ry. Ho - ly, ho - ly, ho - ly, cry;
ev - ery land, Count - less as the o - cean's sand!
with thy word; Be thy sav - ing work re - stored,
is thy will; All things now are pos - si - ble;

Ho - ly, ho - ly, ho - ly cry, And praise the Lamb!
Count - less as the o - cean's sand! To praise the Lamb.
Be thy sav - ing work re - stored, Thou bleed - ing Lamb.
All things now are pos - si - ble; It shall be done.

5. Thus may we each moment feel;
   Love him, serve him, praise him still,
   Till we meet on Zion's hill,
   Till we meet on Zion's hill,
   To praise the Lamb.

6. Savior, let thy kingdom come;
   Now the man of sin consume,
   Bring the blest millennium,
   Bring the blest millennium,
   Exalted Lamb!

165   O Little Town of Bethlehem

Phillips Brooks   **Lewis H. Redner**

Simply ♩=96

1. O little town of Bethlehem, How still we see thee lie.
2. For Christ is born of Mary; And gathered all above,
3. How silently, how silently, The wondrous gift is given!

Above thy deep and dreamless sleep The silent stars go by;
While mortals sleep, the angels keep Their watch of wondering love.
So God imparts to human hearts The blessings of his heaven.

Yet in the dark streets shineth The everlasting Light.
O morning stars, together Proclaim the holy birth;
No ear may hear his coming; But in this world of sin,

The hopes and fears of all the years Are met in thee tonight.
And praises sing to God the King, And peace to men on earth.
Where meek souls will receive him, still The dear Christ enters in.

166 Sweet Hour of Prayer

W. W. Walford
William B. Bradbury

Fervently ♩.=44
mp

1. Sweet hour of prayer! sweet hour of prayer! That calls me from a world of care,
2. Sweet hour of prayer! sweet hour of prayer! Thy wings shall my pe - ti - tion bear

And bids me at my Fa-ther's throne Make all my wants and wish - es known.
To him whose truth and faith - ful-ness En - gage the wait - ing soul to bless.

In sea - sons of dis - tress and grief My soul has oft - en found re - lief
And since he bids me seek his face, Be - lieve his word, and trust his grace,

And oft es-caped the tempt -er's snare By thy re - turn, sweet hour of prayer!
I'll cast on him my ev - er - y care, And wait for thee, sweet hour of prayer!

And oft es-caped the temp - ter's snare By thy re - turn, sweet hour of prayer!
I'll cast on him my ev - ery care, And wait for thee, sweet hour of prayer!

167 Take Courage, Saints, and Faint Not by the Way

James Crystal

Frank W. Asper

Hopefully ♩=69

1. Take cour - age, Saints, and faint not by the way, Though storm clouds
2. The dark - est hour is just be - fore the dawn; Yet who shall
3. 'Tis meet that some should now and then be left To blind - ly
4. No vain a - spir - ing can the soul af - ford; God's search - ing

thick and fast be hov-ering nigh; The sun pro - claims the
doubt the fast ap- proach-ing morn? Or when we see the
grope in life's se - ques-tered shade, To feel their breast of
eyes will ev - ery vice as - sail: The wrong must per - ish

glo - ry of the day, Be - hind the clouds as in the cloud-less sky.
snow-clad hedge and lawn, Who dares to say that spring will ne'er re - turn?
life and hope be - reft, Till all their sins are on the al - tar laid.
like the mis - er's hoard Or as the chaff be - fore the pass - ing gale.

5. God knows the proper path to lead us in.
    And what is best that we should do and know
   To win the victory over death and sin,
    And fit us for the reign of peace below.

6. Let not the heart be sad at trials here,
    But sense how e'en the Savior suffered ill;
   He bore the cruel thorn, the galling spear,
    To glorify his Father's holy will.

168 Sweet Is the Work, My God, My King

Isaac Watts

John J. McClellan

Worshipfully ♩=84

1. Sweet is the work, my God, my King, To praise thy
2. Sweet is the day of sa - cred rest. No mor - tal
3. My heart shall tri - umph in my Lord And bless his
4. But, oh, what tri - umph shall I raise To thy dear

name, give thanks and sing, To show thy love by
care shall seize my breast. O may my heart in
works and bless his word. Thy works of grace, how
name through end - less days, When in the realms of

morn - ing light And talk of all thy truths at night.
tune be found Like Da - vid's harp of sol - emn sound!
bright they shine! How deep thy coun - sels, how di - vine!
joy I see Thy face in full fe - lic - i - ty.

5. Sin, my worst enemy before,
Shall vex my eyes and ears no more.
My inward foes shall all be slain
Nor Satan break my peace again.

6. Then shall I see and hear and know
All I desired and wished below,
And every power find sweet employ
In that eternal world of joy.

There Is Beauty All Around

Fervently ♩=88

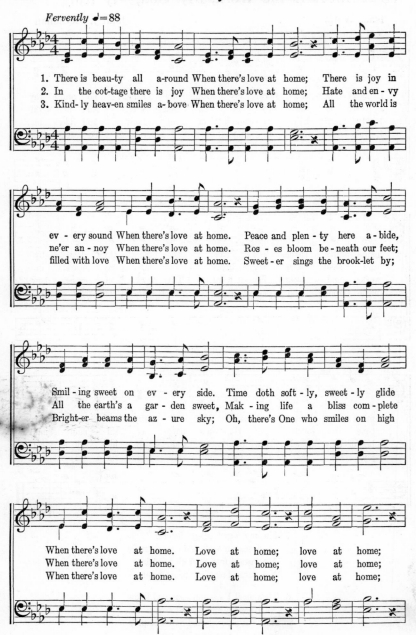

1. There is beau-ty all a-round When there's love at home; There is joy in
2. In the cot-tage there is joy When there's love at home; Hate and en-vy
3. Kind-ly heav-en smiles a-bove When there's love at home; All the world is

ev - ery sound When there's love at home. Peace and plen-ty here a-bide,
ne'er an-noy When there's love at home. Ros - es bloom be-neath our feet;
filled with love When there's love at home. Sweet-er sings the brook-let by;

Smil - ing sweet on ev - ery side. Time doth soft - ly, sweet-ly glide
All the earth's a gar - den sweet, Mak - ing life a bliss com-plete
Bright-er beams the az - ure sky; Oh, there's One who smiles on high

When there's love at home. Love at home; love at home;
When there's love at home. Love at home; love at home;
When there's love at home. Love at home; love at home;

There Is Beauty All Around

Time doth soft - ly, sweet - ly glide When there's love at home.
Mak - ing life a bliss com - plete When there's love at home.
Oh, there's One who smiles on high When there's love at home.

170 Dearest Children, God is Near You

C. L. Walker

J. M. Macfarlane

Not too loud ♩=92

1. Dear - est chil - dren, God is near you Watch - ing o'er you day and night,
2. Dear - est chil - dren, ho - ly an - gels Watch your ac - tions night and day;
3. Chil - dren, God de - lights to teach you By his Ho - ly Spir - it's voice;

And de - lights to own and bless you, If you strive to do what's right.
And they keep a faith - ful rec - ord Of the good and bad you say.
Quick - ly heed its ho - ly prompt - ings, Day by day you'll then re - joice.

He will bless you, He will bless you, If you put your trust in him.
Cher - ish vir - tue! Cher - ish vir - tue! God will bless the pure in heart.
O prove faith - ful, O prove faith - ful To your God and Zi - on's cause.

Now to Heaven Our Prayer

W. G. Hickson

Firmly ♩ = 72

1. Now to heaven our prayer as-cend-ing, God speed the right;
2. Be that prayer a-gain re-peat-ed, God speed the right;
3. Pa-tient, firm, and per-se-ver-ing, God speed the right;

In a no-ble cause con-tend-ing, God speed the right.
Ne'er de-spair-ing, though de-feat-ed, God speed the right.
Ne'er th'e-vent nor dan-ger fear-ing, God speed the right.

Be our zeal in heaven re-cord-ed, With suc-cess on
Like the great and good in sto-ry, If we fail, we
Pains, nor toils, nor tri-als heed-ing, And in heaven's good

earth re-ward-ed, God speed the right, God speed the right.
fail with glo-ry, God speed the right, God speed the right.
time suc-ceed-ing, God speed the right, God speed the right.

172 There Is an Hour of Peace and Rest

H. H. Petersen

1. There is an hour of peace and rest, Un-marred by earth-ly care;
2. The straight and nar-row way to heaven, Where an-gels bright and fair
3. When sail-ing on life's storm-y sea, 'Mid bil-lows of de-spair,
4. When thorns are strewn a-long my path, And foes my feet en-snare,

'Tis when be-fore the Lord I go, And kneel in se-cret prayer.
Are sing-ing to God's praise, is found Through con-stant se-cret prayer.
'Tis sol-ace to my soul to know God hears my se-cret prayer.
My Sav-ior to my aid will come, If sought in se-cret prayer.

May my heart be turned to pray, Pray in se-cret day by day,

May my heart be turned to pray, Pray in se-cret day by day,

That this boon to mor-tals given, May u-nite my soul with heaven.

That this boon to mor-tals given,

173 They the Builders of the Nation

Ida R. Alldredge · **Alfred M. Durham**

With spirit ♩=100

1. They the build-ers of the na-tion, Blaz-ing trails a-long the way;
2. Ser-vice ev-er was their watch-cry; Love be-came their guid-ing star;
3. As an en-sign to the na-tion, They un-furled the flag of truth,

Step-ping stones for gen-er-a-tions, Were their deeds of ev-ery day.
Cour-age, their un-fail-ing bea-con, Ra-di-at-ing near and far.
Pil-lar, guide, and in-spi-ra-tion To the hosts of wait-ing youth;

Build-ing new and firm foun-da-tions, Push-ing on the wild fron-tier,
Ev-ery day some bur-den lift-ed, Ev-ery day some heart to cheer,
Hon-or, praise, and ven-er-a-tion To the found-ers we re-vere!

Forg-ing on-ward, ev-er on-ward, Bless-ed, hon-ored Pi-o-neer!
Ev-ery day some hope the bright-er, Bless-ed, hon-ored Pi-o-neer!
List our song of ad-o-ra-tion, Bless-ed, hon-ored Pi-o-neer!

174 There's Sunshine in My Soul Today

E. E. Hewitt

John R. Sweney

Joyously ♩ = 88

1. There's sun-shine in my soul to-day, More glo - ri - ous and bright
2. There's mu - sic in my soul to-day, A car - ol to my King,
3. There's spring-time in my soul to-day, For when the Lord is near,
4. There's glad - ness in my soul to-day, And hope and praise and love,

Than glows in an - y earth-ly sky, For Je - sus is my light.
And Je - sus lis - ten-ing can hear The songs I can - not sing.
The dove of peace sings in my heart, The flowers of grace ap - pear.
For bless - ings which he gives me now, For joys "laid up" a - bove.

Oh, there's sun - shine, bless - ed sun - shine,
sun - shine in the soul, bless - ed sun - shine in the soul.

When the peace - ful, hap - py mo - ments roll,
hap - py mo - ments roll;

When Je - sus shows his smil-ing face, There is sun-shine in the soul.

175 Who's on The Lord's Side?

H. Cornaby

Arr. by George Careless

Sincerely ♩. = 76

1. Who's on the Lord's side? Who? Now is the time to show;
2. We serve the liv - ing God, And want his foes to know
3. The stone cut with - out hands To fill the earth must grow;
4. The powers of earth and hell In rage di - rect the blow

We ask it fear - less - ly: Who's on the Lord's side? Who?
That if but few, we're great; Who's on the Lord's side? Who?
Who'll help to roll it on? Who's on the Lord's side? Who?
That's aimed to crush the work; Who's on the Lord's side? Who?

We wage no com - mon war, Cope with no com - mon foe;
We're go - ing on to win, Nor fear must blanch the brow;
Our en - sign to the world Is float - ing proud - ly now;
Truth, life, and lib - er - ty, Free - dom from death and woe,

The en - e - my's a - wake; Who's on the Lord's side? Who?
The Lord of hosts is ours; Who's on the Lord's side? Who?
No cow - ard bears our flag; Who's on the Lord's side? Who?
Are stakes we're fight - ing for; Who's on the Lord's side? Who?

Who's on The Lord's Side?

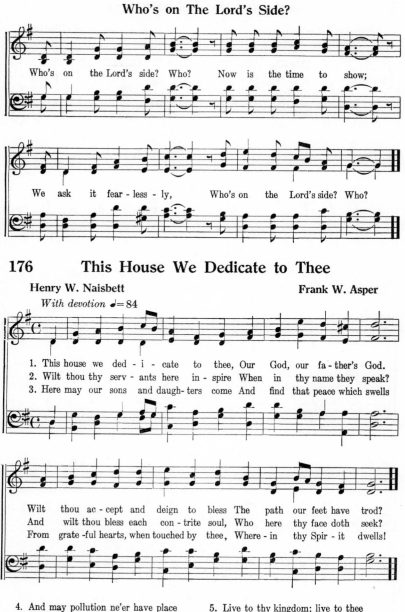

Who's on the Lord's side? Who? Now is the time to show;

We ask it fear - less - ly, Who's on the Lord's side? Who?

176   This House We Dedicate to Thee

Henry W. Naisbett   Frank W. Asper

With devotion ♩=84

1. This house we ded - i - cate to thee, Our God, our fa - ther's God.
2. Wilt thou thy serv - ants here in - spire When in thy name they speak?
3. Here may our sons and daugh- ters come And find that peace which swells

Wilt thou ac - cept and deign to bless The path our feet have trod?
And wilt thou bless each con - trite soul, Who here thy face doth seek?
From grate-ful hearts, when touched by thee, Where- in thy Spir - it dwells!

4. And may pollution ne'er have place
   Within this shrine we give;
   And in it through the years to come,
   Awake the dead to live;

5. Live to thy kingdom; live to thee
   While life shall pass away;
   Then greet again with praise and song,
   In heaven's eternal day.

Thanks for the Sabbath School

William Willes

James R. Murray

Joyously ♩=104

1. Thanks for the Sab-bath School. Hail to the day When e-vil and er-ror are flee-ing a-way. Thanks for our teach-ers who la-bor with care That we in the light of the gos-pel may share.
2. Now in the morn-ing of life let us try Each vir-tue to cher-ish, all vice to de-cry; Strive with the no-ble in deeds that ex-alt And bat-tle with en-er-gy each child-ish fault.
3. May we en-deav-or through life's de-vious way To watch and be ear-nest; true wis-dom dis-play; Try to o'er-come each temp-ta-tion and snare, There-by full sal-va-tion e-ter-nal-ly share.

Join in the ju-bi-lee; min-gle in song; Join in the joy of the Sab-bath School throng. Great be the glo-ry of

Thanks for the Sabbath School

those who do right, Who o-ver-come e-vil, in good take de-light.

178 God Loved Us, So He Sent His Son

Edward P. Kimball   Alexander Schreiner

Thoughtfully ♩ = 52

1. God loved us, so he sent his Son, Christ
2. He came as man, though Son of God, And
3. Oh, love ef - ful - gent, love di - vine! What

Je - sus, the a - ton - ing one, To show us by the
bowed him - self be - neath the rod. He died in ho - ly
debt of grat - i - tude is mine! That in his of - fering

path he trod The one and on - ly way to God.
in - no - cence, A bro - ken law to re - com - pense.
I have part And hold a place with - in his heart.

4. In word and deed he doth require
   My will to his, like son to sire,
   Be made to bend, and I as son,
   Learn conduct from the Holy One.

5. This sacrament doth represent
   His blood and body for me spent.
   Partaking now is deed for word
   That I remember him, my Lord.

179 The Day Dawn Is Breaking

Joseph L. Townsend

William Clayson

Joyfully ♩ = 132

1. The day-dawn is break-ing, The world is a-wak-ing, The clouds of night's darkness are flee-ing a-way; The world-wide com-mo-tion, From o-cean to o-cean, Now her-alds the time of the beau-ti-ful day.

2. In man-y a tem-ple The Saints will as-sem-ble, And la-bor as sav-iors of dear ones a-way; Then hap-py re-un-ion, And sweet-est com-mun-ion We'll have with our friends in the beau-ti-ful day.

3. Still let us be do-ing, Our les-sons re-view-ing, Which God has re-vealed for our walk in his way; And then, won-drous sto-ry, The Lord in his glo-ry Will come in his power in the beau-ti-ful day.

4. Then pure and su-per-nal, Our friend-ship e-ter-nal, With Je-sus we'll live, and his coun-sels o-bey Un-til ev-ery na-tion Will join in sal-va-tion, And wor-ship the Lord of the beau-ti-ful day.

♩. = 50

Beau-ti-ful day of peace and rest, Bright be thy
Beau-ti-ful day of peace and rest,

The Day Dawn Is Breaking

dawn   from east to   west;   Hail   to thine   ear - liest
Bright be thy dawn   from east to west;   Hail to thine ear-liest

wel-come   ray,   Beau - ti - ful,   bright,   mil - len - nial   day.
wel-come   ray,   Beau - ti - ful, bright, mil - len - nial   day.

180   We Give Thee But Thine Own

W. Walsham How   From Cantica Laudis

Simply ♩=84

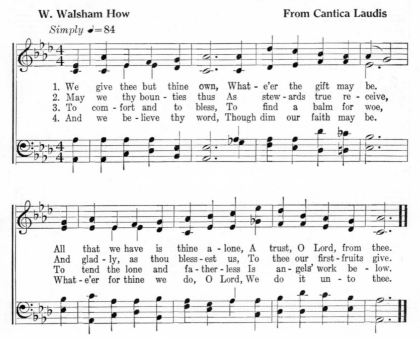

1. We   give   thee but   thine   own,   What - e'er   the   gift   may   be.
2. May   we   thy boun - ties   thus   As   stew - ards   true   re - ceive,
3. To   com - fort and   to   bless,   To   find   a   balm for   woe,
4. And   we   be - lieve thy   word, Though dim   our   faith may   be.

All   that we have   is   thine a - lone,   A   trust, O   Lord, from   thee.
And   glad - ly, as   thou   bless - est us,   To   thee our   first - fruits   give.
To   tend   the lone and   fa - ther - less   Is   an - gels' work   be - low.
What - e'er   for thine   we   do, O   Lord, We   do   it   un - to   thee.

181

Thou Dost Not Weep Alone

Eliza R. Snow

George Careless

Solemnly ♩ = 76

1. Thou dost not weep to weep a - lone;
2. But lo! what joy sa - lutes our grief!
3. It soothes our sor - row, says to thee,
4. 'Tis well with the de - part - ed one;

The broad be - reave - ment seems to fall Un - heed - ed and un -
Bright rain-bows crown the tear - ful gloom; Hope, hope e - ter - nal,
The Lord in chas - tening comes to bless; God is thy God, and
His heaven-lit lamp was shin - ing bright, And when his mor - tal

felt by none: He was be - loved, be - loved by all.
brings re - lief; Faith sounds a tri - umph o'er the tomb.
he will be A fa - ther to the fa - ther - less.
day went down, His spir - it fled where reigns no night.

5. 'Tis meet to die as he has died,
He smiled amid death's conquered gloom.
While angels waited by his side,
To bear a kindred spirit home.

6. Vain are the trophies wealth can give!
His memory needs no sculptor's art;
He's left a name—his virtues live,
'Graved on the tablets of the heart.

182 Hail to the Brightness of Zion's Glad Morning

Thomas Hastings   Edwin F. Parry

Joyfully ♩=100

1. Hail to the bright - ness of Zi - on's glad morn - ing,
2. Hail to the bright - ness of Zi - on's glad morn - ing,
3. Lo! in the des - ert the rich flowers are spring - ing;
4. Hark! from all lands, from the isles of the o - cean,

Joy to the lands that in dark - ness have lain!
Long by the proph - ets of Is - rael fore - told!
Streams, ev - er co - pious, are glid - ing a - long;
Praise to Je - ho - vah as - cend - ing on high;

Hushed be the ac - cents of sor - row and mourn - ing;
Hail to the mil - lions from bond - age re - turn - ing!
Loud from the moun - tain - tops ech - oes are ring - ing;
Fall - en the en - gines of war and com - mo - tion,

Zi - on in tri - umph be - gins her glad reign.
Gen - tiles and Jews the glad vi - sion be - hold.
Wastes rise in ver - dure and min - gle in song.
Shouts of sal - va - tion are rend - ing the sky.

183 Awake! O Ye People, the Savior is Coming

William W. Phelps   Samuel B. Mitton

Earnestly ♩=100

1. A - wake! O ye peo - ple, the Sav - ior is com - ing;
2. Be read - y, O is - lands, the Sav - ior is com - ing;

He'll sud - den - ly come to his tem - ple, we hear;
He'll bring a - gain Zi - on, the proph - ets de - clare;

Re - pent - ance is need - ed of all that are liv - ing,
Re - pent of your sins, and have faith in re - demp - tion,

To gain them a lot of in - her - i - tance near.
To gain you a lot of in - her - i - tance there.

Awake! O Ye People, the Savior is Coming

To - day will soon pass and that un - known to - mor - row
A voice to the na - tions in sea - son is giv - en,

May leave man - y souls in a more dread - ful state
Pre - pare, oh, pre - pare for the king - dom's new birth,

Than came by the flood, or that fell on Go - mor - rah—
To call the e - lect from the four winds of heav - en;

Yea, weep - ing and wail - ing when grief is too late.
For Je - sus is com - ing to reign up - on earth.

184 The Time is Far Spent

Eliza R. Snow

With emphasis ♩=72

1. The time is far spent, there is lit-tle re-main-ing To pub-lish glad-ti-dings by sea and by land. Then has-ten, ye her-alds, go for-ward pro-claim-ing: Re-pent, for the king-dom of heav-en's at hand. Re-pent, for the king-dom of heav-en's at hand.

2. Shrink not from your du-ty how-ev-er un-pleas-ant, But fol-low the Sav-ior, your pat-tern and friend. Our lit-tle af-flic-tions, though pain-ful at pres-ent, Ere long, with the right-eous, in glo-ry will end. Ere long, with the right-eous, in glo-ry will end.

3. What though, if the fa-vor of Ah-man pos-sess-ing, This world's bit-ter hate you are called to en-dure, The an-gels are wait-ing to crown you with bless-ings! Go, breth-ren, be faith-ful, the prom-ise is sure. Go, breth-ren! be faith-ful, the prom-ise is sure.

4. Be fixed in your pur-pose, for Sa-tan will try you; The weight of your call-ing he per-fect-ly knows; Your path may be thorn-y, but Je-sus is nigh you; His arm is suf-fi-cient, though de-mons op-pose. His arm is suf-fi-cient, though de-mons op-pose.

'Mid Pleasures and Palaces

John Howard Payne

Sir Henry Bishop

With devotion ♩ = 46

1. 'Mid pleas-ures and pal - a - ces though we may roam, Be it
2. An ex - ile from home, splen-dor daz - zles in vain; Oh,

ev - er so hum - ble, there's no place like home; A charm from the
give me my low - ly thatched cot - tage a - gain; The birds sing-ing

skies seems to hal - low us there, Which, seek through the world, is ne'er
gai - ly, that came at my call; Oh, give me that peace of mind,

met with else - where. Home, home, sweet, sweet home, Be it
dear - er than all.

ev - er so hum - ble, there's no place like home.

186 To Nephi, Seer of Olden Time

Joseph L. Townsend

William Clayson

Gladly ♩ = 84

1. To Nephi, seer of olden time, A vision came from God, Wherein the holy word sublime, Was shown an iron rod.
2. While on our journey here below, Beneath temptation's power, Through mists of darkness we must go, In peril every hour.
3. And when temptation's power is nigh, Our pathway clouded o'er, Upon the rod we can rely, And heaven's aid implore.

Hold to the rod, the iron rod; 'Tis strong, and bright, and true; The iron rod is the word of God, 'Twill safely guide us through.

4. And, hand o'er hand, the rod along,
Through each succeeding day,
With earnest prayer and hopeful song,
We'll still pursue our way.

5. Afar we see the golden rest
To which the rod will guide,
Where, with the angels bright and blest,
Forever we'll abide.

187 'Tis Sweet to Sing the Matchless Love

George Manwaring

Ebenezer Beesley

Reverently ♩. = 48

1. 'Tis sweet to sing the match-less love Of Him who left his home a-bove,
2. 'Tis good to meet each Sab-bath day, And, in His own ap-point-ed way,
3. O hap-py hour! com-mun-ion sweet! When chil-dren, friends and teach-ers meet,

And came to earth—O won-drous plan—To suf-fer, bleed and die for man!
Par-take the em-blems of his death, And thus re-new our love and faith.
And in re-mem-brance of his grace, U-nite in sweet-est songs of praise.

'Twas Je-sus died on Cal-va-ry, That all thro' him might ran-somed be;

Then sing ho-san-nas to his name: Let heav'n and earth his love pro-claim.

188 Truth Reflects Upon Our Senses

Eliza R. Snow

C. D. Tillman

Thoughtfully ♩ = 60

1. Truth re-flects up-on our sens-es, Gos-pel light re-veals to some;
2. Je - sus said, "Be meek and low - ly," For 'tis high to be a judge;
3. Once I said un - to an-oth - er, In thine eye there is a mote,

If there still should be of - fens - es, Woe to them by whom they come!
If I would be pure and ho - ly, I must love with-out a grudge
If thou art a friend, a broth - er, Hold, and let me pull it out.

Judge not, that ye be not judg - ed, Was the coun - sel Je - sus gave;
It re - quires a con-stant la - bor All his pre-cepts to o - bey.
But I could not see it fair - ly, For my sight was ver - y dim,

Meas - ure giv - en, large or grudg-ed, Just the same you must re - ceive.
If I tru - ly love my neigh-bor, I am in the nar - row way.
When I came to search more clear-ly, In mine eye there was a beam.

Truth Reflects Upon Our Senses

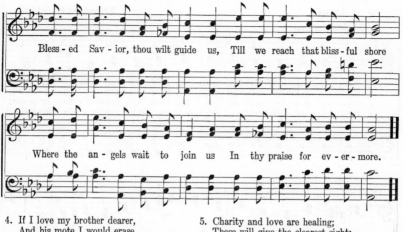

Bless - ed Sav - ior, thou wilt guide us, Till we reach that bliss - ful shore

Where the an - gels wait to join us In thy praise for ev - er - more.

4. If I love my brother dearer,
And his mote I would erase,
Then the light should shine the clearer,
For the eye's a tender place.
Others I have oft reproved,
For an object like a mote,
Now I wish this beam removed,
Oh, that tears would wash it out!

5. Charity and love are healing;
These will give the clearest sight;
When I saw my brother's failing,
I was not exactly right.
Now I'll take no further trouble;
Jesus' love is all my theme;
Little motes are but a bubble
When I think upon the beam.

189 Truth Eternal

Parley P. Pratt

Alexander Schreiner

Joyously ♩ = 84

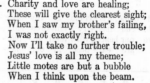

1. Truth e - ter - nal, truth di - vine, In thine an - cient ful - ness shine!
2. Truth a - gain re - stored to earth, O - pened with a proph - et's birth.
3. Truth shall tri - umph as the light Chas - es far the mist - y night.

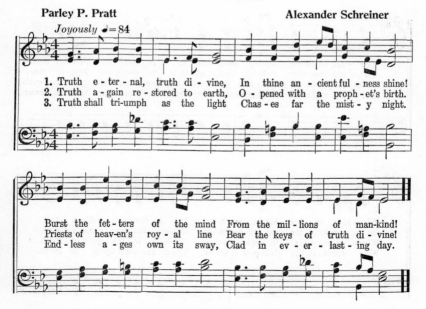

Burst the fet - ters of the mind From the mil - lions of man - kind!
Priests of heav - en's roy - al line Bear the keys of truth di - vine!
End - less a - ges own its sway, Clad in ev - er - last - ing day.

190 Welcome, Welcome Sabbath Morning

R. B. Baird

Ebenezer Beesley

Brightly ♩=80

1. Wel - come, wel-come, Sab-bath morn - ing, Now we rest from ev - ery care;
2. Hark! the Sab-bath bells are ring - ing. Hear the ech - oes all a - round;
3. Here we bow in meek de - vo - tion; Here we sing God's ho - ly praise;
4. Here we meet with friends and neigh- bors; Par - ents too are in the throng;

Wel - come, wel - come is thy dawn - ing, Ho - ly Sabbath, day of prayer.
List! the mer - ry chil-dren sing - ing! What a pleas-ing, joy - ful sound!
Here our hearts, with fond e - mo - tion, Seek to learn his ho - ly ways.
We are ear - nest in our la - bors. To God's king-dom we be - long.

Lov - ing teach-ers kind-ly greet us As we meet in Sun-day School
Ev - ery ten -der note en -treats us, Bids us come, nor long -er stay,
From the books of rev - e - la - tion We are taught while yet in youth.
Tri - als make our faith grow strong-er; Truth is no - bler than a crown;

Where they la - bor hard to teach us By the Sav-ior's gold-en rule.
On our way the mu - sic greets us; Has-ten; has-ten; come a - way.
Words of heaven-ly in - spi - ra - tion Guide us in the path of truth.
We will brave the tem-pest long - er, Though the world up-on us frown.

Welcome, Welcome Sabbath Morning

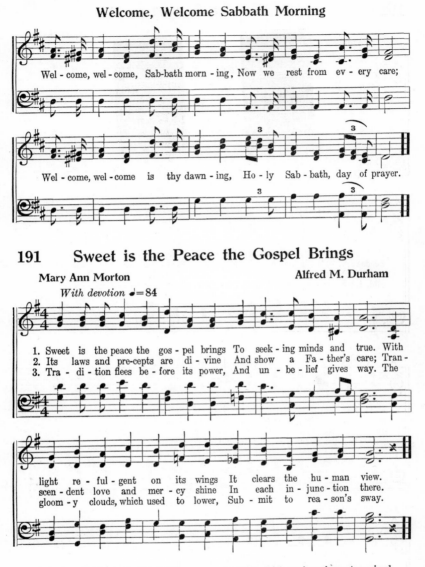

Wel-come, wel-come, Sab-bath morn-ing, Now we rest from ev-ery care;

Wel-come, wel-come is thy dawn-ing, Ho-ly Sab-bath, day of prayer.

191 Sweet is the Peace the Gospel Brings

Mary Ann Morton

Alfred M. Durham

With devotion ♩=84

1. Sweet is the peace the gos-pel brings To seek-ing minds and true. With
2. Its laws and pre-cepts are di-vine And show a Fa-ther's care; Tran-
3. Tra-di-tion flees be-fore its power, And un-be-lief gives way. The

light re-ful-gent on its wings It clears the hu-man view.
scen-dent love and mer-cy shine In each in-junc-tion there.
gloom-y clouds, which used to lower, Sub-mit to rea-son's sway.

4. May we who know the Sacred Name
From every sin depart,
Then will the Spirit's constant flame
Preserve us pure in heart.

5. Ere long the tempter's power will cease,
And sin no more annoy,
No wrangling sects disturb our peace,
Or mar our heartfelt joy.

6. That which we have in part received
Will be in part no more,
For he, in whom we all believe
To us will all restore.

7. In patience, then, let us possess
Our souls till he appear,
On to our mark of calling press.
Redemption draweth near.

192   We Are Sowing

H. A. Tuckett

Steadily ♩=72

1. We are sow-ing, dai-ly sow-ing Count-less seeds of good and ill,
2. Seeds that fall a-mid the still-ness Of the lone-ly moun-tain glen;
3. Seeds that lie un-changed, un-quick-ened, Life-less on the teem-ing mold;
4. Thou who know-est all our weak-ness, Leave us not to sow a-lone!

Scat-tered on the lev-el low-land, Cast up-on the wind-y hill;
Seeds cast out in crowd-ed plac-es, Trod-den un-der foot of men;
Seeds that live and grow and flour-ish When the sow-er's hand is cold.
Bid thine an-gels guard the fur-rows Where the pre-cious grain is sown,

Seeds that sink in rich, brown fur-rows, Soft with heav-en's gra-cious rain;
Seeds, by i-dle hearts for-got-ten, Flung at ran-dom on the air;
By a whis-per sow we bless-ings; By a breath we scat-ter strife;
Till the fields are crowned with glo-ry, Filled with mel-low, ri-pened ears,

Seeds that rest up-on the sur-face Of the dry, un-yield-ing plain.
Seeds, by faith-ful souls re-mem-bered, Sown in tears and love and prayer.
In our words and looks and ac-tions Lie the seeds of death and life.
Filled with fruit of life e-ter-nal From the seed we sowed in tears.

193   We Meet Again in Sabbath School

George Manwaring   Ebenezer Beesley

Joyfully ♩=112

1. We meet a-gain in Sab-bath school On this the Lord's own day,
2. We meet a-gain, yes, glad-ly meet, To learn the will of God,
3. O hap-py day! on which we meet With friends and teach-ers dear,

Where joy-ful glad-ness is the rule, And love doth bear its sway;
For wis-dom seek-ing, that our feet May walk the nar-row road:
And in this ev-er sweet re-treat Their bless-ed teach-ings hear;

Where all may join in songs of praise To him who reigns a-bove,
O Fa-ther, let thy spir-it dwell In ev-ery will-ing heart,
With pre-cious truths our minds are stored, The gos-pel plan made plain,

And thank-ful hearts and voic-es raise, For his re-deem-ing love.
That we may love and serve thee well, And ne'er from thee de-part.
Each Sab-bath day with one ac-cord O let us meet a-gain.

194 We're Marching On To Glory

John M. Chamberlain   John M. Chamberlain

Marching Movement ♩=104

1. We're march-ing on to glo - ry, We're work-ing for our crown,
2. Then day by day we're march-ing, To heav - en we are bound;
3. Then with the ran - somed chil - dren That throng the star - ry throne,

We'll make our ar - mor bright - er, And nev - er lay it down.
Each good act brings us near - er That home where we'll be crowned.
We'll praise our Lord and Sav - ior, His power and mer - cy own.

We're march - ing, march- ing home - ward, To that bright land a - far;

We work for life e - ter - nal, It is our guid - ing star.

Redeemer of Israel

Adapted by
William W. Phelps

Freeman Lewis

Steadily ♩=84

1. Re - deem - er of Is - rael, Our on - ly de - light, On
2. We know he is com - ing To gath - er his sheep And
3. How long we have wan - dered As stran - gers in sin, And
4. As chil - dren of Zi - on, Good ti - dings for us. The

whom for a bless - ing we call, Our shad - ow by day,
lead them to Zi - on in love; For why in the val -
cried in the des - ert for thee! Our foes have re - joiced
to - kens al - read - y ap - pear. Fear not, and be just,

And our pil - lar by night, Our King, our De - liv - erer, our all!
ley Of death should they weep Or in the lone wil - der - ness rove?
When our sor - rows they've seen, But Is - rael will short - ly be free.
For the king - dom is ours. The hour of re - demp - tion is near.

5. Restore, my dear Savior, the light of thy face;
   Thy soul-cheering comfort impart;
   And let the sweet longing for thy holy place
   Bring hope to my desolate heart.

6. He looks! and ten thousands of angels rejoice,
   And myriads wait for his word;
   He speaks! and eternity, filled with his voice,
   Re-echoes the praise of the Lord.

196   We Thank Thee, O God, for a Prophet

William Fowler

Mrs. Norton

Brightly ♩=76

1. We thank thee, O God, for a proph-et To guide us in these lat-ter days. We thank thee for send-ing the gos-pel To light-en our minds with its rays. We thank thee for ev-e-ry bless-ing Be-stowed by thy boun-te-ous hand. We feel it a

2. When dark clouds of trou-ble hang o'er us And threat-en our peace to de-stroy, There is hope smil-ing bright-ly be-fore us, And we know that de-liv-erance is nigh. We doubt not the Lord nor his good-ness. We've proved him in days that are past. The wick-ed who

3. We'll sing of his good-ness and mer-cy. We'll praise him by day and by night, Re-joice in his glo-ri-ous gos-pel, And bask in its life-giv-ing light. Thus on to e-ter-nal per-fec-tion The hon-est and faith-ful will go, While they who re-

We Thank Thee, O God, for a Prophet

plea- sure to serve thee, And love to o - bey thy com - mand.
fight a - gainst Zi - on Will sure - ly be smit - ten at last.
ject this glad mes - sage Shall nev - er such hap - pi - ness know.

197   What Glorious Scenes Mine Eyes Behold

Ebenezer Beesley

Marked ♩=84

1. What glo - rious scenes mine eyes be - hold! What won - ders burst up -
2. Good news to earth have an - gels borne, Which fills our souls with
3. The scat - tered sheep, who once were sold In dark - ness o'er the
4. Now Is - rael, long op - pressed and grieved In ev - ery land, in

on my view! When E - phraim's rec - ords I un - fold, All
joy and peace; Good ti - dings com - fort those who mourn And
moun - tains far, Shall now re - turn un - to their fold, And
ev - ery clime, Shall hear the word of God and live; This

things ap - pear di - vine - ly new, All things ap - pear di - vine - ly new.
bring the cap - tive full re - lease, And bring the cap - tive full re - lease.
there their wait - ing hearts pre - pare, And there their wait - ing hearts pre - pare.
is the time, the cho - sen time, This is the time, the cho - sen time.

198 When First the Glorious Light of Truth

William Clayton

Fervently ♩=108

1. When first the glo-rious light of truth Burst forth in this last age, How
2. How man-y on Mis-sou-ri's plain Lie prone in death's em-brace. Pure
3. And in Nau-voo, that cit-y where A tem-ple cheered the brave, A
4. Our Pa-tri-arch and Proph-et, too, Were mas-sa-cred; they bled To

few there were en-rolled their names Up-on its sa-cred page! And of those
hon-est souls, too good to live In such a wick-ed place! And are they
mul-ti-tude of saint-ed souls Have found a rest-ful grave. And there they
seal their tes-ti-mo-ny and Were num-bered with the dead. Ah, tell me,

few how man-y Have passed from earth a-way And in the grave are
left for-ev-er Be-neath the si-lent clay? Ah, no; they are but
now are sleep-ing, But shall not sleep al-way, For soon they'll share the
are they sleep-ing? Me-thinks I hear them say: "Death's i-cy chains are

sleep-ing Till the res-ur-rec-tion day! Till the res-ur-rec-tion
sleep-ing Till the res-ur-rec-tion day! Till the res-ur-rec-tion
glo-ries Of a res-ur-rec-tion day! Of a res-ur-rec-tion
burst-ing! 'Tis the res-ur-rec-tion day! 'Tis the res-ur-rec-tion

When First the Glorious Light of Truth

day! And in the grave are sleep-ing Till the res-ur-rec-tion day!
day! Ah, no; they are but sleep-ing Till the res-ur-rec-tion day!
day! For soon they'll share the glo-ries Of a res-ur-rec-tion day!
day! Death's i - cy chains are burst-ing! 'Tis the res-ur-rec-tion day!"

5. And here in these sweet peaceful vales
The shafts of death are hurled,
And many faithful Saints are called
Unto a better world.
And friends are ofttimes weeping
For friends who've passed away,
And in their graves are sleeping
Till the resurrection day!

6. Why should we mourn because we leave
These scenes of toil and pain?
Oh, happy change, the righteous go
Celestial crowns to gain!
And soon we all shall follow
To realms of endless day
And taste the joys and glories
Of a ressurection day!

199 When in the Wondrous Realms Above

Frank I. Kooyman

Alexander Schreiner

Serenely ♩=84

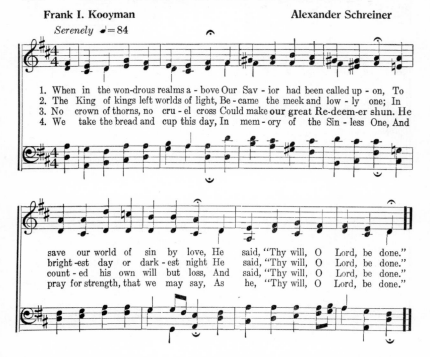

1. When in the won-drous realms a - bove Our Sav - ior had been called up - on, To
2. The King of kings left worlds of light, Be - came the meek and low - ly one; In
3. No crown of thorns, no cru - el cross Could make our great Re-deem-er shun. He
4. We take the bread and cup this day, In mem - ory of the Sin - less One, And

save our world of sin by love, He said, "Thy will, O Lord, be done."
bright-est day or dark-est night He said, "Thy will, O Lord, be done."
count-ed his own will but loss, And said, "Thy will, O Lord, be done."
pray for strength, that we may say, As he, "Thy will, O Lord, be done."

200 When the Rosy Light of Morning

R. B. Baird

R. B. Baird

Brightly ♩=108

1. When the ros - y light of morn - ing Soft - ly beams a-bove the hill;
2. For a good and glo - rious pur - pose Thus we meet each Sab - bath day,
3. Let us then press bold - ly on-ward, Prove our-selves as sol - diers true;

And the birds, sweet heaven-ly song-sters, Ev - ery dell with mu - sic fill,
Each one striv - ing for sal - va - tion Through the Lord's ap-point - ed way.
He will lead us, he will guide us. Come, there's work for all to do.

Fresh from slum - ber we a - wak - en; Sun-shine makes the heart so gay;
Ear - nest toil will be re - ward - ed; Zeal - ous hearts need not re - pine;
Nev - er tir - ing, nev - er doubt - ing, Bold - ly strug - gling to the end,

Na - ture breathes her sweet-est fra - grance On the ho - ly Sab - bath day.
God will not with-hold his bless - ings From the ea - ger, seek-ing mind.
In the world, though foes as - sail us, God will sure - ly be our friend.

When the Rosy Light of Morning

Then a - way, haste a - way; Come a - way to the Sun-day School;
Then a - way, haste a - way

Then a - way, do not de - lay; Come a - way to the Sun-day School.

201 There is a Green Hill Far Away

Cecil Frances Alexander

John H. Gower

Simply ♩ = 88

1. There is a green hill far a - way With - out a cit - y wall,
2. We may not know, we can - not tell What pains he had to bear,
3. There was no oth - er good e - nough To pay the price of sin.
4. O dear - ly, dear - ly, has he loved! And we must love him too

Where the dear Lord was cru - ci - fied, Who died to save us all.
But we be - lieve it was for us He hung and suf - fered there.
He on - ly could un - lock the gate Of heaven and let us in.
And trust in his re - deem - ing blood And try his works to do.

202 When Upon Life's Billows

J. Oatman, Jr.

E. O. Excell

Brightly ♩=88

1. When up-on life's bil-lows you are tem-pest-tossed, When you are dis-cour-aged, think-ing all is lost, Count your man-y bless-ings; name them one by one, And it will sur-prise you what the Lord has done.
2. Are you ev-er bur-dened with a load of care? Does the cross seem heav-y you are called to bear? Count your man-y bless-ings; ev-er-y doubt will fly, And you will be sing-ing as the days go by.
3. When you look at oth-ers with their lands and gold, Think that Christ has prom-ised you his wealth un-told. Count your man-y bless-ings; mon-ey can-not buy Your re-ward in heav-en nor your home on high.
4. So a-mid the con-flict, wheth-er great or small, Do not be dis-cour-aged; God is o-ver all. Count your man-y bless-ings; an-gels will at-tend, Help and com-fort give you to your jour-ney's end.

Count your bless-ings; Name them one by one. Count your
Count your man-y bless-ings; Name them one by one. Count your man-y

When Upon Life's Billows

bless-ings; See what God hath done. Count your bless-ings;
bless-ings, See what God hath done; Count your man-y bless-ings,

rit. *a tempo*

Name them one by one. Count your man-y bless-ings; See what God hath done.

203 We Love Thy House, O God

William Bullock   Leroy J. Robertson

Reverently ♩ = 76

1. We love thy house, O God, Where - in thine hon - or dwells, The
2. It is the house of prayer Where - in thy ser - vants meet, And
3. We love the word of life, The word that tells of peace, Of

joy of thine a - bode All earth - ly joy ex - cels.
thou, O Lord, art there, Thy cho - sen flock to greet.
com - fort in the strife, Of joys that nev - er cease.

204 Thy Spirit, Lord, Has Stirred Our Souls

Frank I. Kooyman

Alexander Schreiner

Fervently ♩ = 60

1. Thy Spir - it, Lord, has stirred our souls, And by its
2. "Did not our hearts with - in us burn?" We know the

in - ward shin - ing glow We see a - new our sa - cred
Spir - it's fire is here. It makes our souls for ser - vice

goals And feel thy near - ness here be - low. No burn - ing
yearn; It makes the path of du - ty clear. Lord, may it

bush near Si - na - i Could show thy pres - ence, Lord, more nigh.
prompt us, day by day, In all we do, in all we say.

We'll Sing the Songs of Zion

William G. Mills

Felix Mendelssohn

With simplicity ♩ = 69

1. We'll sing the songs of Zi - on, Though now in dis - tant lands,
2. O Zi - on! long pre - dict - ed By Seers and Saints of old;
3. When Zi - on reached the moun-tains, They gave their gold - en store,
4. From Zi - on's fa - vored val - ley, Shines gos - pel light and grace,

Our harps shall not be ly - ing Un - touched by skill - ful hands.
The bless - ings they de - pict - ed And beau - ties we be - hold;
And all the limp - id foun - tains Did heal - ing vir - tues pour.
And mil - lions soon will ral - ly A - round her gath - ering place,

The winds in flit - ting breez - es Will sweep the sound - ing string,
Thy walls are sure sal - va - tion, And all thy gates are praise,
Where reigned but gloom - y sad - ness, And earth seemed in re - pose,
Where ev - ery law of heav - en, Whose coun - cils do de - sign

And tune its loft - y prais - es, If Saints neg - lect to sing.
A peace-ful hab - i - ta - tion, In these the lat - ter days.
Re - sounds the song of glad - ness, And blos-soms forth the rose.
To save us, will be giv - en With - in her sa - cred shrine.

206 The World Has Need of Willing Men

Will L. Thompson

Will L. Thompson

Energetically ♩ = 104

1. The world has need of will-ing men, Who wear the work-er's seal;
2. The Church has need of help-ing hands And hearts that know and feel;
3. Then don't stand i-dly look-ing on; The fight with sin is real;
4. Then work and watch and fight and pray With all thy might and zeal;

Come, help the good work move a-long; Put your shoul-der to the wheel.
The work to do is here for you; Put your shoul-der to the wheel.
It will be long but must go on; Put your shoul-der to the wheel.
Push ev-ery wor-thy work a-long; Put your shoul-der to the wheel.

Put your shoul-der to the wheel; push a-long;

push a-long,

Do your du-ty with a heart full of song. We

full of song

The World Has Need of Willing Men

all have work; let no one shirk; Put your shoul-der to the wheel.

207   Rejoice, Ye Saints of Latter-days

Mabel Jones Gabbott

Frank W. Asper

With exultation ♩=116

1. Re - joice, ye Saints of lat - ter days; Lift up your hearts in songs of
2. A - gain is reared from earth's deep sod A tem - ple to the Most High
3. Oh, work-men, rear it ten - der - ly In per - fect form and sym - e -
4. Oh, Saints, re - joice in this great day And wor - ship him in his own

praise; An - oth - er tem - ple to our God Now stands up on this cho - sen
God; A house of prayer, a place of peace, Where en - vy, hate, and greed will
try. Let love be in this ho - ly place; Let no crude act or word ef -
way, For thus his king-dom will go forth Un - til his tem-ples fill the

sod, A house of ho - li - ness and love To him who sits en-throned a - bove.
cease, Where men will serve un-self - ish - ly Their kin-dred dead and set them free.
face This sa - cred ed - i - fice of prayer; Oh, build it true with ut - most care.
earth; Then will the heav-ens sing a - bove, And Christ de-scend to reign in love.

208   You Can Make the Pathway Bright

Helen Dungan   J. M. Dungan

Brightly ♩=92

1. You can make the path-way bright, Fill the soul with heav-en's light,
2. You can speak the gen-tle word To the heart with an-ger stirred,
3. You can do a kind-ly deed To your neigh-bor in his need,
4. You can live a hap-py life In this world of toil and strife,

If there's sun-shine in your heart; Turn-ing dark-ness in-to day,
If there's sun-shine in your heart; Though it seems a lit-tle thing,
If there's sun-shine in your heart; And his bur-den you will share
If there's sun-shine in your heart; And your soul will glow with love

As the shad-ows fly a-way, If there's sun-shine in your heart to-day.
It will heav-en's bless-ings bring, If there's sun-shine in your heart to-day.
As you lift his load of care, If there's sun-shine in your heart to-day.
From the per-fect Light a-bove, If there's sun-shine in your heart to-day.

If there's sun-shine in your heart, You can
sun-shine in your heart,

You Can Make the Pathway Bright

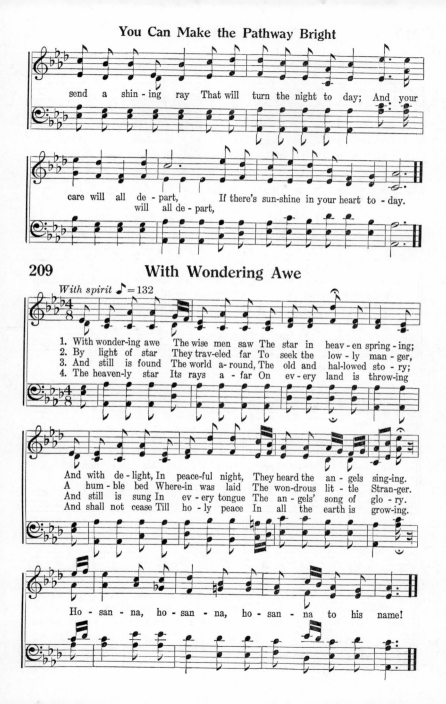

send a shin-ing ray That will turn the night to day; And your

care will all de - part,
will all de - part,

If there's sun-shine in your heart to - day.

209 ## With Wondering Awe

With spirit ♪ = 132

1. With wonder-ing awe The wise men saw The star in heav - en spring-ing;
2. By light of star They trav-eled far To seek the low - ly man - ger,
3. And still is found The world a-round, The old and hal-lowed sto - ry;
4. The heaven-ly star Its rays a - far On ev - ery land is throw-ing

And with de - light, In peace-ful night, They heard the an - gels sing-ing.
A hum - ble bed Where-in was laid The won-drous lit - tle Stran-ger.
And still is sung In ev - ery tongue The an - gels' song of glo - ry.
And shall not cease Till ho - ly peace In all the earth is grow-ing.

Ho - san - na, ho - san - na, ho - san - na to his name!

210 We Are All Enlisted

William B. Bradbury

Martial ♩=108

1. We are all en-list-ed till the con-flict is o'er— Hap-py are we!
2. Hark! the sound of bat-tle sound-ing loud-ly and clear— Come join the ranks!
3. Fight-ing for a king-dom, and the world is our foe— Hap-py are we!

Hap-py are we! Sol-diers in the ar-my, there's a bright crown in store;
Come join the ranks! We are wait-ing now for sol-diers; who'll vol-un-teer?
Hap-py are we! Glad to join the ar-my, we will sing as we go;

We shall win and wear it by and by. Haste to the bat-tle,
Ral-ly round the stan-dard of the cross. Hark! 'tis our Cap-tain
We shall gain the vic-to-ry by and by. Dan-gers may gath-er—

quick to the field, Truth is our hel-met, buck-ler, and shield. Stand by our col-ors—
calls you to-day; Lose not a mo-ment, make no de-lay! Fight for our Sav-ior,
why should we fear? Je-sus, our Lead-er, ev-er is near. He will pro-tect us,

We Are All Enlisted

proud - ly they wave—We're joy - ful - ly, joy - ful - ly march-ing to our home.
come, come a - way! We're joy - ful - ly, joy - ful - ly march-ing to our home.
com - fort and cheer: We're joy - ful - ly, joy - ful - ly march-ing to our home.

We are all en - list - ed till the con - flict is o'er— Hap - py are

we! Hap - py are we! Sol - diers in the ar - my, there's a

bright crown in store; We shall win and wear it by and by.

211 Ye Chosen Twelve, To You are Given

Parley P. Pratt

A. M. Fox

With deliberation ♩=60

1. Ye cho-sen Twelve, to you are given The keys of this last
2. First to the Gen-tile sound the news Through-out Col-um-bia's
3. Let Eur-ope's towns and cit-ies hear The gos-pel ti-dings

min-is-try, To ev-ery na-tion un-der heaven, To ev-ery
hap-py land, And then, be-fore it reach the Jews, And then, be-
an-gels bring; Let Gen-tile na-tions far and near, Let Gen-tile

na-tion un-der heaven, From land to land, from sea to sea.
fore it reach the Jews, Pre-pare on Eur-ope's shores to stand.
na-tions far and near Pre-pare their hearts his praise to sing.

4. Both Africa's and India's plains
   Must hear the tidings as they roll
   Where darkness rules and sorrow reigns
   And tyranny has held control.

5. Give ear, ye isles in every zone,
   For every land must hear the sound!
   And tongues and nations long unknown
   Since they were lost shall soon be found.

6. And then again shall Asia hear,
   Where angels first the news revealed,
   Eternity the record bear,
   And earth a joyful tribute yield.

7. The nations catch the pleasing sound,
   And Jew and Gentile swell the strain.
   Hosanna o'er the earth resound;
   Messiah then will come to reign.

212 Zion Stands With Hills Surrounded

Thomas Kelly   A. C. Smyth

Sturdily ♩ = 92

1. Zi - on stands with hills sur - round - ed— Zi - on, kept by
2. Ev - ery hu - man tie may per - ish; Friend to friend un-
3. In the fur - nace God may prove thee, Thence to bring thee

power di - vine. All her foes shall be con - found - ed,
faith - ful prove; Moth - ers cease their own to cher - ish;
forth more bright, But can nev - er cease to love thee;

Though the world in arms com - bine. Hap - py Zi - on,
Heaven and earth at last re - move. But no chang - es,
Thou art pre - cious in his sight. God is with thee,

Hap - py Zi - on, What a fa - vored lot is thine!
But no chang - es, Can at - tend Je - ho - vah's love.
God is with Thee; Thou shalt tri - umph in his might.

213 The Spirit of God Like a Fire

William W. Phelps

With exultation ♩=100

1. The Spir-it of God like a fire is burn-ing!
2. The Lord is ex-tend-ing the Saints' un-der-stand-ing,
3. We'll call in our sol-emn as-sem-blies in spir-it,
4. How bless-ed the day when the lamb and the li-on

1. The lat-ter-day glo-ry be-gins to come forth; The
2. Re-stor-ing their judg-es and all as at first. The
3. To spread forth the king-dom of heav-en a-broad, That
4. Shall lie down to-geth-er with-out an-y ire, And

1. vi-sions and bless-ings of old are re-turn-ing, And
2. knowl-edge and pow-er of God are ex-pand-ing, The
3. we through our faith may be-gin to in-her-it The
4. Eph-raim be crowned with his bless-ing in Zi-on, As

1. an-gels are com-ing to vis-it the earth.
2. veil o'er the earth is be-gin-ning to burst. We'll sing and we'll
3. vi-sions and bless-ings and glo-ries of God.
4. Je-sus de-scends with his char-iot of fire!

The Spirit of God Like a Fire

shout with the ar - mies of heav - en, Ho - san - na, ho - san - na to

God and the Lamb! Let glo - ry to them in the high - est be

giv - en, Hence-forth and for - ev - er; A - men and a - men!

214 Praise God From Whom All Blessings Flow

Thomas Ken

Louis Bourgeois
Genevan Psalter

Well marked ♩ = 54

Praise God from whom all bless - ings flow; Praise him, all crea-tures here be - low;

Praise him a - bove, ye heaven-ly host; Praise Fa - ther, Son, and Ho - ly Ghost.

Today, While the Sun Shines

Evan Stephens

Vigorously ♩=100

1. To - day, while the sun shines, work with a will; To-
2. To - day seek the treas - ure bet - ter than gold; The
3. To - day seek for good - ness, vir - tue, and truth, As

day all your du - ties with pa - tience ful - fil; To-
peace and the joy that are found in the fold; To-
crown of your life and the grace of your youth; To-

day, while the birds sing, har - bor no care,
day, seek the gems that shine in the heart.
day, while the heart beats, live to be true,

Call life a good gift, call the world fair.
While here we la - bor, choose the good part.
Con - stant and faith - ful all the way through.

To - day, to - day, work with a will; To - day, to - day,

Today, While the Sun Shines

your du-ties ful-fil; To-day, to-day, work while you

may. There is no to-mor-row, but on-ly to-day.

216   With All the Power of Heart and Tongue

Isaac Watts   Lowell M. Durham

Majestic $\quad = 66$

1. With all the power of heart and tongue, I'll praise my
2. I'll sing thy truth and mer-cy, Lord; I'll sing the
3. To God I cried when trou-bles rose; He heard me
4. A-midst a thou-sand snares I stand, Up-held and

Mak-er in my song; An-gels shall hear the notes I'll
won-ders of thy word; Not all thy works and names be-
and sub-dued my foes; He did my ris-ing fears con-
guid-ed by thy hand; Thy words my faint-ing soul re-

raise, Ap-prove the song and join the praise.
low So much thy power and glo-ry show.
trol, And strength dif-fused through all my soul.
vive, And keep my dy-ing faith a-live.

217 While of These Emblems We Partake

John Nicholson   Alexander Schreiner

Reverently ♩=78

1. While of these em - blems we par - take In Je - sus'
2. For us the blood of Christ was shed, For us on
3. The law was bro - ken; Je - sus died That jus - tice
4. But rise tri - um - phant from the tomb, And in e -

name and for his sake, Let us re - mem - ber and be
Cal - vary's cross he bled, And thus dis - pelled the aw - ful
might be sat - is - fied, That man might not re - main a
ter - nal splen - dor bloom, Freed from the power of death and

sure Our hearts and hands are clean and pure.
gloom That else were this cre - a - tion's doom.
slave Of death, of hell, or of the grave,
pain, With Christ, the Lord, to rule and reign.

218 We'll Sing All Hail to Jesus' Name

R. Alldridge   Joseph Coslett

Fervently ♩=80

1. We'll sing all hail to Je - sus' name And praise and hon - or give
2. He passed the por - tals of the grave; Sal - va - tion was his song;
3. He seized the keys of death and hell And bruised the ser - pent's head;
4. The bread and wa - ter rep - re - sent His sac - ri - fice for sin;

We'll Sing All Hail to Jesus' Name

To him who bled on Cal - vary's hill And died that we might live.
He called up - on the sin - bound soul To join the heaven-ly throng.
He bid the pris - on doors un - fold, The grave yield up her dead.
Ye Saints par - take and tes - ti - fy Ye do re-mem - ber him.

5. The sacrament the soul inspires
And calms the human breast,
Points to the time when faithful Saints
Shall enter into rest.

6. Then hail, all hail, to such a Prince
Who saves us by his blood!
He's marked the way and bids us tread
The path that leads to God.

219   I Heard the Bells on Christmas Day

Henry W. Longfellow   J. Baptiste Calkin

With contemplation ♩=76

1. I heard the bells on Christ - mas day Their
2. I thought how, as the day had come, The
3. And in de - spair I bowed my head: "There

old fa - mil - iar car - ols play; And wild and sweet the
bel - fries of all Chris - ten - dom Had rolled a - long th'un -
is no peace on earth," I said, "For hate is strong and

words re - peat Of peace on earth, good will to men.
bro - ken song Of peace on earth, good will to men.
mocks the song Of peace on earth, good will to men."

4. Then pealed the bells more loud and deep:
"God is not dead, nor doth he sleep;
The wrong shall fail the right prevail,
With peace on earth, good will to men."

5. Till, ringing, singing, on its way,
The world revolved from night to day,
A voice, a chime, a chant sublime,
Of peace on earth, good will to men!

220 Prayer Is the Soul's Sincere Desire

James Montgomery

George Careless

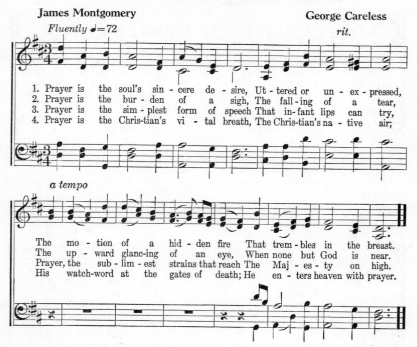

Fluently ♩ = 72

rit.

1. Prayer is the soul's sin - cere de - sire, Ut - tered or un - ex - pressed,
2. Prayer is the bur - den of a sigh, The fall - ing of a tear,
3. Prayer is the sim - plest form of speech That in - fant lips can try,
4. Prayer is the Chris-tian's vi - tal breath, The Chris-tian's na - tive air;

a tempo

The mo - tion of a hid - den fire That trem - bles in the breast.
The up - ward glanc-ing of an eye, When none but God is near.
Prayer, the sub - lim - est strains that reach The Maj - es - ty on high.
His watch-word at the gates of death; He en - ters heaven with prayer.

5. Prayer is the contrite sinner's voice,
Returning from his ways,
While angels in their songs rejoice,
And cry, "Behold, he prays!"

6. The Saints in prayer appear as one
In word and deed and mind,
While with the Father and the Son
Their fellowship they find.

7. Nor prayer is made on earth alone:
The Holy Spirit pleads,
And Jesus at the Father's throne,
For sinners intercedes.

8. Oh, thou by whom we come to God,
The Life, the Truth, the Way!
The path of prayer thyself hast trod;
Lord, teach us how to pray.

221 Upon the Cross of Calvary

Vilate Raile

Leroy J. Robertson

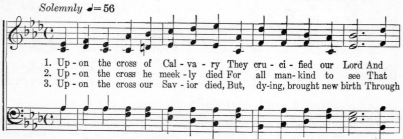

Solemnly ♩ = 56

1. Up - on the cross of Cal - va - ry They cru - ci - fied our Lord And
2. Up - on the cross he meek - ly died For all man - kind to see That
3. Up - on the cross our Sav - ior died, But, dy-ing, brought new birth Through

Upon the Cross of Calvary

sealed with blood the sac - ri - fice That sanc - ti - fied his word.
death un - locks the pas - sage - way In - to e - ter - ni - ty.
res - ur - rec - tion's mir - a - cle To all the sons of earth.

222 While Shepherds Watched Their Flocks by Night

Nahum Tate

Yorkshire Traditional Carol

With spirit ♩ = 72

1. While shepherds watched their flocks by night, All seated on the ground, The an-gel of the
2. "To you, in Da-vid's town this day, Is born of Da-vid's line The Sav - ior who is
3. Thus spake the ser-aph and forthwith Appeared a shining throng Of an - gels praising

Lord came down, And glo - ry shone a - round."Fear not," said he, for might-y dread Had
Christ the Lord; And this shall be the sign: The heaven-ly Babe you there shall find To
God, who thus Addressed their joyful song: "All glo - ry be to God on high And

seized their troubled mind;"Glad tid-ings of great joy I bring To you and all man-kind."
hu - man view displayed, All meanly wrapped in swathing bands, And in a man-ger laid."
on the earth be peace. Good will henceforth from heaven to men Begin and never cease."

223
All Hail the Glorious Day
(Choir)

Joel H. Johnson

Evan Stephens

Marcato ♩ = 100

1. All hail the glo-rious day, By proph-ets long fore-told, When, with har-mo-nious lay, The sheep of Is-rael's fold On Zi - on's hill His praise pro - claim, And shout ho - san - na to his name.

2. When Is-rael from a - far And Ju - dah scat-tered wide Shall to their land re - pair, And there in peace a - bide, Di - rect - ed by Je - ho - vah's hand, Shall dwell in peace in Zi - on's land.

3. From Zi - on's heaven-ly mount Shall heal - ing wa - ters flow, And near this ho - ly fount Will trees im - mor - tal grow Whose heaven - ly balm the king - doms feel, Whose leaves will all the na - tions heal.

4. Jerusalem shall be
Our great Redeemer's throne,
O'er all the earth and sea,
His glory be made known;
Messiah, kings and nations greet
And lay their honors at his feet.

5. Strike, strike the golden lyre,
And ye his angels sing,
Let joy your bosoms fire
And heaven with glory ring;
From earth and air and sea and skies
Let our Redeemer's praise arise.

224 An Angel From on High
(Choir)

Parley P. Pratt

John Tullidge

1. An an-gel from on high The long, long si-lence broke,
2. Sealed by Mo-ro-ni's hand, It has for a-ges lain
3. It speaks of Jo-seph's seed And makes the rem-nant known

De-scend-ing from the sky, These gra-cious words he spoke:
To wait the Lord's com-mand, From dust to speak a-gain.
Of na-tions long since dead, Who once had dwelt a-lone.

with motion ♩=104

"Lo, in Cu-mo-rah's lone-ly hill A sa-cred rec-ord lies con-cealed;
It shall a-gain to light come forth To ush-er in Christ's reign on earth;
The ful-ness of the gos-pel, too, Its pag-es will re-veal to view;

Lo, in Cu-mo-rah's lone-ly hill, A sa-cred rec-ord lies con-cealed."
It shall a-gain to light come forth To ush-er in Christ's reign on earth.
The ful-ness of the gos-pel, too, Its pag-es will re-veal to view.

4. The time is now fulfilled,
The long expected day;
Let earth obedience yield
And darkness flee away;
Remove the seals; be wide unfurled
Its light and glory to the world.
Remove the seals; be wide unfurled
Its light and glory to the world.

5. Lo, Israel filled with joy
Shall now be gathered home;
Their wealth and means employ
To build Jerusalem,
While Zion shall arise and shine
And fill the earth with truth divine,
While Zion shall arise and shine.
And fill the earth with truth divine.

225 Arise, O Glorious Zion

(Choir)

William G. Mills

George Careless

Brightly ♩ = 104

1. A - rise, O glo - rious Zi - on, Thou joy of lat - ter days,
2. Let faith - ful Saints be rear - ing The cit - y of our Lord,
3. The tem - ple long ex - pect - ed Shall stand on Zi - on's hill,
4. What though the world in mal - ice De - spise these might - y things,

Whom count-less Saints re - ly on To gain a rest - ing place.
On moun-tain tops ap - pear - ing, Ac - cord - ing to his word.
By will - ing hearts e - rect - ed, Who love Je - ho - vah's will.
We'll build the roy - al pal - ace To serve the King of kings,

A - rise and shine in splen - dor A - mid the world's deep night,
A sought - out hab - i - ta - tion By men of truth and faith,
Let earth, her wealth be - stow - ing, A - dorn his ho - ly seat,
Where ho - ly men a - noint - ed To know his sov - ereign will,

For God, thy sure de - fend - er, Is now thy life and light.
A cov - ert of sal - va - tion From ig - no - rance and death.
For na - tions great shall flow in To wor - ship at his feet.
Each or - di - nance ap - point - ed To save us, will re - veal.

Arise, O Glorious Zion

5. From Zion's favored dwelling
The gospel issues forth,
The covenant revealing
To gather all the earth;
And Saints, the message bringing
To all the sons of men,
With the redeemed, shall, singing
To Zion come again.

6. O hear the proclamation
And fly as on the wind!
For righteous indignation
Shall desolate mankind!
Then, Zion, men shall prize thee
And bow before thy shrine;
And they who now despise thee
Shall own thy light divine.

7. Through painful tribulation
We walk the narrow road
And battle with temptation,
To gain that blest abode.
But patient, firm endurance
With glory in our view
The Spirit's bright assurance
Will bring us conquerors through.

8. O grant, Eternal Father,
That we may faithful be,
With all the just to gather,
And thy salvation see!
Then, with the hosts of heaven,
We'll sing the immortal theme:
To him be glory given,
Whose blood did us redeem.

226   While of These Emblems We Partake
(Choir)

John Nicholson

S. McBurney

Reverently ♩=66

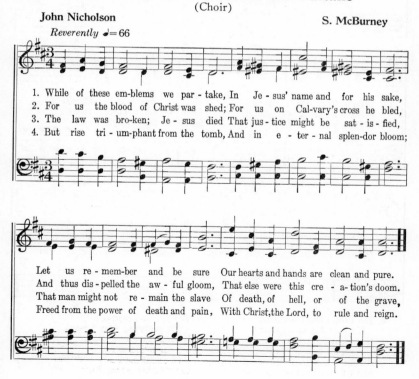

1. While of these em-blems we par - take, In Je - sus' name and for his sake,
Let us re - mem-ber and be sure Our hearts and hands are clean and pure.

2. For us the blood of Christ was shed; For us on Cal-vary's cross he bled,
And thus dis - pelled the aw - ful gloom, That else were this cre - a-tion's doom.

3. The law was bro-ken; Je - sus died That jus-tice might be sat - is - fied,
That man might not re - main the slave Of death, of hell, or of the grave,

4. But rise tri - um-phant from the tomb, And in e - ter - nal splen-dor bloom;
Freed from the power of death and pain, With Christ, the Lord, to rule and reign.

227 Arise, My Soul, Arise
(Choir)

Wesley's Collection

George Careless

Fervently ♩=92

1. A - rise, my soul, a - rise, Shake off thy guilt - y fears;
2. He ev - er lives a - bove For me to in - ter - cede;
3. Five bleed - ing wounds He bears, Re - ceived on Cal - va - ry.

The bleed - ing sac - ri - fice In my be - half ap - pears;
His all - re - deem - ing love, His pre - cious blood to plead;
They pour ef - fec - tual prayers; They strong - ly plead for me;

Be - fore the throne my sure - ty stands.
His blood a - toned for all our race
"For - give him, oh, for - give!" they cry.

My name is writ - ten on his hands.
And sprin - kles now the throne of grace.
"Nor let the ran - somed sin - ner die!"

4. The Father hears him pray,
   His dear Annointed One;
He cannot turn away
   From his beloved Son;
His Spirit answers to the blood
And tells me I am born of God.

5. To God I'm reconciled;
   His pardoning voice I hear;
He owns me for his child;
   I can no longer fear.
With confidence I now draw nigh,
And "Father, Abba, Father," cry.

228 Author of Faith, Eternal Word

(Choir)

Wesley's Collection   George Careless

Smoothly ♩ = 72

1. Au - thor of faith, E - ter - nal Word,
2. To thee our hum - ble hearts a - spire,
3. By faith we know thee strong to save;
4. To him that in thy name be - lieves,

Whose Spir - it breathes the ac - tive flame. Faith, like its
And ask the gift un - speak - a - ble. In - crease in
Save us, a pres - ent Sav - ior thou! What - e'er we
E - ter - nal life with thee is given! Un - to him -

Fin - ish - er and Lord, To - day as yes - ter -
us the kin - dled fire; In us the work of
hope, by faith we have, Fu - ture and past sub -
self he all re - ceives, Par - don and ho - li -

day the same, To - day as yes - ter - day the same.
faith ful - fil; In us the work of faith ful - fil.
sist - ing now, Fu - ture and past sub - sist - ing now.
ness and heaven, Par - don and ho - li - ness and heaven.

5. The things unknown to feeble sense;
   Unseen by reason's glimmering ray,
   With strong, commanding evidence,
   Their heavenly origin display.

6. Faith lends its realizing light,
   The clouds disperse; the shadows **fly**;
   Th' invisible appears in sight;
   And God is seen by mortal eye.

229 Awake, Ye Saints of God, Awake!
(Choir)

Eliza R. Snow

Evan Stephens

Vigorously ♩ = 96

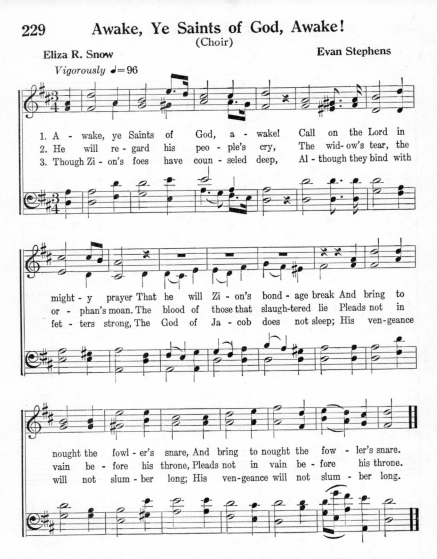

1. A - wake, ye Saints of God, a - wake! Call on the Lord in
2. He will re - gard his peo - ple's cry, The wid- ow's tear, the
3. Though Zi - on's foes have coun - seled deep, Al - though they bind with

might - y prayer That he will Zi - on's bond - age break And bring to
or - phan's moan. The blood of those that slaugh-tered lie Pleads not in
fet - ters strong, The God of Ja - cob does not sleep; His ven-geance

nought the fowl - er's snare, And bring to nought the fow - ler's snare.
vain be - fore his throne, Pleads not in vain be - fore his throne.
will not slum - ber long; His ven-geance will not slum - ber long.

4. Then let your souls be stayed on God,
A glorious scene is drawing nigh;
Though tempests gather like a flood,
The storm, though fierce, will soon pass by.

5. With constant faith and fervent prayer,
With deep humility of soul,
With steadfast mind and heart prepare,
To see th' eternal purpose roll.

6. Our God in judgement will come near;
His mighty arm he will make bare.
For Zion's sake he will appear;
Then, O ye Saints, awake, prepare!

7. Awake to righteousness; be one.
Or, saith the Lord, "You are not mine!"
Yea, like the Father and the Son,
Let all the Saints in union join.

230 Behold the Great Redeemer Die
(Choir)

Eliza R. Snow

George Careless

With solemnity ♩=66

1. Be - hold the great Re - deem - er die, A bro - ken law to
2. While guilt - y men his pains de - ride, They pierce his hands and
3. Al - though in ag - o - ny he hung, No mur-muring word es -
4. "Fa - ther, from me re - move this cup. Yet, if thou wilt, I'll

sat - is - fy. He dies a sac - ri - fice for sin; He dies a
feet and side; And with in - sult - ing scoffs and scorns, And with in-
caped his tongue. His high com - mis - sion to ful - fil, His high com-
drink it up; I've done the work thou gav - est me; I've done the

sac - ri - fice for sin That man may live and glo - ry win.
sult - ing scoffs and scorns They crown his head with plat - ted thorns.
mis - sion to ful - fil, He mag - ni - fied his Fa - ther's will.
work thou gav - est me; Re - ceive my Spir - it un - to thee."

5. He died, and at the awful sight
The sun in shame withdrew its light!
Earth trembled, and all nature sighed,
In dread response, "A God has died!"

6. He lives—he lives, we humbly now
Around these sacred symbols bow,
And seek, as Saints of latter-days,
To do his will and live his praise.

231 Before Thee, Lord, I Bow My Head

(Choir)

Joseph H. Dean

Joseph H. Dean

With deep feeling ♩ = 72

1. Be - fore thee, Lord,   I bow my head   And thank thee
2. Do thou, O Lord,   an - noint mine eyes   That I may
3. Look up, my soul,   be not cast down;   Keep not thine

1. Be - fore thee, Lord,   I bow my head

for   what has been said.   My soul vi - brates;
see   and win the prize.   My heart is broke;
eyes   up - on the ground.   Break off the shack -

And thank thee for   what has been said.   My soul vi -

my poor heart sings   When thy sweet Spir - it strikes the strings.
mine eyes are wet;   Oh, help me, Lord,   lest I for - get.
les of the earth.   Re - ceive, my soul,   the spir - it's birth.

brates;   my poor heart sings   When thy sweet Spir-it strikes the strings.

How sweet thy word I've heard this day!   Be thou my
So may my soul be filled with light   That I may
And now as I go forth a - gain   To min - gle

Before Thee, Lord, I Bow My Head

guide, oh, Lord, I pray. May I in pa-
see and win the fight, And then at last
with my fel - low men, Stay thou near by

May I in

tience do my part. Seal thou the word up - on my heart.
ex - alt - ed be, In peace and rest, oh, Lord, with thee.
my steps to guide That I may in thy love a - bide.

pa - tience do my part, Seal thou the word

232 As the Dew From Heaven Distilling
(Choir)

Parley P. Pratt

Joseph J. Daynes

Smoothly ♩=69

1. As the dew from heaven dis-till-ing Gent-ly on the grass de-scends
2. Let thy doc-trine, Lord, so gra-cious, Thus de-scend-ing from a-bove,
3. Lord, be-hold this con - gre - ga - tion; Pre - cious prom-is-es ful-fil;
4. Let our cry come up be-fore thee; Thy sweet Spir-it shed a-round,

And re - vives it, thus ful - fill - ing What thy prov - i - dence in - tends,
Blest by thee, prove ef - fi - ca - cious To ful - fil thy work of love.
From thy ho - ly hab - i - ta - tion Let the dews of life dis - til.
So the peo - ple shall a - dore thee And con - fess the joy - ful sound.

233 Blessed Are They That Have the Faith
(Choir)

Herbert Auerbach

Anthony C. Lund

Fluently ♩=92

1. Bless - ed are they that have the faith, For they are cho - sen of the Lord. The glo - ries of the prom - ised land Shall be their por - tion and re - ward.

2. 'Twas Ne - phi in the old - en days En - joyed this gift of faith su - preme. Re - call what might - y deeds he wrought. Have faith, Ye Saints; Faith can re - deem.

3. Faith is a rock, stead - fast, se - cure. Who builds there - on he build - eth well. Let faith thy pil - lar ev - er be. Then 'midst the saint - ed shall ye dwell.

Ye Saints, have faith and con - stant be. When skies grow dark and hopes de - cline, Then let your

Blessed Are They That Have the Faith

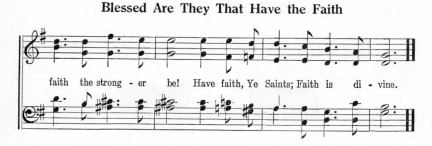

faith the strong - er be! Have faith, Ye Saints; Faith is di - vine.

234 Great Is the Lord; 'Tis Good to Praise
(Choir)

Eliza R. Snow   Ebenezer Beesley

With dignity ♩=63

1. Great is the Lord; 'tis good to praise His high and ho - ly name:
2. We'll praise him for our hap - py lot On this much fa - vored land,
3. We'll praise him for more glo - rious things Than lan - guage can ex - press;

Well may the Saints in lat - ter days His won - drous love pro - claim.
Where truth and right - eous - ness are taught By his di - vine com - mand.
The "Ev - er - last - ing Gos - pel" brings The soul to bless - ed - ness.

4. The Comforter is sent again;
   His power the Church attends,
   And with the faithful will remain
   Till Jesus Christ descends.

5. We'll praise him for a Prophet's voice,
   His people's steps to guide;
   In this we do and will rejoice,
   Though all the world deride.

6. Praise him! the time, the chosen time
   To favor Zion's come;
   And all the Saints from every clime
   Will soon be gathered home.

7. The opening seals announce the day
   Of light and truth restored,
   When all in one triumphant lay
   Will join to praise the Lord.

235 Cast Thy Burden Upon the Lord

(Choir)

Felix Mendelssohn

Quietly ♩ = 63

Cast thy bur-den up-on the Lord, And he shall sus-tain thee.

He nev-er will suf-fer the right-eous to fall. He is at thy

right hand. Thy mer-cy, Lord, is great And far a-bove the

heavens. Let none be made a-sham-ed that wait up-on thee.

236 Captain of Israel's Host

(Choir)

Wesley's Collection

Gioacchino Rossini

Broadly ♩· = 54

1. Cap-tain of Is-rael's host, and Guide Of all who seek the
2. By thy un-err-ing Spir-it led, We shall not in the

land a - bove, Be-neath the shad - ow we a - bide, The
des - ert stray. We shall no oth - er guid - ance need Nor

cloud of thy pro-tect - ing love, Our strength, thy grace, our
miss our prov - i - den - tial way, As far from dan - ger

rule, thy word, Our end, the glo - ry of the Lord.
as from fear, While love, al-might - y love, is near.

237 Come, Dearest Lord
(Choir)

Isaac Watts

Evan Stephens

Suppliantly ♩ = 72

1. Come, dear - est Lord, de - scend and dwell By faith and love, in ev - er - y breast. Then shall we know and taste and feel The joys that can - not be ex - pressed, The joys that can - not be ex - pressed.

2. Come, fill our hearts with in - ward strength; Make our en - larg - ing souls pos - sess And learn the height and breadth and length And depth of thine un - meas - ured grace, And depth of thine un - meas - ured grace.

3. Now to the God, whose power can do More than our thoughts or wish - es know, Be ev - er - last - ing hon - or done, By all the Church; through Christ, his Son, By all the Church, through Christ, his Son.

238 Come, Let Us Sing an Evening Hymn

(Choir)

William W. Phelps

Tracy Y. Cannon

Calmly ♩=69

1. Come, let us sing an eve - ning hymn
2. Yea, let us sing a sa - cred song
3. O thank the Lord for grace and gifts
4. For ev - ery line we have re - ceived,

To calm our minds for rest, And each one try, with
To close the pass - ing day, With one ac - cord call
Re - newed in lat - ter days, For truth and light to
To turn our hearts a - bove, For ev - ery word and

sin - gle eye, To praise the Sav - ior best.
on the Lord, And ev - er watch and pray.
guide us right In wis - dom's pleas - ant ways;
ev - ery good That fill our souls with love.

5. O let us raise a holier strain,
   For blessings great as ours.
   And be prepared while angels guard
   Us through our slumbering hours.

6. O may we sleep and wake in joy,
   While life with us remains,
   And then go home beyond the tomb,
   Where peace forever reigns.

239 Break Forth, O Beauteous Heavenly Light
(Choir)

Johann Schop

Johann Schop

With dignity ♩=58

Break forth, O beau-teous heaven-ly light, And ush - er in the morn - ing. Ye shep - herds, shrink not with af-fright But hear the an - gel's warn - ing. This child, this lit - tle help - less Boy shall be our con - fi - dence and joy, The powers of hate o'er - throw - ing, At last our peace be - stow - ing.

240 Come, Thou Glorious Day of Promise

(Choir)

Alex Neibaur

A. C. Smyth

With breadth ♩=63

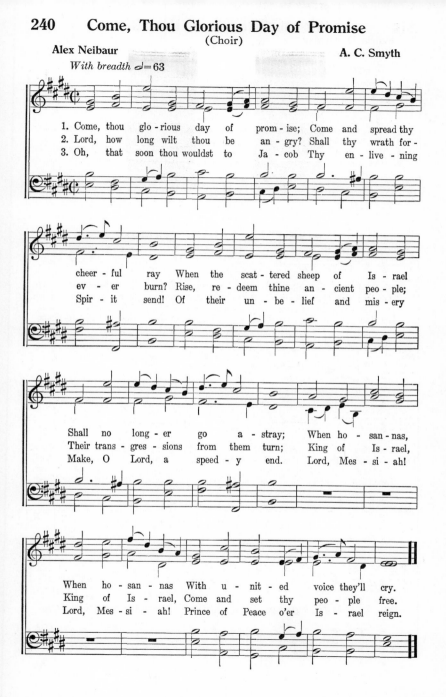

1. Come, thou glo-rious day of prom-ise; Come and spread thy cheer-ful ray When the scat-tered sheep of Is-rael Shall no long-er go a-stray; When ho-san-nas, When ho-san-nas With u-nit-ed voice they'll cry.

2. Lord, how long wilt thou be an-gry? Shall thy wrath for-ev-er burn? Rise, re-deem thine an-cient peo-ple; Their trans-gres-sions from them turn; King of Is-rael, King of Is-rael, Come and set thy peo-ple free.

3. Oh, that soon thou wouldst to Ja-cob Thy en-live-ning Spir-it send! Of their un-be-lief and mis-er-y Make, O Lord, a speed-y end. Lord, Mes-si-ah! Lord, Mes-si-ah! Prince of Peace o'er Is-rael reign.

241 For the Strength of the Hills

Felicia D. Hemans
Altered by Edward L. Sloan
(Choir)
Evan Stephens

Energetically ♩=88

1. For the strength of the hills we bless thee, Our God, our fa-thers' God;
2. At the hands of foul op-press-ors, We've borne and suf-fered long;
3. Thou hast led us here in safe-ty Where the moun-tain bul-wark stands
4. Here the wild bird swift-ly darts on His quar-ry from the heights,

Thou hast made thy chil-dren might-y By the touch of the moun-tain sod;
Thou hast been our help in weak-ness, And thy power hath made us strong;
As the guar-dian of the loved ones Thou hast brought from man-y lands.
And the red un-tu-tored In-dian Seek-eth here his rude de-lights;

Thou hast led thy cho-sen Is-rael To free-dom's last a-bode.
A-mid ruth-less foes out-num-bered, In wea-ri-ness we trod;
For the rock and for the riv-er, The val-ley's fer-tile sod;
But the Saints for thy com-mun-ion Have sought the moun-tain sod:

For the strength of the hills we bless thee, Our God, our fa-thers' God.

For the Strength of the Hills

5. We are watchers of a beacon
Whose light must never die;
We are guardians of an altar
'Midst the silence of the sky.
Here the rocks yield founts of courage,
Struck forth as by thy rod;
For the strength of the hills we bless thee,
Our God, our fathers' God.

6. For the shadow of thy presence,
Our camp of rocks o'erspread;
For the canyons' rugged defiles
And the beetling crags o'erhead;
For the snows and for the torrents,
And for our burial sod;
For the strength of the hills we bless thee,
Our God, our fathers' God.

242 Again We Meet Around the Board
(Choir)

Eliza R. Snow

George Careless

Reverently ♩ = 72

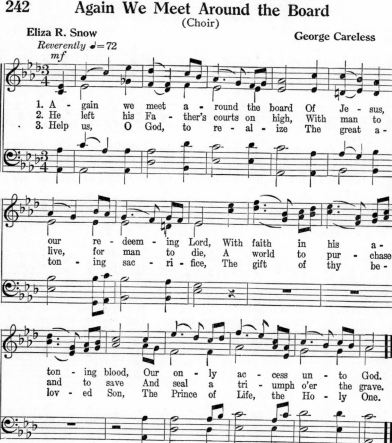

1. A - gain we meet a - round the board Of Je - sus, our re - deem - ing Lord, With faith in his a - ton - ing blood, Our on - ly ac - cess un - to God.

2. He left his Fa - ther's courts on high, With man to live, for man to die, A world to pur - chase and to save And seal a tri - umph o'er the grave.

3. Help us, O God, to re - al - ize The great a - ton - ing sac - ri - fice, The gift of thy be - lov - ed Son, The Prince of Life, the Ho - ly One.

4. We're his, who has the purchase made;
His life, his blood, the price he paid;
We're his, to do his sacred will,
And his requirements all fullfill.

5. Jesus, the great fac-simile
Of the Eternal Diety,
Has stooped to conquer, died to save
From sin and sorrow and the grave.

6. Bless us, O Lord, for Jesus' sake;
O may we worthily partake
These emblems of the flesh and blood
Of our Redeemer, Savior, God.

243 Glorious Things Are Sung of Zion
(Choir)

William W. Phelps

Joseph J. Daynes

Cheerfully ♩ = 72

1. Glo - rious things are sung of Zi - on, E - noch's cit - y seen of old,
2. There they shunned the power of Sa - tan And, ob - served ce - les - tial laws;
3. Then the towers of Zi - on glit - tered Like the sun in yon - der skies,
4. When the Lord re - turns with Zi - on, And we hear the watch - man cry,

Where the right - eous, be - ing per - fect, Walked with God in streets of gold.
For in A - dam - on - di - Ah - man Zi - on rose where E - den was.
And the wick - ed stood and trem - bled, Filled with won - der and sur - prise.
Then we'll sure - ly be u - nit - ed, And we'll all see eye to eye.

Love and vir - tue, faith and wis - dom, Grace and gifts were all com - bined;
When be - yond the power of e - vil, So that none could cov - et wealth,
Then their faith and works were per - fect. Lo, they fol - lowed their great Head!
Then we'll min - gle with the an - gels, And the Lord will bless his own.

As him - self each loved his neigh - bor; All were one in heart and mind.
One con - tin - ual feast of bless - ings Crowned their days with peace and health.
So the cit - y went to heav - en, And the world said, "Zi - on's fled!"
Then the earth will be as E - den, And we'll know as we are known.

Glorious Things Are Sung of Zion

As him - self each loved his neigh - bor; All were one in heart and mind.
One con - tin - ual feast of bless - ings Crowned their days with peace and health.
So the cit - y went to heav - en, And the world said, "Zi - on's fled!"
Then the earth will be as E - den, And we'll know as we are known.

244 **Glorious Things of Thee Are Spoken**
(Choir)

John Newton

J. S. Hanecy

Brightly ♩=84

1. Glo - rious things of thee are spo - ken, Zi - on, ci - ty of our God!
2. On the Rock of A - ges found - ed, What can shake our sure re - pose?
3. See! the streams of liv - ing wa - ters, Spring - ing from ce - les - tial love,

He whose word can - not be bro - ken Choose thee for his own a - bode.
With sal - va - tion's wall sur - round - ed, Thou may'st smile on all thy foes.
Well sup - ply the sons and daugh - ters, And all fear of drought re - move.

4. Round each habitation hovering,
See the cloud and fire appear
For a glory and a covering,
Showing that the Lord is near.

5. Blest inhabitants of Zion,
Purchased by the Savior's blood;
Jesus, whom their souls rely on,
Makes them kings and priests to God.

6. While in love his Saints he raises,
With himself to reign as King;
All, as priests, his solemn praises
For thank-offerings freely bring.

7. Fading are all worldly treasures
With their boasted pomp and show;
Heavenly joys and lasting pleasures
None but Zion's children know.

245 Does the Journey Seem Long?

(Choir)

Joseph Fielding Smith

George D. Pyper

Softly and tenderly ♩=63

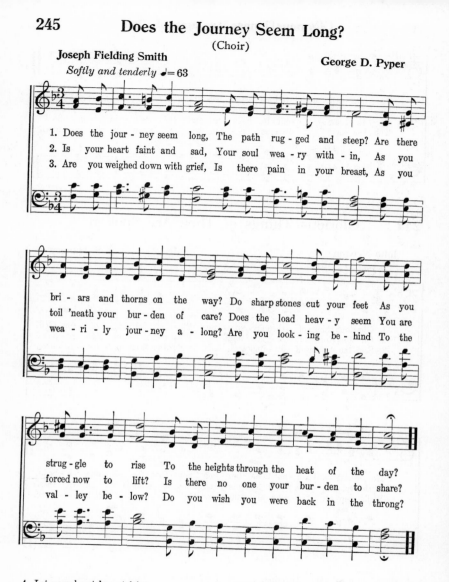

1. Does the jour-ney seem long, The path rug-ged and steep? Are there
2. Is your heart faint and sad, Your soul wea-ry with-in, As you
3. Are you weighed down with grief, Is there pain in your breast, As you

bri-ars and thorns on the way? Do sharp stones cut your feet As you
toil 'neath your bur-den of care? Does the load heav-y seem You are
wea-ri-ly jour-ney a-long? Are you look-ing be-hind To the

strug-gle to rise To the heights through the heat of the day?
forced now to lift? Is there no one your bur-den to share?
val-ley be-low? Do you wish you were back in the throng?

4. Let your heart be not faint
   Now the journey's begun;
   There is One who still beckons to you.
   Look upward in gladness
   And take hold of his hand,
   He will lead you to heights that are new,

5. A land holy and pure
   Where all trouble doth end,
   And your life shall be free from all sin,
   Where no tears shall be shed
   For no sorrows remain;
   Take his hand and with him enter in.

God Is In His Holy Temple

(Choir)

Frank W. Asper

Reverently ♩=84

1. God is in his ho - ly tem - ple. Earth - ly thoughts, be si - lent now,
2. God is in his ho - ly tem - ple, In the pure and ho - ly mind,

While with rev-erence we as - sem - ble And be - fore his pres - ence bow.
In the rev -erent heart and sim - ple; In the soul from sense re - fined.

He is with us, now and ev - er, When we call up - on his name,
Ban - ish then each base e - mo - tion. Lift us up, O Lord, to thee;

Aid - ing ev - ery good en - deav - or, Guid - ing ev - ery up - ward aim.
Let our souls, in pure de - vo - tion, Tem - ples for thy wor - ship be.

Go, Ye Messengers of Glory
(Choir)

John Taylor

Leroy J. Robertson

Joyously ♩ = 72

1. Go, ye mes-sen-gers of glo-ry; Run, ye leg-ates of the skies; Go and tell the pleas-ing sto-ry That a glo-rious an-gel flies; Great and might-y, Great and might-y, With a mes-sage from the skies.

2. Go to ev-ery tribe and na-tion; Vis-it ev-ery land and clime; Sound to all the proc-la-ma-tion; Tell to all the truth sub-lime: That the gos-pel, That the gos-pel Does in an-cient glo-ry shine.

3. Go, to all the gos-pel car-ry; Let the joy-ful news a-bound; Go till ev-ery na-tion hear you, Jew and Gen-tile greet the sound. Let the gos-pel, Let the gos-pel Ech-o all the earth a-round.

4. Bear-ing seed of heaven-ly vir-tue, Scat-ter it o'er all the earth; Go! Je-ho-vah will sup-port you, Gath-er all the sheaves of worth. Then, with Je-sus, Then, with Je-sus Reign in glo-ry on the earth.

248 Great God, Attend While Zion Sings

(Choir)

Isaac Watts

Joseph J. Daynes

Solemnly ♩ = 69

1. Great God, at-tend while Zi-on sings The joy that from thy pres-ence springs. To spend one day with thee on earth Ex-ceeds a thou-sand days of mirth.

2. Might I en-joy the mean-est place With-in thy house, O God of grace. Not tents of ease nor thrones of power Should tempt my feet to leave thy door.

3. God is our sun; he makes our day. God is our shield; He guards our way From all as-saults of hell and sin, From foes with-out and fears with-in.

4. All needful grace will God bestow
And crown that grace with glory too;
He gives us all things and withholds
No blessings due to upright souls.

5. Our God, our King whose sovereign sway
The glorious hosts of heaven obey,
(And devils at thy presence flee)
Blest is the man that trusts in thee!

249   Hark, Ten Thousand Thousand Voices

Raffles   (Choir)   Joseph J. Daynes

Energetically ♩=100

1. Hark, ten thou-sand thou-sand voic-es Sing the song of ju - bi - lee!
2. Wid - er now and loud-er ris-ing Swells and soars the loft - y strain,
3. Then in loft-ier, sweet-er num-bers We shall sing Im - man-uel's praise.

Earth, through all her tribes, re - joic-es, Broke her long cap - tiv - i - ty.
Earth's un-num-bered tongues com - pris-ing. Hark! the Con-queror's praise a - gain.
Free from all that now en - cum-bers No - bler songs our voic - es raise.

Hail, Im-man - uel! Great De-liv - erer! Hail Im - man - uel! praise to thee!
Hail, Im-man - uel! Great De-liv - erer! Stones shall speak if we re - frain;
Hail, Im-man - uel! Great De-liv - erer! Live for - ev - er in our lays,

Now, the theme, in peal-ing thun-ders, Through the un - i - verse is rung;
Thus, while heart and pulse are beat-ing, To his name let praise a - rise,
While our crowns of glo - ry cast-ing At his feet in rap - ture lost,

Now in gen - tler tones, the won-ders Of re - deem - ing grace are sung.
Till from earth the soul, re - treat-ing, Joins the cho - rus of the skies.
We, in an-thems ev - er - last-ing, Min - gle with the an - gel host.

Hark, Ten Thousand Thousand Voices

4. But till that great consummation,
That bright Sabbath of mankind,
Till each distant tribe and nation
Taste the bliss by God designed,
Speed the gospel! Let its tidings
Gladden every human mind!
Be its silver trumpets sounded;
Let the joyous echoes roll
Till a sea of bliss unbounded
Spreads on earth from pole to pole!

5. Then shall come the great Messiah,
In millennial glory crowned;
Israel's hope, and earth's desire,
Now triumphant and renowned.
Hail, Messiah! Reign forever!
Heaven to earth reflects the sound.
Heaven and earth with all their regions,
At his footstool prostrate fall;
Heaven and earth with all their legions
Crown Immanuel Lord of all!

250 The Happy Day Has Rolled On
(Choir)

Philo Dibble

Ebenezer Beesley

Brightly ♩ = 69

1. The hap-py day has roll-ed on. The truth re-stored is now made known. The prom-ised an-gel's come a-gain To in-tro-duce Mes-si-ah's reign.

2. The gos-pel trump a-gain is heard. The truth from dark-ness has ap-peared. The lands, which long be-night-ed lay, Have now be-held a glo-rious day:

3. The day by proph-ets long fore-told, The day which A-bram did be-hold, The day that Saints de-sired so long, When God his strange work would per-form:

4. The day when Saints a-gain shall hear The voice of Je-sus in their ear, And an-gels, who a-bove do reign, Come down to con-verse hold with men.

251 Again, Our Dear Redeeming Lord
(Choir)

Theodore E. Curtis

Alfred M. Durham

Andante, with feeling ♩=84

1. A - gain, our dear re - deem - ing Lord, We meet in thy be -
2. In to - ken of thy bleed - ing flesh And of thy blood so

lov - ed name, While from the foun - tains of thy love, Thy Spir - it
free - ly spent, We meet a - round thy ta - ble now And take thy

kin - dles like a flame. For all the an - guish of thy soul,
ho - ly sac - ra - ment. We seek thy par - don, dear - est Lord,

For thy great gift so full and free, With grate - ful hearts all
And may thy fa - vor too, be sent, While in our hearts we

pen - i - tent, Dear Lord, we do re - mem - ber thee.
turn to thee, Re - newed in faith and cov - e - nant.

252 Hushed Was the Evening Hymn

(Choir)

James D. Burns

Arthur Sullivan

Fluently ♩ = 84

1. Hushed was the ev - ening hymn; the tem - ple courts were dark; The
2. The old man, meek and mild, the priest of Is - rael slept; His
3. O give me Sam - uel's ear, the o - pen ear, O Lord, A -

lamp was burn - ing dim be - fore the sa - cred ark; When sud - den -
watch the tem - ple child, the lit - tle Le - vite kept; And what from
live and quick to hear each whis - per of thy word, Like him to

ly a voice di - vine rang through the si - lence of the shrine.
E - li's sense was sealed, the Lord to Han - nah's son re - vealed.
an - swer at thy call and to o - bey thee first of all.

4. O give me Samuel's heart,
   A lowly heart, that waits,
   Wherein thy house thou art
   Or watches at thy gates,
   By day and night, a heart that still ·
   Moves at the breathing of thy will!

5. O give me Samuel's mind,
   A sweet unmurmuring faith,
   Obedient and resigned
   To thee in life and death,
   That I may read with childlike eyes,
   Truths that are hidden from the wise!

253 Hark! Listen to the Trumpeters

(Choir)

George Careless

In march style ♩= 100

1. Hark, lis-ten to the trum-pet-ers! They sound for vol-un-teers.
2. It sets my heart all in a flame A sol-dier brave to be;
3. To see our ar-mies on pa-rade, How mar-tial they ap-pear!
4. The trump-ets sound, the ar-mies shout, They drive the host of hell,

On Zi-on's bright and flow-ery mount Be-hold the of-fi-cers.
I will en-list, gird on my arms, And fight for lib-er-ty.
All armed and dressed in un-i-form They look like men of war.
How dread-ful is our God, our King, The great Em-man-u-el!

Their hors-es white, their ar-mor bright, With cour-age bold they stand,
We want no cow-ards in our bands Who will our col-ors fly.
They fol-low their great Gen-er-al, The great E-ter-nal Lamb;
Sin-ners, en-list with Je-sus Christ, Th' e-ter-nal Son of God,

En-list-ing sol-diers for their King To march to Zi-on's land.
We call for val-iant-heart-ed men Who're not a-fraid to die.
His gar-ments stained in his own blood, King Je-sus is his name.
And march with us to Zi-on's land, Be-yond the swell-ing flood.

254 I'll Praise My Maker While I've Breath
(Choir)

Isaac Watts

J. G. Fones

Cheerfully ♩=72

1. I'll praise my Mak-er while I've breath; And when my voice is
2. Hap-py the man whose hopes re-ly On Is-rael's God. He
3. The Lord pours eye-sight on the blind. The Lord sup-ports the
4. I'll praise him while he lends me breath; And when my voice is

lost in death, Praise shall em-ploy my no-blest powers. My days of
made the sky And earth and sea, with all their train. His truth for-
faint-ing mind. He sends the lab-oring con-science peace. He helps the
lost in death, Praise shall em-ploy my no-bler powers. My days of

1. Praise shall em-ploy my no-blest powers.

praise shall ne'er be past While life and thought and be-ing last,
ev-er stands se-cure; He saves op-pressed ones, feeds the poor,
stran-ger in dis-tress, The wid-ow, and the fa-ther-less,
praise shall ne'er be past While life and thought and be-ing last,

While life and

While life and thought and be-ing last Or im-mor-tal-i-ty en-dures.
He saves op-pressed ones, feeds the poor, And none shall find his prom-ise vain.
The wid-ow, and the fa-ther-less, And grants the pris-oner sweet re-lease.
While life and thought and be-ing last, Or im-mor-tal-i-ty en-dures.

thought and be-ing last,

255

I Saw a Mighty Angel Fly

(Choir)

George Careless

Gladly ♩ = 84

1. I saw a might-y an-gel fly; To earth he bent his way,
2. Truth is the ti-dings which he bears, The gos-pel's joy-ful sound,
3. He cries and with a might-y voice; Ye na-tions lend an ear,

A mes-sage bear-ing from on high To cheer the sons of day.
To calm our doubts, to chase our fears, And make our joys a-bound.
And isles and con-ti-nents re-joice, The great Re-deem-er's near!

4. He cries. Let every ear attend,
And thrones and empires all!
Fear God, and make the Lord your friend,
The King, the Lord of all!

5. Fear God, and worship him who made
The heavens, earth, and sea.
Fear him on whom your sins were laid,
Who died to make you free.

256

Give Us Room That We May Dwell

(Choir)

Wm. N. B. Shepherd

Simply ♩ = 76

1. "Give us room that we may dwell," Zi-on's chil-dren cry a-loud,
2. Oh, how bright the morn-ing seems! Bright-er from so dark a night,
3. Lo! thy sun goes down no more; God Him-self will be thy light,
4. Zi-on, now a-rise and shine! Lo, thy light from heaven is come!

See their num-bers, how they swell, How they gath-er like a cloud!
Zi-on is, like one who dreams, Filled with won-der and de-light.
All that caused thee grief be-fore, Bur-ied lies in end-less night.
These that crowd from far are thine. Give thy sons and daugh-ters room.

257   If You Could Hie to Kolob

(Choir)

William W. Phelps   Joseph J. Daynes

With contemplation ♩ = 76

1. If you could hie to Ko-lob In the twink-ling of an eye,
2. Or see the grand be-gin-ning, Where space did not ex-tend?
3. The works of God con-tin-ue, And worlds and lives a-bound;

And then con-tin-ue on-ward With that same speed to fly,
Or view the last cre-a-tion, Where Gods and mat-ter end?
Im-prove-ment and pro-gres-sion Have one e-ter-nal round.

D'ye think that you could ev-er, Through all e-ter-ni-ty,
Me-thinks the Spir-it whis-pers, "No man has found 'pure space'."
There is no end to mat-ter; There is no end to space;

Find out the gen-er-a-tion Where Gods be-gan to be?
Nor seen the out-side cur-tains, Where noth-ing has a place.
There is no end to spir-it; There is no end to race.

4. There is no end to virtue;
There is no end to might;
There is no end to wisdom;
There is no end to light.
There is no end to union;
There is no end to youth;
There is no end to priesthood;
There is no end to truth.

5. There is no end to glory;
There is no end to love;
There is no end to being;
There is no death above.
There is no end to glory;
There is no end to love;
There is no end to being;
There is no death above.

258 In Remembrance Of Thy Suffering

(Choir)

Evan Stephens

Evan Stephens

Reverently ♩ = 46
mf

1. In re-mem-brance of thy suf-fering, Lord, these em-blems we par - take,
2. Pur - i - fy our hearts, our Sav - ior; Let us go not far a - stray,
3. When thou com - est in thy glo - ry To this earth to rule and reign,

When thy - self thou gavest an of - fering, Dy - ing for the sin - ner's sake.
That we may be count-ed wor - thy Of thy Spir - it day by day.
And with faith - ful ones par - tak - est Of the bread and wine a - gain,

We've for - giv - en as thou bid - dest All who've tres - passed a - gainst us.
When temp-ta - tions are be - fore us, Give us strength to o - ver - come;
May we be a - mong the num - ber Wor-thy to sur - round the board,

Lord, for - give, as we've for-giv -en, All thou seest a - miss in us.
Al - ways guard us in our wan-d'rings Till we leave our earth- ly home.
And par - take a - new the em-blems Of the suf - ferings of our Lord.

259 Jesus, Lover of My Soul

(Choir)

Charles Wesley

Joseph P. Holbrook

Cheerfully ♩ = 50

1. Je - sus, Lov - er of my soul, Let me to thy bos - om fly,
2. Oth - er ref - uge have I none, Hangs my help - less soul on thee.

While the near - er wa - ters roll, While the tem - pest still is high.
Leave, oh, leave me not a lone, Still sup - port and com - fort me.

Hide me, O my Sav - ior, hide, Till the storm of life is past.
All my trust on thee is stayed; All my help from thee I bring;

Safe in - to the hav - en guide, Oh, re - ceive my soul at last.
Cov - er my de - fense-less head With the shad - ow of thy wing.

260 Lean on My Ample Arm
(Choir)

Theodore E. Curtis

Evan Stephens

Steadily ♩=76

mf

1. Lean on my am - ple arm, Oh, thou de - pressed!
2. Lift up thy tear - ful eyes, Sad heart, to me;

And I will bid the storm Cease in thy breast.
I am the sac - ri - fice Of - fered for thee.

What - e'er thy lot may be,— On life's com - plain - ing sea,
In me thy pain shall cease, In me is thy re - lease,

If thou wilt come to me, Thou shalt have rest.
In me thou shalt have peace E - ter - nal - ly.

p

If thou wilt come to me, Thou shalt have rest.
In me thou shalt have peace E - ter - nal - ly.

261 I'm a Pilgrim; I'm a Stranger
(Choir)

H. H. Petersen

Leroy J. Robertson

Adagio ♩=60

1. I'm a pil - grim; I'm a strang - er Cast up - on the
2. Mist - y va - pors rise be - fore me. Scarce - ly can I
3. O my Fa - ther, I en - treat thee, Let me see thy

rock - y shore Of a land where death - ly dan - ger Surg - es
see the way. Clouds of dark - est hue hang o'er me, And I'm
beck - oning hand; And when stray - ing, may I meet thee, Ere I

with a sul - len roar, Oft des - pair - ing, oft des - pair - ing,
apt to go a - stray With the man - y, with the man - y
join the si - lent band. Guide me, Sav - ior, guide me Sav - ior,

1st and 2nd ten rit.   3   ten. rit.

Lest I reach my home no more.
That are now the vul - ture's prey.
(Omit   ) Safe - ly to the prom - ised land.

262 Let Zion in Her Beauty Rise
(Choir)

Edward Partridge   Lewis D. Edwards

Well marked ♩= 92

1. Let Zi - on in her beau - ty rise; Her light be - gins to shine.
2. Ye her - alds, sound the gold - en trump To earth's re - mot - est bound;
3. That glo - rious rest will then com-mence Which proph-ets did fore - tell,

Ere long her King will rend the skies, Ma - jes - tic and di - vine.
Go spread the news from pole to pole In all the na - tions round:
When Saints will reign with Christ on earth, And in his pres - ence dwell

The gos - pel spread - ing through the land, The gos - pel spread - ing
That Je - sus in the clouds a - bove, That Je - sus in the
A thou - sand years; O glo - rious day! A thou - sand years; O

through the land, The gos - pel spread-ing through the land A peo - ple to pre -
clouds a - bove, That Je - sus in the clouds a - bove, With hosts of an - gels
glo - rious day! A thou-sand years; O glo - rious day! Dear Lord, pre-pare my

Let Zion in Her Beauty Rise

pare To meet the Lord and E-noch's band, Tri - um-phant in the air.
too, Will soon ap-pear his Saints to save, His en - e - mies sub - due.
heart To stand with thee on Zi - on's mount And nev - er more to part.

263 He died! The Great Redeemer Died
(Choir)

Isaac Watts

George Careless

Reverently ♩ = 66

1. He died! the Great Re - deem - er died, And Is - rael's
2. Come, Saints, and drop a tear or two For him who
3. Here's love and grief be - yond de - gree; The Lord of
4. The ris - ing Lord for - sook the tomb. In vain the

daugh - ters wept a - round; A sol - emn dark - ness
groaned be - neath your load; He shed a thou - sand
glo - ry died for men; But lo! what sud - den
tomb for - bade him rise; Che - ru - bic le - gions

veiled the sky; A sud - den trem - bling shook the ground.
drops for you, A thou - sand drops of pre - cious blood.
joys were heard! Je - sus, though dead, re - vived a - gain.
guard him home, And shout him wel - come to the skies.

264 Lo! The Mighty God Appearing

(Choir)

William Goode

Evan Stephens

With animation ♩=100

1. Lo, the might-y God ap - pear - ing; From on high Je - ho - vah speaks!
2. Zi - on, all its light un - fold - ing, God in glo - ry shall dis - play.
3. To the heav'ns his voice as - cend - ing, To the earth be-neath he cries;

East - ern lands the sum - mons hear - ing, O'er the west his thun -der breaks.
Lo! he comes! nor si - lence hold - ing, Fire and clouds pre- pare his way,
Souls im - mor - tal, now de - scend - ing, Let their sleep-ing dust a - rise!

Earth be - hold him! Earth be - hold him! Un - i - ver - sal na - ture shakes;
Tem-pests round him! Tem- pests round him! Has - ten on the dread -ful day;
Rise to judg-ment; Rise to judg-ment; Let thy throne a - dorn the skies.

Earth be - hold him! Earth be-hold him! Un - i - ver - sal na -ture shakes.
Tem-pests round him! Tem-pests round him! Has - ten on the dread-ful day.
Rise to judg - ment; Rise to judg - ment; Let thy throne a - dorn the skies.

4. Gather first my Saints around me,
Those who to my covenants stood—
Those who humbly sought and found me
Through the dying Savior's blood.
Blest Redeemer,
Dearest Sacrifice to God.

5 Now the heavens on high adore him,
And his righteousness declare;
Sinners perish from before him,
But his saints his mercies share.
Just his judgments:
God, himself the judge, is there.

265 Lord, Thou Wilt Hear Me

(Choir)

Isaac Watts

Joseph J. Daynes

Reverently ♩. = 54

1. Lord, thou wilt hear me when I pray. I am for ev - er thine! I fear be - fore thee all the day; O may I nev - er sin, O may I nev - er sin.

2. And while I rest my wea - ry head From cares and busi - ness free, 'Tis sweet con - vers - ing on my bed With my own heart and thee, With my own heart and thee.

3. I pay this eve - ning sac - ri - fice And when my work is done, Great God, my faith, my hope re - lies Up - on thy grace a - lone, Up - on thy grace a - lone.

4. Thus, with my thoughts com - posed to peace, I'll give mine eyes to sleep; Thy hand in safe - ty keeps my days And will my slum - bers keep, And will my slum - bers keep.

266 We're Not Ashamed to Own Our Lord
(Choir)

William W. Phelps   Joseph J. Daynes

Without dragging ♩=100

1. We're not a-shamed to own our Lord And wor-ship him on earth. We
2. When Je - sus comes in burn - ing flame To rec - om-pense the just, The
3. When he comes down from heaven to earth, With all his ho - ly band, Be -
4. He then will give us our "new name" With robes of right-eous - ness, And

love to learn his ho - ly word And know what souls are worth. We
world will know the on - ly name In which the Saints can trust. The
fore cre - a - tion's sec - ond birth, We hope with him to stand. Be
in the new Je - ru - sa-lem E - ter - nal hap - pi - ness. And

We love to learn his ho- ly word,

love to learn his ho - ly word, We love to learn his ho - ly word,
world will know the on - ly name, The world will know the on - ly name,
fore cre - a - tion's sec - ond birth, Be - fore cre - a - tion's sec - ond birth,
in the new Je - ru - sa - lem, And in the new Je - ru - sa - lem,

We love to learn his ho - ly word And know what souls are worth.
The world will know the on - ly name In which the Saints can trust.
Be - fore cre - a - tion's sec - ond birth We hope with him to stand.
And in the new Je - ru - sa - lem E - ter - nal hap - pi - ness.

267 Not Now, But in the Coming Years

(Choir)

Maxwell N. Cornelius

James McGranahan

Tenderly ♩ = 58

1. Not now, but in the com-ing years, It may be in the bet-ter land,
2. We'll catch the bro-ken threads a-gain And fin-ish what we here be-gan;
3. We'll know why clouds in-stead of sun Were o-ver man-y a cher-ished plan,

We'll read the mean-ing of our tears, And there, some-time, we'll un-der-stand.
Heaven will the mys-ter-ies ex-plain, And then, ah then we'll un-der-stand.
Why song has ceased when scarce be-gun; 'Tis there some-time we'll un-der-stand.

Then trust in God through all thy days; Fear not, for he doth hold thy hand;

Though dark thy way, still sing and praise, Some-time, some-time we'll un-der-stand.

4. Why what we long for most of all
Eludes so oft our eager hand,
Why hopes are crushed and castles fall,
Up there, sometime we'll understand.

5. God knows the way; he holds the key;
He guides us with unerring hand;
Sometime with tearless eyes we'll see,
Yes, there, up there we'll understand.

268   O Awake! My Slumbering Minstrel
(Choir)

Eliza R. Snow   Evan Stephens

Brightly ♩.=63

1. O a - wake! my slum-bering min-strel, Let my harp for - get its spell;
2. Strike a chord un - known to sad-ness, Strike and let its num-bers tell
3. Zi - on's wel - fare is my por-tion, And I feel my bos-om swell

Say, O say, in sweet-est ac - cents, Zi - on pros - pers; all is well;
In ce - les - tial tones of glad - ness, Zi - on pros - pers; all is well;
With a warm, di - vine e - mo - tion When she pros - pers; all is well;

Zi - on pros-pers; Zi - on pros - pers; Zi - on pros-pers; all is well.
Zi - on pros-pers; Zi - on pros - pers; Zi - on pros-pers; all is well.
When she pros-pers; When she pros - pers; When she pros-pers; all is well.

4. Zion, lo, thy day is dawning,
Though the darksome shadows swell,
Faith and hope prelude the morning;
Thou art prospering; all is well;
Thou art prospering; Thou art prospering.
Thou art prospering; all is well.

5. Thy swift messengers are treading
The high courts where princes dwell,
And thy glorious light is spreading;
Zion prospers; all is well;
Zion prospers; Zion prospers;
Zion prospers; all is well.

269 The Morning Breaks; the Shadows Flee

(Choir)

Parley P. Pratt

George Careless

Triumphantly ♩=92

1. The morn-ing breaks; the shad-ows flee; Lo, Zi-on's stan-dard
2. The clouds of er-ror dis-ap-pear Be-fore the rays of
3. The Gen-tile ful-ness now comes in, And Is-rael's bless-ings

is un-furled! The dawn-ing of a bright-er day, The dawn-ing
truth di-vine; The glo-ry burst-ing from a-far, The glo-ry
are at hand. Lo, Ju-dah's rem-nant, cleansed from sin, Lo, Ju-dah's

of a brigh-ter day Ma-jes-tic ris - es on the world.
burst-ing from a-far Wide o'er the na - tions soon will shine.
rem - nant, cleansed from sin, Shall in their prom - ised Ca-naan stand.

4. Jehovah speaks! let earth give ear,
   And Gentile nations turn and live.
   His mighty arm is making bare,
   His mighty arm is making bare
   His covenant people to receive.

5. Angels from heaven and truth from earth
   Have met, and both have record borne;
   Thus Zion's light is bursting forth,
   Thus Zion's light is bursting forth
   To bring her ransomed children home.

270
O My Father
(Familiar Tune)
(Choir)

Eliza R. Snow

James McGranahan
Arr. by Evan Stephens

With deep feeling ♩. = 50

SOLO *mf*

1. O my Fa - ther, thou that dwell - est In the
2. For a wise and glo - rious pur - pose Thou hast
3. I had learned to call thee Fa - ther, Through thy
4. When I leave this frail ex - ist - ence, When I

1. O my Fa - ther, thou that dwell - est
2. For a wise and glo - rious pur - pose
3. I had learned to call thee Fa - ther,
4. When I leave this frail ex - ist - ence,

high and glo-rious place! When shall I re - gain thy
placed me here on earth, And with-held the re - col-
Spir - it from on high; But, un - til the Key of
lay this mor tal by, Fa - ther, Moth - er, may I

In the high and glo-rious place! When shall I re - gain thy
Thou hast placed me here on earth, And with-held the re - col-
Through thy Spir - it from on high; But, un - til the Key of
When I lay this mor-tal by, Fa - ther, Moth - er, may I

O My Father

O My Father

271 O Lord of Hosts
(Choir)

A. Dalrymple

George Careless

Suppliantly ♩=66

1. O Lord of hosts, we now in-voke Thy Spir - it most di - vine
2. May we for - ev - er think of thee And of thy suf-ferings sore,
3. Pre - pare our minds that we may see The beau - ties of thy grace,

To cleanse our hearts while we par-take The bro - ken bread, and wine.
En - dured for us on Cal - va - ry, And praise thee ev - er - more.
Sal - va - tion pur-chased on that tree For all who seek thy face.

4. As brethren let us ever live
In fellowship and peace!
Forgive, that God may us forgive,
That love may still increase.

5. May union, peace, and love abound,
And perfect harmony,
And joy in one continual round
Through all eternity.

272 One Sweetly Solemn Thought
(Choir)

Phoebe Cary

R. S. Ambrose

Solemnly ♩=58

Introduction

One Sweetly Solemn Thought

One Sweetly Solemn Thought

fore, Near-er my Fa-ther's house Where the man-y man-sions

be, Near-er the great white throne, Near-er the crys-tal sea,

Near-er the bounds of life where we lay our bur-dens

One Sweetly Solemn Thought

down, lay our bur-dens down, Near - er leav - ing the cross,

Near - er gain-ing the crown. But ly - ing dark-ly be-

tween, Wind-ing a-down through the night,

Is the si - lent, un-known stream That leads at last to the

One Sweetly Solemn Thought

Slowly

273 On The Mountain's Top Appearing

(Choir)

John Kelly

Simply ♩=84

1. On the moun-tain's top ap - pear-ing, Lo, the sa - cred
2. Lo, thy sun is risen in glo - ry! God him - self ap-
3. En - e - mies no more shall trou - ble: All thy wrongs shall

her - ald stands, Wel - come news to Zi - on bear - ing,
pears thy Friend. All thy foes shall flee be - fore thee.
be re - dressed, For thy shame thou shalt have dou - ble,

Zi - on, long in hos - tile lands. Mourn-ing cap - tive!
Hear their boast - ed tri - umphs end. Great de - liv - erance,
In thy Mak - er's fa - vor blest; All thy con - flicts,

Mourn-ing cap - tive! God him - self shall loose thy bands.
Great de - liv - erance Zi - on's King vouch-safes to send.
All thy con - flicts End in an e - ter - nal rest.

274 O Thou, Before the World Began

(Choir)

W. B. Turton

Frank W. Asper

Prayerfully ♩=84

1. O thou, be - fore the world be - gan, Or - dained a Sac - ri -
2. Thy of - fering still con - tin - ues new Be - fore the right - eous
3. O that our faith may nev - er move, But stand un - shak - en

fice for man, And by th' e - ter - nal spir - it made An
Fa - ther's view; Thy - self the Lamb for - ev - er slain; Thy
as thy love, Sure ev - i - dence of things un - seen, Now

of - fering in the sin - ner's stead; Our ev - er - last - ing
priest - hood doth un - changed re - main. Thy years, O God, can
let it pass the years be - tween And view thee bleed - ing

Priest art thou, Plead - ing thy death for sin - ners now.
nev - er fail Nor thy blest work with - in the veil.
on the tree: My Lord, my God, who dies for me.

275 What Voice Salutes the Startled Ear?

(Choir)

Henry W. Naisbitt

Ebenezer Beesley

Solemnly ♩=60

1. What voice sa-lutes the start-led ear And wakes the strick-en heart,
2. This doth not spring from earth-ly soil Nor from its wis-dom grow;
3. Here, where the o-pen bier sus-tains The friend just passed a-way,
4. And so we thank thee, Fa-ther, God; Thy voice will raise the dead,

Yet seems to chide each child-ish fear, And life a-gain im-part?
'Tis not e-voked by stu-dent's toil, Though years hath crowned with snow.
We know that glad re-lief ob-tains From its en-cum-ber-ing clay.
E'en though a thorn-y path they trod Or were by Cal-va-ry led;

Is it an ech-o of the past, To which we si-lent cling?
No! rich ex-per-ience bids this swell, Di-vine its pre-cious ring—
While by the read-y grave we stand, Ex-ult-ing faith we bring—
'Twas there thy Son, our Sav-ior, went, And man by this can sing:

"O grave, where is thy vic-to-ry? O grave, where is thy vic-to-ry?

What Voice Salutes the Startled Ear?

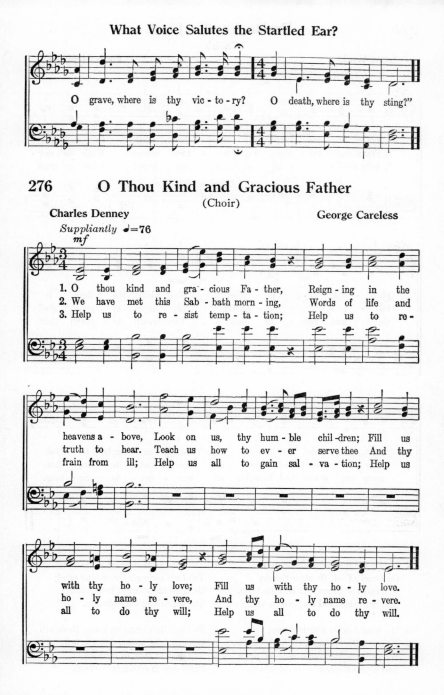

O grave, where is thy vic-to-ry? O death, where is thy sting?"

276　O Thou Kind and Gracious Father
(Choir)

Charles Denney　　　　　　　　　　　　　　George Careless

Suppliantly ♩=76
mf

1. O thou kind and gra-cious Fa-ther, Reign-ing in the
2. We have met this Sab-bath morn-ing, Words of life and
3. Help us to re-sist temp-ta-tion; Help us to re-

heavens a-bove, Look on us, thy hum-ble chil-dren; Fill us
truth to hear. Teach us how to ev-er serve thee And thy
frain from ill; Help us all to gain sal-va-tion; Help us

with thy ho-ly love; Fill us with thy ho-ly love.
ho-ly name re-vere, And thy ho-ly name re-vere.
all to do thy will; Help us all to do thy will.

277 Praise Ye the Lord

(Choir)

Isaac Watts

Evan Stephens

With spirit ♩=84

1. Praise ye the Lord! my heart shall join In work so
2. Praise shall em - ploy my no - blest powers While im - mor -
3. Why should I make a man my trust? Princ - es must

pleas - ant, so di - vine, Now, while the flesh is
tal - i - ty en - dures; My days of praise shall
die and turn to dust; Their breath de - parts; their

my a - bode And when my soul as - cends to God.
ne'er be past While life and thought and be - ing last.
pomp and power And thoughts all van - ish in an hour.

4. Happy the man whose hopes rely
On Israel's God! He made the sky
And earth and seas with all their train,
And none shall find his promise vain.

5. His truth forever stands secure;
He saves th'oppressed; He feeds the poor;
He sends the troubled conscience peace
And grants the captive sweet release.

6. The Lord gives eyesight to the blind,
The Lord supports the sinking mind;
He helps the stranger in distress,
The widow and the fatherless.

7. He loves the Saints; he knows them well
But turns the wicked down to hell;
Thy God, O Zion, ever reigns,
Praise him in everlasting strains.

278 Rest, Rest for the Weary Soul

(Choir)

Henry W. Naisbitt   George Careless

Peacefully ♩=58

1. Rest, rest for the wea-ry soul; Rest, rest for the ach-ing head;
2. Rest, rest for the bat-tle's o'er; Rest, rest for the race is run;
3. Peace, peace where no strife in-trudes, Peace, peace, where no quar-rels come,

Rest, rest on the hill-side, rest With the great un-count-ed dead.
Rest, rest where the gates are closed With each ev-ening's set-ting sun.
Peace, peace, for the end is there Of our wild life's bus-y hum.

4. Peace, peace, the op-pressed are free; Rest, rest, oh, ye wea-ry, rest,
5. Peace, peace, there is mu-sic's sound, Peace, peace, till the ris-ing sun

For the an-gels guard those well Who sleep on their moth-er's breast.
Of the res-ur-rec-tion morn Pro-claims life's vic-tory won.

279

Ring Out, Wild Bells

(Choir)

Alfred Tennyson   **Crawford M. Gates**

With fervor ♩. = 72

1. Ring out, wild bells, to the wild sky, The fly-ing cloud, the
2. Ring out the old; ring in the new; Ring hap-py bells a-
3. Ring in the val-iant men and free, The larg-er heart, the

frost-y light; The year is dy-ing in the night; Ring
cross the snow; The year is go-ing; let him go; Ring
kind-lier hand; Ring out the dark-ness of the land; Ring

out, wild bells, and let him die. The year is dy-ing
out the false; ring in the true. The year is go-ing,
in the Christ that is to be. Ring out the dark-ness

in the night; Ring out, wild bells, and let him die.
let him go; Ring out, the false; ring in the true.
of the land; Ring in the Christ that is to be.

280 Reverently and Meekly Now
(Choir)

Joseph L. Townsend   Ebenezer Beesley

Reverently ♩ = 72

1. Rev - erent - ly and meek-ly now Let thy head most hum - bly bow.
2. In this bread now blest for thee, Em - blem of my bod - y see;
3. Bid thine heart all strife to cease; With thy breth-ren be at peace.
4. At the throne I in - ter - cede. For thee ev - er do I plead.

Think of me, thou ran-somed one; Think what I for thee have done
In this wa - ter or this wine, Em - blem of my blood di - vine.
Oh, for - give, as thou wouldst be E'en for - giv - en now by me.
I have loved thee as thy friend With a love that can - not end.

Instrument

With my blood that dripped like rain, Sweat in ag - o - ny of pain.
Oh, re - mem - ber what was done That the sin - ner might be won.
In the sol - emn faith of prayer Cast up - on me all thy care,
Be o - be - dient, I im-plore, Prayer-ful, watch-ful, ev - er - more,

Voices   1st and 2nd Sopranos

With my bod - y on the tree I have ran - somed e - ven thee.
On the cross of Cal - va - ry I have suf - fered death for thee.
And my spir - it's grace shall be Like a foun - tain un - to thee.
And be con - stant un - to me That thy Sav - ior I may be.

281 Sacred the Place of Prayer and Song

(Choir)

Evan Stephens   Evan Stephens

Peacefully ♩=60

1. Sa - cred the place of prayer and song, The house of sac - ra - ment;
2. Fa - ther, do thou but touch each heart With pure and good de - sire.

How sweet to view the peace - ful throng, So si - lent and con - tent!
Free - ly do thou to us im - part Thy Ho - ly Spir - it's fire.

Each come to taste the pow - er from a - bove,
Then shall we know our sins have been for - given,

The in - spi - ra - tion, and the glow Of ho - ly love.
The cov - e - nants we make with thee Are sealed in heaven.

282   Savior, Redeemer of My Soul
(Choir)

Orson F. Whitney

Evan Stephens

Fervently ♩ = 54

1. Sav - ior, Re-deem - er of my soul, Whose might - y hand hath made me whole, Whose won - drous power hath raised me up, And filled with sweet my bit - ter cup! What tongue my gra - ti - tude can tell, O gra - cious God of Is - ra - el.

2. Nev - er can I re - pay thee, Lord; But I can love thee. Thy pure word, Hath it not been my one de - light, My joy by day, my dream by night? Then let my lips pro - claim it still, And all my life re - flect thy will.

3. O'er - rule mine acts to serve thine ends; Change frown - ing foes to smil - ing friends; Chas - ten my soul till I shall be In per - fect har - mo - ny with thee. Make me more wor - thy of thy love, And fit me for the life a - bove.

283   Up! Arouse Thee, O Beautiful Zion

(Choir)

Emily H. Woodmansee

Leroy J. Robertson

Marcia ♩ = 96

1. Up! a - rouse thee, O beau - ti - ful Zi - on!
2. Up! a - rouse thee, O beau - ti - ful Zi - on!
3. Who should shrink from the glo - ri - ous bat - tle,
4. Lo! des - truc - tion hangs o - ver the na - tions,

Wake, a - wake, hear the war - der's deep cry, For the
Give the mam - mon - care clouds to the wind. When the
With so daz - zling a guer - don in view? If so
Though not seen by the un - ho - ly throng; And death

sea - son of slum - ber hath end - ed; And the spoil - er is
bu - gle's shrill sum - mons is, Ral - ly! They are cow - ards that
base as to herd with the trait - or, It is das - tard! not
will be heard in the ech - oes Of the gath - er - ing,

rit.   *a tempo*

watch - ful and nigh. With cour - age e - late and heart to be
lin - ger be - hind. You've foes to o'er - come in each heart and each
spark - ling for you. Who with nerve strong as steel, and soul that can
om - i - nous storm! Then a - rouse thee, O beau - ti - ful Zi -

Up! Arouse Thee, O Beautiful Zion

284 Softly Beams the Sacred Dawning
(Choir)

John Jaques   George Careless

Andante ♩= 72

1. Soft - ly beams the sa - cred dawn - ing Of the great mil - len - nial morn, And to Saints gives wel - come warn-ing That the day is hast - ing on, That the day is hast - ing on.
2. Splen - did, ris - ing o'er the moun-tains, Glow - ing with ce - les - tial cheer, Stream-ing from e - ter - nal foun-tains, Rays of liv - ing light ap - pear, Rays of liv - ing light ap - pear.
3. Swift - ly flee the clouds of dark - ness, Speed - i - ly the mists re - tire; Na - ture's u - ni - ver - sal black-ness Is con - sumed by heaven - ly fire, Is con - sumed by heaven - ly fire.
4. Yea, the fair sab - bat - ic e - ra, When the world will be at rest, Rap - id - ly is draw-ing near - er; Then all Is - rael will be blest, Then all Is - rael will be blest.

5. Odors sweet the air perfuming,
   Verdure of the purest green;
   In primeval beauty beaming
   Will our native earth be seen.

6. At the resurrection morning,
   We shall all appear as one;
   O what robes of bright adorning
   Will the righteous then put on!

7. None have seen the untold treasures
   Which the Father hath in store,
   Teeming with surpassing pleasures,
   Even life for evermore.

8. Mourn no longer, Saints beloved;
   Brave the dangers, no retreat;
   Neither let your hearts be moved;
   Scorn the trials you may meet.

285 Though Deepening Trials

(Choir)

Eliza R. Snow

George Careless

Cheerfully ♩ = 88

1. Though deep-ening tri - als throng your way, Press on, press on, ye
2. Though out - ward ills a - wait us here, The time at long - est
3. Lift up your hearts in praise to God; Let your re - joic - ings

Saints of God! Ere long the res - ur - rec - tion day Will spread its
is not long Ere Je - sus Christ will re - ap - pear, Sur - round - ed
nev - er cease; Though trib - u - la - tions rage a - broad, Christ says, "In

life and truth a - broad, Will spread its life and truth a - broad.
by a glo - rious throng, Sur - round - ed by a glo - rious throng.
me ye shall have peace," Christ says, "In me ye shall have peace."

4. What though our rights have been assailed?
What though by foes we've been despoiled?
Jehovah's promise has not failed;
Jehovah's purpose is not foiled.

5. His work is moving on apace,
And great events are rolling forth;
The kingdom of the latter days,
The "little stone," must fill the earth.

6. Though Satan rage, 'tis all in vain;
The words the ancient Prophet spoke,
Sure as the throne of God remain;
Nor men nor devils can revoke.

7. All glory to his holy name
Who sends his faithful servants forth
To prove the nations, to proclaim
Salvation's tidings through the earth.

286 Unanswered Yet? The Prayer

(Choir)

Ophelia G. Adams

Charles D. Tillman

Tenderly ♩ = 50

1. Un - an - swered yet? The prayer your lips have plead - ed In ag - o - ny of heart these man - y years? Does faith be - gin to fail, is hope de - part - ing, And think you all in vain those fall - ing tears? Say not the Fa - ther hath not heard your prayer; You shall have your de - sire, some -

2. Un - an - swered yet? Though when you first pre - sent - ed This one pe - ti - tion at the Fa - ther's throne, It seemed you could not wait the time of ask - ing, So ur - gent was your heart to make it known. Though years have passed since then, do not de - spair; The Lord will an - swer you, some -

3. Un - an - swered yet? Nay, do not say un - grant - ed; Per - haps your part is not yet whol -ly done; The work be - gan when first your prayer was ut - tered, And God will fin - ish what he has be - gun. If you will keep the spir - it burn - ing there, His glo - ry you shall see, some -

4. Un - an - swered yet? Faith can - not be un - an - swered; Her feet were firm - ly plant-ed on the rock; A - mid the wild-est storm prayer stands un - daunt - ed, Nor quails be - fore the loud - est thun - der shock. She knows Om - nip - o - tence has heard her prayer, And cries, "It shall be done," some -

Unanswered Yet? The Prayer

Rit.   *Ad lib.*

time, some - where, You shall have your de - sire, some-time,   some-where.
time, some - where, The Lord will an- swer you, some-time,   some-where.
time, some - where, His glo - ry you shall see, some-time,   some-where.
time, some - where, And cries, "It shall be done," some-time,   some-where.

287 Lord of All Being, Throned Afar
(Choir)

Oliver Wendell Holmes

Leroy J. Robertson

Majestically ♩=52

1. Lord of all be - ing, throned a - far, Thy glo - ry
2. Sun of our life, thy quick- ening ray Sheds on our
3. Our mid - night is thy smile with - drawn; Our noon - tide

flames from sun and star, Cen - ter and soul of
path the glow of day; Star of our hope, thy
is thy gra - cious dawn; Our rain - bow arch, thy

ev - ery sphere, Yet to each lov - ing heart how near!
sof - tened light Cheers the long watch - es of the night.
mer - cy's sign; All, save the clouds of sin, are thine.

4. Lord of all life, below, above,
Whose light is truth, whose warmth is love,
Before thy ever-blazing throne
We ask no luster of our own.

5. Grant us thy truth to make us free,
And kindle hearts that burn for thee
Till all thy living altars claim
One holy light, one heavenly flame.

Ye Children of Our God

(Choir)

Parley P. Pratt

George Careless

Reverently ♩=69

1. Ye chil-dren of our God, Ye Saints of lat-ter days, Sur-
2. He gives his flesh and blood, Our souls to pur-i-fy, And
3. We do re-mem-ber him, His sor-row, pain, and death, And
4. He tri-umphed o'er the grave And then as-cend-ed high, Where

round the ta-ble of our Lord, Sur-round the ta-ble of our
bless-es us with ev-ery good, And bless-es us with ev-ery
how with power he rose a-gain, And how with power he rose a-
throned in power he sits to save, Where throned in power he sits to

Lord, And join to sing his praise, And join to sing his praise.
good, And thus he brings us nigh, And thus he brings us nigh.
gain, Tri-um-phant from the earth, Tri-um-phant from the earth.
save And bring the sin-ner nigh, And bring the sin-ner nigh.

5. He soon will come again,
   And with his people taste
   The marriage supper of the Lamb,
   With his own presence blest.

6. Arrayed in spotless white,
   We'll then each other greet,
   And see Messiah throned in might,
   And worship at his feet.

289

The Voice of God Again Is Heard

(Choir)

Evan Stephens

Evan Stephens

Majestically ♩=63

1. The voice of God a - gain is heard. The si - lence has been bro - ken. The curse of dark - ness is with - drawn. The Lord from heaven hath spo - ken. Re - joice, ye liv - ing and ye dead! Re - joice, for your sal - va - tion Be - gins a - new this hap - py morn Of fi - nal dis - pen - sa - tion.

2. O mes - sen - gers of truth, go forth, Pro - claim the gos - pel sto - ry. Go forth the na - tions to pre - pare To greet the King of glo - ry. Shout we ho - san - na, shout a - gain Till all cre - a - tion blend - ing Shall join in one great grand a - men Of an - thems nev - er end - ing.

Ye Simple Souls Who Stray

(Choir)

Wesley's Collection

Evan Stephens

Calmly ♩ = 69

1. Ye sim - ple souls who stray Far from the path of peace,
2. Mad - ness and mis - er - y Ye count our life be - neath,
3. So wretch-ed and ob - scure, The man whom ye de - spise,
4. Rich - es un - search - a - ble In Je - sus' love we know,

That lone - ly, un - fre - quent-ed way To life and hap - pi -
And noth - ing great or good can see Or glo - rious in our
So fool - ish, im - po - tent, and poor, A - bove your scorn we
And pleas - ures spring - ing from the well Of life our souls o'er -

ness, Why will ye fol - ly love And throng the down - ward road,
death; As on - ly born to grieve, Be - neath your feet we lie,
rise. We through the Ho - ly Ghost Can wit - ness bet - ter things,
flow. The Spir - it we re - ceive Of wis - dom, grace, and power:

And hate the wis - dom from a - bove, And mock the sons of God?
And ut - ter - ly con - temned we live And un - la - ment -ed die.
For he, whose blood is all our boast, Has made us priests and kings.
And though 'mid scenes of woe we live, Re - joic - ing ev - er -more.

Ye Simple Souls Who Stray

5. Angels our servants are
   And keep in all our ways;
   And in their watchful hands they bear
   The sacred sons of grace;
   Unto that heavenly bliss
   They all our steps attend,
   And God himself our Father is,
   And Jesus is our Friend.

6. With him we walk in white;
   We in his image shine;
   Our robes are robes of glorious light,
   Our righteousness divine.
   On all the kings of earth
   With pity we look down;
   And claim, in virtue of our birth,
   A never-fading crown.

291   A Voice Hath Spoken From the Dust
(Choir)

J. Marinus Jensen   J. J. Keeler

Joyously ♩ = 100

1. A voice hath spo-ken from the dust, Its mes-sage pure with-out al-loy Of treas-ured hope, and sa-cred trust. O "Men are that they might have joy."
2. Should sor-row come, we'll not de-spair, For he would not that men should pine; The grief that comes we'll learn to bear Un-til a-gain the sun doth shine.
3. Be-fore the Lord then hum-bly go; His mes-sage will our spir-its buoy; On us his bless-ings he'll be-stow, For "Men are that they might have joy."

292 The Wintry Day, Descending to Its Close
(Choir)

Orson F. Whitney   Edward P. Kimball

Calmly ♩=63
mf

1. The win - try day, de - scend-ing to its close, In - vites all
2. I can - not go to rest but lin - ger still In med - i -
3. A - way be - yond the prair-ies of the West Where ex - iled
4. The wil - der - ness, that naught be - fore would yield, Is now be -

wea - ried na - ture to re - pose, And shades of night are
ta - tion at my win - dow sill, While, like the twink - ling
Saints in sol - i - tude were blest; Where in - dus - try the
come a fer - tile, fruit - ful field. Where roamed at will the

fall - ing dense and fast Like sa - ble cur - tains clos - ing o'er the
stars in heav - en's dome, Come one by one sweet mem - o - ries of
seal of wealth has set A - mid the peace - ful vales of Des - er -
sav - age In - dian band, The tem - pled cit - ies of the Saints now

past. Pale through the gloom the new - ly fall - en snow Wraps in a
home. And wouldst thou ask me where my fan - cy roves To re - pro -
et, Un - heed - ing still the fierc-est blasts that blow, With tops en -
stand. And sweet re - li - gion in its pur - i - ty In - vites all

The Wintry Day, Descending to Its Close

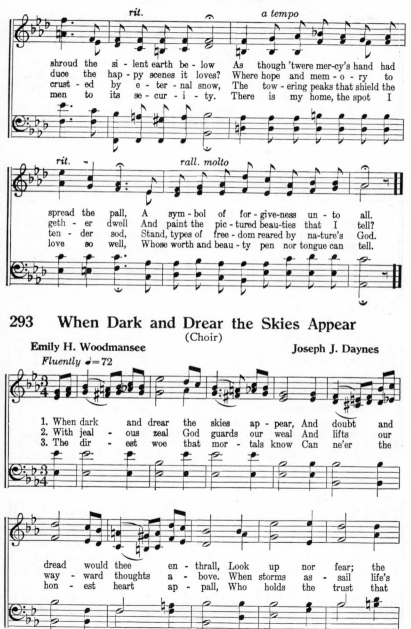

rit.   *a tempo*

shroud the si - lent earth be - low As though 'twere mer-cy's hand had
duce the hap - py scenes it loves? Where hope and mem - o - ry to
crust - ed by e - ter - nal snow, The tow - ering peaks that shield the
men to its se - cur - i - ty. There is my home, the spot I

rit.   *rall. molto*

spread the pall, A sym - bol of for - give-ness un - to all.
geth - er dwell And paint the pic - tured beau-ties that I tell?
ten - der sod, Stand, types of free - dom reared by na-ture's God.
love so well, Whose worth and beau - ty pen nor tongue can tell.

293   When Dark and Drear the Skies Appear
(Choir)

Emily H. Woodmansee   Joseph J. Daynes

Fluently ♩ = 72

1. When dark and drear the skies ap - pear, And doubt and
2. With jeal - ous zeal God guards our weal And lifts our
3. The dir - est woe that mor - tals know Can ne'er the

dread would thee en - thrall, Look up nor fear; the
way - ward thoughts a - bove. When storms as - sail life's
hon - est heart ap - pall, Who holds the trust that

When Dark and Drear the Skies Appear

day   is   near;   And   Prov - i - dence   is   o - ver   all.
bark   so   frail,   We   seek   the   ha - ven   of   his   love.
God   is   just,   And   Prov - i - dence   is   o - ver   all.

From   heaven a - bove,   his   light   and love,   God   giv - eth
And   when our eyes   tran - scend   the skies,   His   gra - cious
Should foes in - crease   to   mar   our peace,   Frus - trat - ed

free - ly   when   we   call.   Our   ut - most   need   is
pur - pose   is   com - plete.   No   more   the   night   dis -
all   their   plans   shall   fall.   Our   ut - most   need   is

rit.

oft   de - creed,   And   Prov - i - dence   is   o - ver   all.
tracts   our   sight;   The   clouds   are   all   be - neath   our   feet.
oft   de - creed,   And   Prov - i - dence   is   o - ver   all.

294 I Wander Through the Stilly Night

(Choir)

Theodore E. Curtis

Hugh W. Dougall

Moderato ♩= 84

1. I wan - der through the still - y night, When sol - i - tude is
2. When I am filled with strong de - sire, And ask a boon of
3. It mat - ters not what may be - fall, What threat-ening hand hangs

ev - ery-where. A - lone, be - neath the star - ry light And yet I
Him, I see No mir - a - cle of liv - ing fire But what I
o - ver me, He is my ram - part through it all, My ref - uge

know that God is there. I kneel up - on the grass and pray,
ask flows in - to me. And when the tem - pest rag - es high
from mine en - e - my. Come un - to him all ye de - prest;

An an - swer comes with - out a voice. It takes my bur - den
I feel no arm a - round me thrust, But ev - ery storm goes
Ye err - ing souls whose eyes are dim, Ye wea - ry ones who

all a - way And makes my ach - ing heart re - joice.
roll - ing by When I re - pose in him my trust.
long for rest, Come un - to him! come un - to him!

295 When Christ Was Born in Bethlehem
(Choir)

Henry W. Longfellow   Ebenezer Beesley

With spirit ♩ = 108

1. When Christ was born in Beth - le - hem, 'Twas night, but seemed the
2. Then peace was spread through-out the land; The li - on fed be -
3. As shep-herds watched their flocks by night, An an - gel, bright-er

noon of day; The stars, whose light Was pure and bright, Shone with un - wav-ering
side the lamb; And with the kid To pas - ture led The spot-ted leop-ard
than the sun, Ap - peared in air, And gent - ly said, "Fear not, be not a -

poco rit.   *a tempo*

ray, Shone with un - wav-ering ray; But one, one glo - rious star, But
fed, The spot - ted leop - ard fed; In peace the calf and bear, In
fraid, Fear not, be not a - fraid. For lo! be - neath your eyes, For

rit.

one, one glo - rious star Guid - ed the east-ern ma - gi from a - far.
peace the calf and bear, The wolf and lamb re-posed to - geth - er there.
lo! be-neath your eyes Earth has be - come a smil - ing par - a - dise!"

The Seer, Joseph, The Seer

(Choir)

John Taylor

Neukomm
Arr. by Ebenezer Beesley

Allegro moderato ♩. = 60

1. The Seer, the Seer, Jo - seph, the Seer!
2. Of no - ble seed, of heav - en - ly birth,
3. The Saints, the Saints, his on - ly pride!
4. He's free! he's free! the Proph - et's free!

Tenor Solo

I'll sing of the Proph - et ev - er dear, the Proph - et ev - er
He came to bless the sons of earth, to bless the sons of
For them he lived, for them he died; he lived, for them he
He is where he will ev - er be, where he will ev - er

dear;
earth;
died;
be,

His e - qual
With keys by
Their joys were
Be - yond the

The Seer, Joseph, The Seer

now   can-not be found   By   search-ing the   wide world a-round.
the   Al- might-y given, He   opened the full   rich stores of heaven;
his,   their sor-rows too. He   loved the Saints; he   loved Nau-voo.
reach   of mobs and strife, He   rests un-harmed in end - less life.

With   Gods   he   soared   in the   realms   of day,
O'er the world   that was wrapped in   sa - ble night,
Un - changed   in death,   with a   Sav - ior's love,
His   home's   in the sky;   he   dwells with the Gods

Chorus

And   men   he taught the   heaven-ly way, And   men   he taught the
Like the sun he spread his   gold - en light, Like the sun he spread his
He   pleads their cause in the courts a - bove. He   pleads their cause in the
Far   from the fu - ri-ous rage of mobs, Far   from the fu - ri-ous

The Seer, Joseph, The Seer

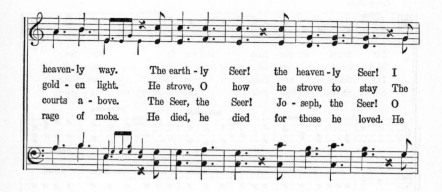

heaven-ly way. The earth - ly Seer! the heaven - ly Seer! I
gold - en light. He strove, O how he strove to stay The
courts a - bove. The Seer, the Seer! Jo - seph, the Seer! O
rage of mobs. He died, he died for those he loved. He

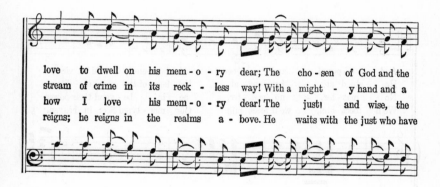

love to dwell on his mem - o - ry dear; The cho - sen of God and the
stream of crime in its reck - less way! With a might - y hand and a
how I love his mem - o - ry dear! The just, and wise, the
reigns; he reigns in the realms a - bove. He waits with the just who have

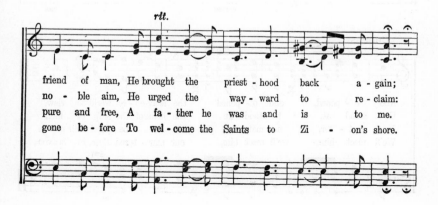

rit.

friend of man, He brought the priest - hood back a - gain;
no - ble aim, He urged the way - ward to re - claim:
pure and free, A fa - ther he was and is to me.
gone be - fore To wel - come the Saints to Zi - on's shore.

The Seer, Joseph, The Seer

He gazed on the past and the fu - ture, too,
'Mid foam - ing bil - lows of an - gry strife,
Let fiends now rage, in their dark hour—
Shout, shout, ye Saints! this boon is given;

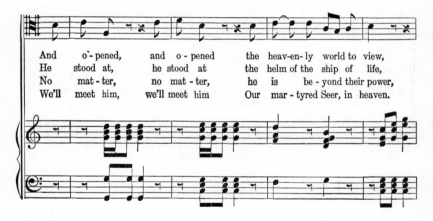

And o - pened, and o - pened the heav-en-ly world to view,
He stood at, he stood at the helm of the ship of life,
No mat - ter, no mat - ter, he is be - yond their power,
We'll meet him, we'll meet him Our mar - tyred Seer, in heaven.

CHORUS

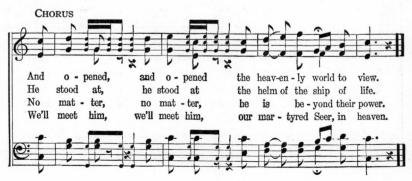

And o - pened, and o - pened the heav-en-ly world to view.
He stood at, he stood at the helm of the ship of life.
No mat - ter, no mat - ter, he is be - yond their power.
We'll meet him, we'll meet him, our mar - tyred Seer, in heaven.

297   Behold, the Mountain of the Lord

(Choir)

Logan

Joseph J. Daynes

Joyously ♩=100

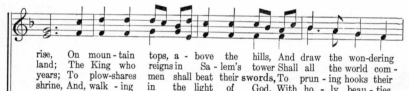

1. Be - hold, the moun - tain of the Lord In lat - ter days shall
2. The rays that shine from Zi - on's hill Shall light - en ev - ery
3. No strife shall rage, nor hos - tile feuds Dis - turb those peace - ful
4. Come, then, O house of Ja - cob, come, To wor - ship at His

rise, On moun - tain tops, a - bove the hills, And draw the won-dering
land; The King who reigns in Sa - lem's tower Shall all the world com -
years; To plow-shares men shall beat their **swords,** To prun - ing hooks their
shrine, And, walk - ing in the light of God, With ho - ly beau - ties

eyes, And draw the won - dering eyes. To this the joy - ful
mand, Shall all the world com - mand. A - mong the na - tions
spears, To prun - ing hooks their spears. No long - er host en -
shine, With ho - ly beau - ties shine. Come, then, O house of

na - tions, round, All tribes and tongues, shall flow; "Up
he shall judge, His judg - ments truth shall guide, His
count - ering host, Shall crowds of slain de - plore; They'll
Ja - cob, come, To wor - ship at His shrine, And

Behold, the Mountain of the Lord

to the hill of God," they'll say, "And to his house, we'll go."
scep-tre shall pro-tect the just; And quell the sin-ner's pride.
hang the trum-pet in the hall, And stud-y war no more.
walk-ing in the light of God, With ho-ly beau-ties shine.

298

The Lord Imparted from Above
(Choir)

Eliza R. Snow

George Careless

Moderately ♩=100

1. The Lord im-part-ed from a-bove The "Word of
2. Have we not been di-vine-ly taught To heed its
3. Has self-de-ni-al grown a task? Or has that
4. O, that the Saints would all re-gard Each gra-cious

Wis-dom" for our bless-ing, But shall it un-to
voice, and high-ly prize it? Then who shall once in-
word been vain-ly spo-ken? Or why, I fain would
word that God has giv-en. And prize the fa-vor

man-y prove A gift that is not worth pos-sess-ing?
dulge the thought, It can be bet-ter to de-spise it?
hum-bly ask, Why is that word so of-ten bro-ken?
of the Lord A-bove all things be-neath the heav-en!

299   What Was Witnessed in the Heavens?

(Choir)

John S. Davis   Evan Stephens

Joyously ♩. = 72

1. What was wit-nessed in the heav-ens? Why, an an-gel earth-ward bound.
2. Had we not be-fore the gos-pel? Yes; it came of old to men.
3. Where so long has been the gos-pel? Did it pass from earth a-way?

Had he some-thing with him bring-ing? Yes, the gos-pel, joy-ful sound!
Then what is this lat-ter gos-pel? 'Tis the first one come a-gain.
Yes; 'twas tak-en back to heav-en Till should dawn a bright-er day.

It was to be preached in pow-er On the earth, the an-gel said,
This was preached by Paul and Pet-er And by Je-sus Christ, the Head;
What be-came of those de-part-ed, Know-ing not the gos-pel plan?

rit.

To all men, all tongues and na-tions That up-on its face are spread.
This we lat-ter Saints are preach-ing. We their foot-steps wish to tread.
In the spir-it world they'll hear it; God is just to ev-ery man.

An Angel From on High

(Male Chorus)

Parley P. Pratt

John Tullidge

Quietly ♪=92

1. An an - gel from on high The long, long si - lence broke;
2. Sealed by Mo - ro - ni's hand, It has for a - ges lain,
3. It speaks of Jo - seph's seed And makes the rem - nant known

De - scend - ing from the sky, These gra - cious words he spoke:
To wait the Lord's com - mand From dust to speak a - gain.
Of na - tions long since dead, Who once had dwelt a - lone.

♩=104

"Lo, in Cu - mo - rah's lone - ly hill, A sa - cred re - cord lies con-cealed.
It shall a - gain to light come forth To ush - er in Christ's reign on earth.
The ful-ness of the gos - pel, too, Its pag - es will re - veal to view.

Lo, in Cu - mo-rah's lone - ly hill, A sa - cred re - cord lies con-cealed."
It shall a - gain to light come forth To ush - er in Christ's reign on earth.
The ful-ness of the gos - pel, too, Its pag - es will re - veal to view.

4. The time is now fulfilled, The long expected day;
   Let earth obedience yield, And darkness flee away.
   Remove the seals; be wide unfurled Its light and glory to the world.
   Remove the seals; be wide unfurled Its light and glory to the world.

5. Lo, Israel filled with joy Shall now be gathered home,
   Their wealth and means employ To build Jerusalem:
   While Zion shall arise and shine And fill the earth with truth divine,
   While Zion shall arise and shine And fill the earth with truth divine.

301 Brightly Beams Our Father's Mercy

(Male Chorus)

Philip Paul Bliss

Philip Paul Bliss

Fluently ♩ = 76

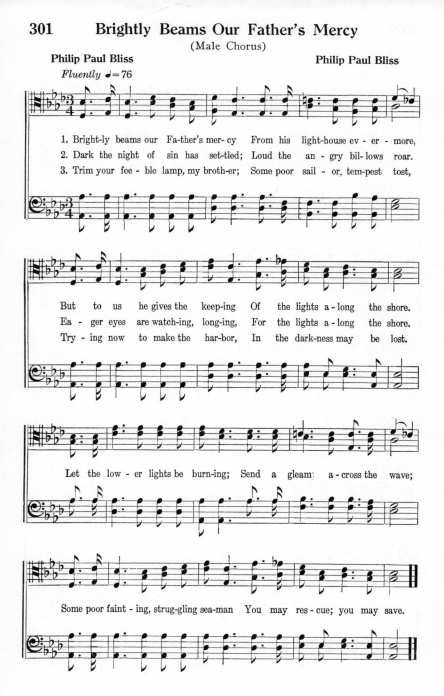

1. Bright-ly beams our Fa-ther's mer-cy From his light-house ev - er - more,
2. Dark the night of sin has set-tled; Loud the an - gry bil-lows roar.
3. Trim your fee - ble lamp, my broth-er; Some poor sail - or, tem-pest tost,

But to us he gives the keep-ing Of the lights a - long the shore.
Ea - ger eyes are watch-ing, long-ing, For the lights a - long the shore.
Try - ing now to make the har-bor, In the dark-ness may be lost.

Let the low - er lights be burn-ing; Send a gleam a - cross the wave;

Some poor faint - ing, strug-gling sea-man You may res - cue; you may save.

302 Come, All Ye Sons of God

(Men's Voices)

T. Davenport   O. P. Huish

Boldly ♩ = 63

1. Come, all ye sons of God, who have re-ceived the priest-hood;
2. Come, all ye scat-tered sheep, and lis-ten to your Shep-herd,
3. Re-pent and be bap-tized, and have your sins re-mit-ted,
4. And when your grief is o'er and end-ed your af-flic-tion,

Go spread the gos-pel wide, and gath-er in his peo-ple;
While you the bless-ings reap, which long have been pre-dict-ed;
And get the Spir-it's zeal; O then you'll be u-nit-ed;
Your spir-its then will soar to a-wait the res-ur-rec-tion;

The lat-ter day work has be-gun, to gath-er scat-tered
By proph-ets long it's been fore-told, He'll gath-er you in-
Go cast up-on him all your care; He will re-gard your
And then his pres-ence you'll en-joy, in heaven-ly bliss your

Is-rael in, And bring them back to Zi-on to praise the Lamb.
to his fold, And bring you home to Zi-on to praise the Lamb.
hum-ble prayer, And bring you home to Zi-on to praise the Lamb.
time em-ploy, A thou-sand years in Zi-on to praise the Lamb.

303 Come, All Ye Sons of Zion

(Men's Voices)

William W. Phelps

John Tullidge

Enthusiastically ♩=104

1. Come, all ye sons of Zi - on, And let us praise the Lord;
2. Come, ye dis-persed of Ju - dah, Join in the theme and sing,
3. Re - joice, re - joice, O Is - rael, And let your joys a - bound!
4. Then gath - er up for Zi - on, Ye Saints through-out the land,

His ran - somed are re - turn - ing Ac - cord - ing to his word;
With har - mo - ny un - ceas - ing, The prais - es of our King,
The voice of God shall reach you Wher - ev - er you are found
And clear the way be - fore you, As God shall give com - mand.

In sa - cred song and glad - ness They walk the nar - row way,
Whose arm is now ex - tend - ed, On which the world may gaze,
And call you back from bond - age, That you may sing his praise
Though wick-ed men and dev - ils Ex - ert their power, 'tis vain,

And thank the Lord who brought them To see the lat - ter day.
To gath - er up the right - eous In these the lat - ter days.
In Zi - on and Je - ru - salem, In these the lat - ter days.
Since he who is e - ter - nal Has said you shall ob - tain.

304   Come, O Thou King of Kings

(Male Chorus)

Parley P. Pratt

Boldly ♩=92

1. Come, O thou King of kings; We've wait-ed long for thee, With heal-ing in thy wings To set thy peo-ple free; Come, thou de-sire of na-tions, Come, thou de-sire, come, thou de-sire of na-tions, Let Is-rael now be gath-ered home.

2. Come, make an end to sin And cleanse the earth by fire, And right-eous-ness bring in, That Saints may tune the lyre With songs of joy a hap-pier strain, With songs of joy, with songs of joy, a hap-pier strain, To wel-come in thy peace-ful reign.

3. Ho-san-nas now shall sound From all the ran-somed throng, And glo-ry ech-o round A new tri-um-phal song; The wide ex-panse of heav-en fill The wide ex-panse, the wide ex-panse of heav-en fill With an-thems sweet from Zi-on's hill.

4. Hail! Prince of life and peace!
Thrice welcome to thy throne!
While all the chosen race
Their Lord and Savior own.
The heathen nations bow the knee,
And every tongue sounds praise to thee.

305 Come, Come, Ye Saints

(Male Chorus)

William Clayton
Old English Tune

Resolutely ♩=66

1. Come, come, ye Saints, no toil nor la-bor fear; But with joy wend your way;
2. Why should we mourn or think our lot is hard? 'Tis not so; all is right.
3. We'll find the place which God for us pre-pared, Far a-way in the West.
4. And should we die be-fore our jour-ney's through, Hap-py day! all is well!

Though hard to you this jour-ney may ap-pear, Grace shall be as your day.
Why should we think to earn a great re-ward, If we now shun the fight?
Where none shall come to hurt or make a-fraid; There the Saints will be blessed.
We then are free from toil and sor-row, too; With the just we shall dwell.

'Tis bet-ter far for us to strive, Our use-less cares from us to drive;
Gird up your loins; fresh cour-age take, Our God will nev-er us for-sake;
We'll make the air with mu-sic ring, Shout prais-es to our God and King;
But if our lives are spared a-gain To see the Saints their rest ob-tain,

Do this, and joy your hearts will swell — All is well, all is well!
And soon we'll have this tale to tell — All is well, all is well!
A-bove the rest these words we'll tell — All is well, all is well!
O how we'll make this cho-rus swell — All is well, all is well!

Come, Let Us Anew

(Men's Voices)

Charles Wesley

James Lucas

Resolutely ♩=72

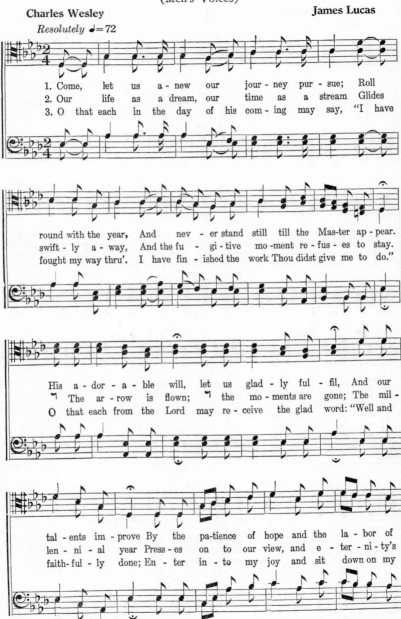

1. Come, let us a - new our jour - ney pur - sue; Roll round with the year, And nev - er stand still till the Mas - ter ap - pear. His a - dor - a - ble will, let us glad - ly ful - fil, And our tal - ents im - prove By the pa - tience of hope and the la - bor of

2. Our life as a dream, our time as a stream Glides swift - ly a - way, And the fu - gi - tive mo - ment re - fus - es to stay. The ar - row is flown; the mo - ments are gone; The mil - len - ni - al year Press - es on to our view, and e - ter - ni - ty's

3. O that each in the day of his com - ing may say, "I have fought my way thru'. I have fin - ished the work Thou didst give me to do." O that each from the Lord may re - ceive the glad word: "Well and faith - ful - ly done; En - ter in - to my joy and sit down on my

Come, Let Us Anew

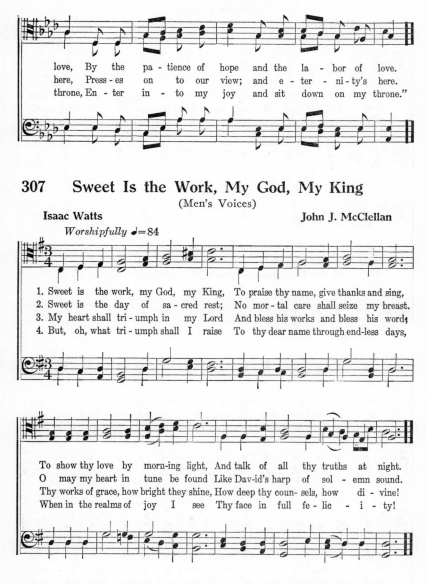

love, By the pa-tience of hope and the la-bor of love.
here, Press-es on to our view; and e-ter-ni-ty's here.
throne, En-ter in-to my joy and sit down on my throne."

307 Sweet Is the Work, My God, My King
(Men's Voices)

Isaac Watts

John J. McClellan

Worshipfully ♩=84

1. Sweet is the work, my God, my King, To praise thy name, give thanks and sing,
2. Sweet is the day of sa-cred rest; No mor-tal care shall seize my breast.
3. My heart shall tri-umph in my Lord And bless his works and bless his word;
4. But, oh, what tri-umph shall I raise To thy dear name through end-less days,

To show thy love by morn-ing light, And talk of all thy truths at night.
O may my heart in tune be found Like Dav-id's harp of sol-emn sound.
Thy works of grace, how bright they shine, How deep thy coun-sels, how di-vine!
When in the realms of joy I see Thy face in full fe-lic-i-ty!

5. Sin, my worst enemy before,
   Shall vex my eyes and ears no more;
   My inward foes shall all be slain
   Nor Satan break my peace again.

6. Then shall I see and hear and know
   All I desired and wished below;
   And every power find sweet employ
   In that eternal world of joy.

308 Come, Ye Children of the Lord

(Men's Voices)

James H. Wallis

Joyously ♩=108

1. Come, ye chil - dren of the Lord, Let us sing with one ac - cord;
2. O how joy - ful it will be, When our Sav - ior we shall see!
3. All ar-rayed in spot - less white, We will dwell 'mid truth and light;

Let us raise a joy - ful strain! To our Lord who soon will reign
When in splen-dor he'll de - scend. Then all wick - ed - ness will end.
We will sing the songs of praise; We will shout in joy - ous lays;

On this earth when it shall be Cleansed from all in - iq - ui - ty;
O what songs we then will sing To our Sav - ior, Lord and King!
Earth shall then be cleansed from sin, Ev - ery liv - ing thing there - in

When all men from sin will cease, And will live in love and peace.
O what love will then bear sway, When our fears shall flee a - way.
Shall in love and beau - ty dwell; Then with joy each heart will swell.

309 Jesus, My Savior True

(Male Chorus)

O. P. Huish

O. P. Huish

Fervently ♪ = 104

1. Je - sus, my Sav - ior true, Guide me to thee;
2. Through this dark world of strife, Guide me to thee;
3. When strife and sin a - rise, Guide me to thee;
4. When si - lent death draws near, Guide me to thee;

Help me thy will to do; Guide me to thee;
Teach me a bet - ter life; Guide me to thee;
When tears be - dim my eyes, Guide me to thee;
Calm thou my trem - bling fear; Guide me to thee;

E'en in the dark - est night, As in the morn - ing bright,
Let thy re - deem - ing power Be with me ev - ery hour;
When hopes are crushed and dead, When earth - ly joys are fled,
Let me thy mer - cy prove; Let thy en - dur - ing love

Be thou my bea - con light; Guide me to thee.
Be thou my safe - ty tower; Guide me to thee.
Thy glo - ry 'round me shed; Guide me to thee.
Guide me to heaven a - bove; Guide me to thee.

310   For the Strength of the Hills

(Men's Voices)

Felicia D. Hemans
Altered by Edward L. Sloan

Evan Stephens

Energetically ♩=88

1. For the strength of the hills we bless thee, Our God, our fa - ther's God. Thou hast made thy chil - dren might - y By the touch of the moun - tain sod. Thou hast led thy cho - sen Is - ra - el To free - dom's last a - bode.

2. At the hands of foul op - press - ors We've borne and suf - fered long. Thou hast been our help in weak - ness, And thy power hath made us strong. A - mid ruth - less foes, out - num - bered, In wea - ri - ness we trod.

3. Thou hast led us here in safe - ty Where the moun - tain bul - wark stands, As the guar - dian of the loved ones Thou hast brought from man - y lands. For the rock and for the riv - er, The val - ley's fer - tile sod,

4. Here the wild bird swift - ly darts on His quar - ry from the heights, And the red un - tu - tored In - dian Seek - eth here his rude de - lights; But the Saints for thy com - mun - ion Have sought the moun - tain sod.

For the Strength of the Hills

For the strength of the hills we bless thee, Our God, our fa - thers' God.

311
Jesus, Lover of My Soul
(Male Chorus)

Charles Wesley

Joseph P. Holbrook

With devotion ♩ = 108

mf

1. Je - sus, Lov - er of my soul, Let me to thy bos - om fly,
2. Oth - er ref - uge have I none, Hangs my help - less soul on thee;

While the near - er wa - ters roll, While the tem - pest still is high.
Leave, oh, leave me not a - lone; Still sup - port and com - fort me.

f

Hide me, O my Sav - ior, hide, Till the storm of life is past;
All my trust on thee is stayed; All my help from thee I bring.

Safe in - to the ha - ven guide; Oh, re - ceive my soul at last.
Cov - er my de - fense-less head With the shad - ow of thy wing.

312 High on the Mountain Top
(Men's Voices)

Joel H. Johnson

Ebenezer Beesley

Vigorously ♩=60

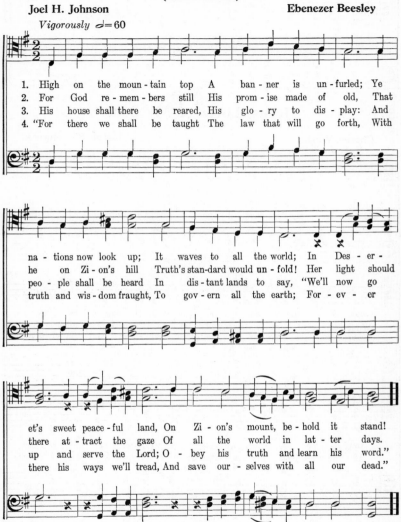

1. High on the moun-tain top A ban-ner is un-furled; Ye na-tions now look up; It waves to all the world; In Des-er-et's sweet peace-ful land, On Zi-on's mount, be-hold it stand!

2. For God re-mem-bers still His prom-ise made of old, That he on Zi-on's hill Truth's stan-dard would un-fold! Her light should there at-tract the gaze Of all the world in lat-ter days.

3. His house shall there be reared, His glo-ry to dis-play: And peo-ple shall be heard In dis-tant lands to say, "We'll now go up and serve the Lord; O-bey his truth and learn his word."

4. "For there we shall be taught The law that will go forth, With truth and wis-dom fraught, To gov-ern all the earth; For-ev-er there his ways we'll tread, And save our-selves with all our dead."

5. Then hail to Deseret!
A refuge for the good,
And safety for the great,
If they but understood
That God with plagues will shake the world
Till all its thrones shall down be hurled.

6. In Deseret doth truth
Rear up its royal head;
Though nations may oppose,
Still wider it shall spread;
Yes, truth and justice, love and grace,
In Deseret find ample place.

How Firm a Foundation

(Men's Voices)

Kirkham

Stately ♩=104

1. How firm a foundation, Ye Saints of the Lord, Is laid for your faith in his excellent word! What more can he say than to you he has said, You who unto Jesus, you who unto Jesus, You who unto Jesus for refuge have fled.

2. In every condition, In sickness, in health, In poverty's vale or abounding in wealth, At home or abroad, on the land or the sea, As thy days may demand, as thy days may demand, As thy days may demand so thy succor shall be.

3. Fear not, I am with thee, O be not dismayed, For I am thy God and will still give thee aid; I'll strengthen thee, help thee and cause thee to stand, Upheld by my righteous, upheld by my righteous, Upheld by my righteous, omnipotent hand.

4. When through the deep waters I call thee to go,
The rivers of sorrow shall not thee o'erflow,
For I will be with thee, thy troubles to bless,
And sanctify to thee, and sanctify to thee,
And sanctify to thee thy deepest distress.

5. When through fiery trials thy pathway shall lie,
My grace, all sufficient, shall be thy supply;
The flame shall not hurt thee; I only design
Thy dross to consume, thy dross to consume,
Thy dross to consume and thy gold to refine.

Do What Is Right

(Men's Voices)

E. Kaillmark

With marked accent ♩ = 100

1. Do what is right; the day-dawn is break-ing, Hail-ing a
2. Do what is right; the shack-les are fall-ing; Chains of the
3. Do what is right; be faith-ful and fear-less; On-ward, press

fu - ture of free - dom and light; An - gels a - bove us are
bonds-men no long - er are bright; Light- ened by hope soon they'll
on - ward, the goal is in sight; Eyes that are wet now ere

si - lent notes tak - ing Of ev - ery ac - tion; Do what is right!
cease to be gall-ing; Truth go - eth on - ward; Do what is right!
long will be tear - less; Bless-ings a - wait you In do - ing what's right.

Do what is right; let the con - se-quence fol - low; Bat - tle for

free - dom in spir - it and might; And with stout hearts look ye

Do What Is Right

forth till to-mor-row; God will pro-tect you; Then do what is right.

315   Jehovah, Lord of Heaven and Earth

(Men's Voices)

Oliver Holden

Boldly ♩=88

1. Je - ho - vah, Lord of heaven and earth, Thy word of truth pro - claim!
2. We long to see thy Church in - crease, Thy own new king-dom grow,
3. Roll on thy work in all its power! The dis - tant na-tions bring!
4. One gen - eral cho - rus then shall rise From men of ev - ery tongue,

O may it spread from pole to pole, Till all shall know thy name.
That all the earth may live in peace, And heaven be seen be - low.
In thy new king-dom may they stand, And own thee, God and King.
And songs of joy sa - lute the skies, By ev - ery na - tion sung.

O may it spread from pole to pole, Till all shall know thy name.
That all the earth may live in peace, And heaven be seen be - low.
In thy new king - dom may they stand, And own thee, God and King.
And songs of joy sa - lute the skies, By ev - ery na - tion sung.

316 How Great the Wisdom and the Love

(Men's Voices)

Eliza R. Snow

Thomas McIntyre

Calmly ♩=66

1. How great the wis - dom and the love That
2. His pre - cious blood he free - ly spilt; His
3. By strict o - be - dience Je - sus won The
4. He marked the path and led the way, And

filled the courts on high And sent the Sav - ior
life he free - ly gave, A sin - less sac - ri -
prize with glo - ry rife: "Thy will, O God, not
ev - ery point de - fines, To light and life and

from a - bove To suf - fer, bleed, and die!
fice for guilt, A dy - ing world to save.
mine be done," A - dorned his mor - tal life.
end - less day, Where God's full pres - ence shines.

5. How great, how glorious and complete
Redemption's grand design,
Where justice, love, and mercy meet
In harmony divine!

6. In memory of the broken flesh,
We eat the broken bread;
And witness with the cup, afresh,
Our faith in Christ our Head.

317 I Know That My Redeemer Lives

(Men's Voices)

Samuel Medley

Lewis D. Edwards

With Devotion ♩=62

Sing Melody in Unison

1. I know that my Re-deem-er lives. What com-fort this sweet sen-tence gives!
2. He lives to grant me rich sup-ply. He lives to guide me with his eye.
3. He lives, my kind, wise, heaven-ly friend. He lives and loves me to the end.
4. He lives, all glo-ry to his name! He lives, my Sav-ior, still the same;

He lives, he lives, who once was dead. He lives, my ev-er-liv-ing head.
He lives to com-fort me when faint. He lives to hear my soul's com-plaint.
He lives, and while he lives I'll sing, He lives, my Proph-et, Priest, and King.
O sweet the joy this sen-tence gives: "I know that my Re-deem-er lives!"

Tenors

He lives to bless me with his love. He lives to plead for me a-bove.
He lives to si-lence all my fears. He lives to wipe a-way my tears.
He lives and grants me dai-ly breath; He lives, and I shall con-quer death.
He lives, all glo-ry to his name! He lives, my Sav-ior, still the same;

Basses

He lives, my hun-gry soul to feed. He lives to bless in time of need.
He lives to calm my trou-bled heart. He lives, all bless-ings to im-part.
He lives my man-sion to pre-pare. He lives to bring me safe-ly there.
O sweet the joy this sen-tence gives: "I know that my Re-deem-er lives!"

318 It May Not Be on the Mountain Height

(Men's Voices)

Mary Brown   Carrie E. Rounsefell

Sincerely ♩. = 52

1. It may not be on the moun-tain height Or o-ver the storm-y sea; It may not be at the bat-tle's front My Lord will have need of me; But if by a still, small voice he calls To paths that I do not know, I'll an-swer, dear Lord, with my

2. Per-haps to-day there are lov-ing words Which Je-sus would have me speak; There may be now in the paths of sin Some wan-der-er whom I should seek; O Sav-ior, if thou wilt be my guide, Though dark and rug-ged the way, My voice shall ech-o the

3. There's sure-ly some-where a low-ly place In earth's har-vest fields so wide, Where I may la-bor through life's short day For Je-sus the Cru-ci-fied; So trust-ing my all to thy ten-der care, And know-ing thou lov-est me, I'll do thy will with a

It May Not Be on the Mountain Height

hand in thine: I'll go where you want me to go.

mes-sage sweet: I'll say what you want me to say. I'll go where you

heart sin-cere; I'll be what you want me to be.

want me to go, dear Lord, O - ver moun-tain, or plain, or sea;

I'll say what you want me to say, dear Lord,

I'll be what you want me to be.

319 Glory to God on High

(Men's Voices)

James Allen

Felice Giardini

Praisingly ♩ = 92

1. Glo - ry to God on high! Let heaven and
2. Je - sus, our Lord and God, Bore sin's tre -
3. Let all the hosts a - bove Join in one

earth re - ply; Praise ye his name.
men - dous load; Praise ye his name!
song of love, Prais - ing his name;

His love and grace a - dore, Who all our sor - rows bore;
Tell what his arm has done; What spoils from death he won;
To him as - crib - ed be Hon - or and maj - es - ty

Sing a - loud ev - er - more, Wor - thy the Lamb!
Sing his great name a - lone, Wor - thy the Lamb!
Through all e - ter - ni - ty: Wor - thy the Lamb!

320 I Need Thee Every Hour

(Male Chorus)

Annie S. Hawkes

Robert Lowry

Tenderly ♩ = 60

1. I need thee ev - ery hour, Most gra - cious Lord;
2. I need thee ev - ery hour, Stay thou near by;
3. I need thee ev - ery hour, In joy or pain;
4. I need thee ev - ery hour, Most ho - ly One;

No ten - der voice like thine Can peace af - ford.
Temp - ta - tions lose their power When thou art nigh.
Come quick - ly and a - bide, Or life is vain.
O make me thine in - deed, Thou bless - ed Son!

I need thee; O I need thee; Ev - ery hour I need thee!

O bless me now, my Sav - ior, I come to thee.

321 The Lord is My Shepherd

(Male Chorus)

23rd Psalm

Thomas Koschat

Worshipfully ♩=60

1. The Lord is my Shep-herd; no want shall I know; I feed in green pas-tures; safe fold-ed I rest; He lead-eth my soul where the still wa-ters flow, Re-stores me when wan-dering, re-deems when op-pressed; Re-stores me when wan-dering, re-deems when op-pressed.

2. Thru the val-ley and shad-ow of death though I stray, Since thou art my Guard-ian, no e-vil I fear; Thy rod shall de-fend me; thy staff be my stay; No harm can be-fall with my Com-fort-er near; No harm can be-fall with my Com-fort-er near.

3. In the midst of af-flic-tion my ta-ble is spread; With bless-ings un-meas-ured my cup run-neth o'er; With per-fume and oil thou a-noint-est my head; Oh, what shall I ask of thy prov-i-dence more? Oh, what shall I ask of thy prov-i-dence more?

322 Lord Dismiss Us With Thy Blessing

(Men's Voices)

John Faucett   Jean Jacques Rousseau

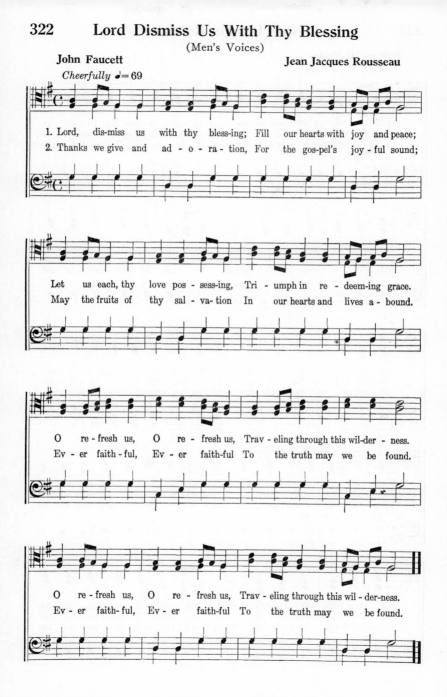

1. Lord, dismiss us with thy bless-ing; Fill our hearts with joy and peace;
2. Thanks we give and ad-o-ra-tion, For the gos-pel's joy-ful sound;

Let us each, thy love pos-sess-ing, Tri-umph in re-deem-ing grace.
May the fruits of thy sal-va-tion In our hearts and lives a-bound.

O re-fresh us, O re-fresh us, Trav-eling through this wil-der-ness.
Ev-er faith-ful, Ev-er faith-ful To the truth may we be found.

O re-fresh us, O re-fresh us, Trav-eling through this wil-der-ness.
Ev-er faith-ful, Ev-er faith-ful To the truth may we be found.

323 Now Let Us Rejoice

(Men's Voices)

William W. Phelps

Cheerfully ♩ = 104

1. Now let us re - joice in the day of sal - va - tion; No long - er as stran-gers on earth need we roam. Good ti - dings are sound -ing to us and each na - tion; And short - ly the hour of re-demp-tion will come; When all that was prom-ised the Saints will be giv - en, And none will mo - lest them from morn un - til even, And earth will ap - pear as the

2. We'll love one an - oth - er and nev - er dis - sem - ble, But cease to do e - vil and ev - er be one; And when the un - god - ly are fear -ing and trem - ble, We'll watch for the day when the Sav - ior will come; When all that was prom-ised the Saints will be giv - en, And none will mo - lest them from morn un - til even, And earth will ap - pear as the

3. In faith we'll re - ly on the arm of Je - ho - vah, To guide through these last days of trou - ble and gloom, And af - ter the scourg - es and har-vest are o - ver, We'll rise with the just when the Sav - ior doth come. Then all that was prom-ised the Saints will be giv - en, And they will be crowned with the an - gels of heaven, And earth will ap - pear as the

Now Let Us Rejoice

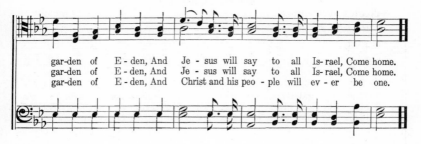

gar-den of E - den, And Je - sus will say to all Is- rael, Come home.
gar-den of E - den, And Je - sus will say to all Is- rael, Come home.
gar-den of E - den, And Christ and his peo - ple will ev - er be one.

324 Prayer Is the Soul's Sincere Desire
(Men's Voices)

James Montgomery   George Careless

Fluently ♩=72

1. Prayer is the soul's sin - cere de - sire, Ut - tered or un - ex-pressed,
2. Prayer is the bur - den of a sigh, The fall - ing of a tear,
3. Prayer is the sim - plest form of speech, That in - fant lips can try,
4. Prayer is the Chris - tian's vi - tal breath, The Chris-tian's na - tive air,

The mo - tion of a hid - den fire That trem - bles in the breast.
The up - ward glanc - ing of an eye, When none but God is near.
Prayer the sub - lim - est strains that reach The Maj - es - ty on high.
His watch-word at the gates of death; He en - ters heav'n with prayer.

5. Prayer is the contrite sinner's voice,
   Returning from his ways.
   While angels in their songs rejoice,
   And cry, "Behold, he prays!"

6. The Saints in prayer appear as one
   In word and deed and mind,
   While with the Father and the Son
   Their fellowship they find.

7. Nor prayer is made on earth alone;
   The Holy Spirit pleads,
   And Jesus, at the Father's throne,
   For sinners intercedes.

8. Oh, thou by whom we come to God,
   The Life, the Truth, the Way!
   The path of prayer thyself hast trod;
   Lord, teach us how to pray.

325 O Ye Mountains High

(Men's Voices)

Charles W. Penrose

Old melody

Brightly ♩ = 69

1. O ye moun-tains high, where the clear blue sky Arch-es o-ver the vales of the free, Where the pure breez-es blow and the clear stream-lets flow, How I've longed to your bos-om to flee! O Zi-on! dear Zi-on! land of the free, Now my own moun-tain

2. Though the great and the wise all thy beau-ties de-spise, To the hum-ble and pure thou art dear. Though the haught-y may smile and the wick-ed re-vile, Yet we love thy glad ti-dings to hear. O Zi-on! dear Zi-on! home of the free, Though thou wert forced to

3. In thy moun-tain re-treat, God will strength-en thy feet; With-out fear of thy foes thou shalt tread; And their sil-ver and gold, as the proph-ets have told, Shall be brought to a-dorn thy fair head. O Zi-on! dear Zi-on! home of the free, Soon thy tow-ers shall

4. Here our voic-es we'll raise, and we'll sing to thy praise, Sa-cred home of the proph-ets of God; Thy de-liv-erance is nigh; thy op-pres-sors shall die; And thy land shall be free-dom's a-bode. O Zi-on! dear Zi-on! land of the free, In thy tem-ples we'll

O Ye Mountains High

home, un-to thee I have come. All my fond hopes are cen-tered in thee.
fly to thy cham-bers on high, Yet we'll share joy and sor-row with thee.
shine with a splen-dor di-vine, And e-ter-nal thy glo-ry shall be.
bend; all thy rights we'll de-fend; And our home shall be ev-er with thee.

326 ## Praise to the Man
(Men's Voices)

William W. Phelps

Brightly ♩ = 76

1. Praise to the man who com-muned with Je-ho-vah! Je-sus a-
2. Praise to his mem-ory, he died as a mar-tyr! Hon-ored and
3. Great is his glo-ry and end-less his priest-hood; Ev-er and
4. Sac-ri-fice brings forth the bless-ings of heav-en; Earth must a-

noint-ed "that Proph-et and Seer." Bless-ed to o-pen the
blest be his ev-er great name! Long shall his blood, which was
ev-er the keys he will hold; Faith-ful and true, he will
tone for the blood of that man; Wake up the world for the

last dis-pen-sa-tion; Kings shall ex-tol him, and na-tions re-vere.
shed by as-sas-sins, Plead un-to heaven while the earth lauds his fame.
en-ter his king-dom, Crowned in the midst, of the proph-ets of old.
con-flict of jus-tice. Mil-lions shall know broth-er Jos-eph" a-gain.

Praise to the Man

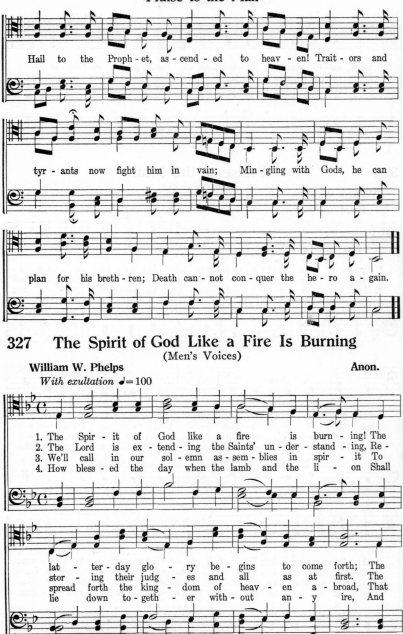

Hail to the Proph-et, as-cend-ed to heav-en! Trait-ors and

tyr-ants now fight him in vain; Min-gling with Gods, he can

plan for his breth-ren; Death can-not con-quer the he-ro a-gain.

327 The Spirit of God Like a Fire Is Burning
(Men's Voices)

William W. Phelps   Anon.

With exultation ♩=100

1. The Spir - it of God like a fire is burn - ing! The
2. The Lord is ex - tend - ing the Saints' un - der - stand - ing, Re -
3. We'll call in our sol - emn as - sem - blies in spir - it To
4. How bless - ed the day when the lamb and the li - on Shall

lat - ter-day glo - ry be - gins to come forth; The
stor - ing their judg - es and all as at first. The
spread forth the king - dom of heav - en a - broad, That
lie down to - geth - er with - out an - y ire, And

The Spirit of God Like a Fire Is Burning

vis - ions and bless - ings of old are re - turn - ing, And
knowl - edge and pow - er of God are ex - pand - ing; The
we through our faith may be - gin to in - her - it The
Eph - raim be crowned with his bless - ing in Zi - on, As

an - gels are com - ing to vis - it the earth.
veil o'er the earth is be - gin - ning to burst.
vi - sions and bless - ings and glo - ries of God.
Je - sus de - scends with his char - iots of fire.

We'll sing, and we'll shout with the ar - mies of heav - en: Ho - san - na, ho -

san - na to God and the Lamb! Let glo - ry to them in the

high-est be giv - en, Hence-forth and for - ev - er; a - men and a - men!

328 Sweet Hour of Prayer

(Men's Voices)

William W. Walford

William B. Bradbury

Fervently ♩.=44

mf

1. Sweet hour of prayer, sweet hour of prayer! That calls me from a world of care, And bids me at my Father's throne Make all my wants and wishes known. In seasons of distress and grief My soul has often found relief And oft escaped the tempter's snare By thy return, sweet hour of prayer!

2. Sweet hour of prayer, sweet hour of prayer! Thy wings shall my petition bear To him whose truth and faithfulness Engage the waiting soul to bless. And since he bids me seek his face, Believe his word and trust his grace, I'll cast on him my every care And wait for thee, sweet hour of prayer!

Sweet Hour of Prayer

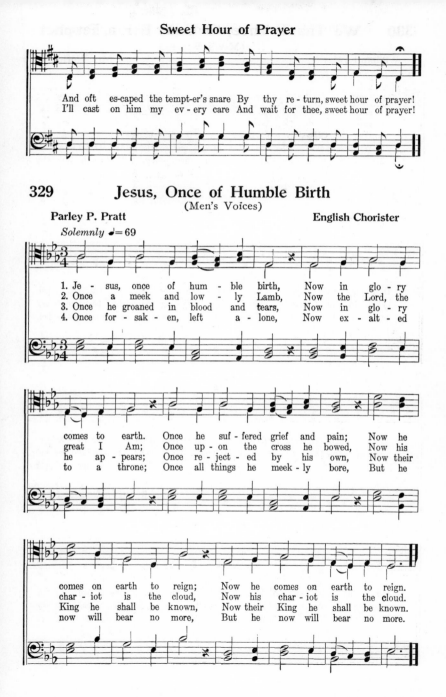

And oft es-caped the tempt-er's snare By thy re-turn, sweet hour of prayer!
I'll cast on him my ev-ery care And wait for thee, sweet hour of prayer!

329   Jesus, Once of Humble Birth
(Men's Voices)

Parley P. Pratt   English Chorister

Solemnly ♩ = 69

1. Je - sus, once of hum - ble birth, Now in glo - ry comes to earth. Once he suf - fered grief and pain; Now he comes on earth to reign; Now he comes on earth to reign.
2. Once a meek and low - ly Lamb, Now the Lord, the great I Am; Once up - on the cross he bowed, Now his char - iot is the cloud, Now his char - iot is the cloud.
3. Once he groaned in blood and tears, Now in glo - ry he ap - pears; Once re - ject - ed by his own, Now their King he shall be known, Now their King he shall be known.
4. Once for - sak - en, left a - lone, Now ex - alt - ed to a throne; Once all things he meek - ly bore, But he now will bear no more, But he now will bear no more.

330 We Thank Thee, O God, For a Prophet

(Men's Voices)

William Fowler

Mrs. Norton

Brightly ♩ = 76

1. We thank thee, O God, for a proph - et To guide us in these lat - ter days. We thank thee for send - ing the gos - pel To light - en our minds with its rays. We thank thee for ev - er - y bless - ing Be - stowed by thy boun - te - ous hand. We feel it a

2. When dark clouds of trou - ble hang o'er us And threat - en our peace to de - stroy, There is hope smil - ing bright - ly be - fore us, And we know that de - liv-erance is nigh. We doubt not the Lord nor his good - ness; We've proved him in days that are past; The wick - ed who

3. We'll sing of his good-ness and mer - cy. We'll praise him by day and by night, Re - joice in his glo - ri - ous gos - pel, And bask in its life - giv - ing light. Then on to e - ter - nal per - fec - tion The hon - est and faith- ful will go, While they who re -

We Thank Thee, O God, For a Prophet

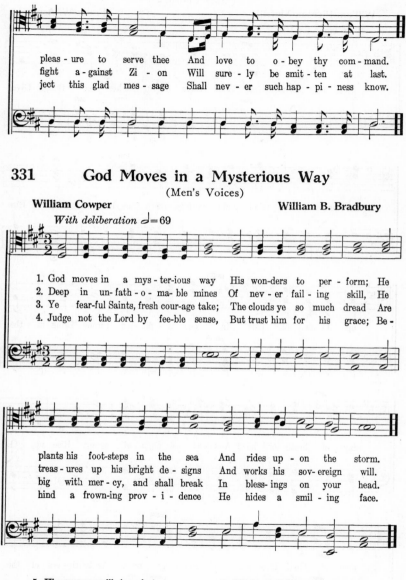

pleas - ure   to   serve thee   And   love   to   o - bey   thy   com - mand.
fight   a - gainst   Zi - on   Will   sure - ly   be smit - ten   at   last.
ject   this glad   mes - sage   Shall   nev - er   such hap - pi - ness   know.

331 God Moves in a Mysterious Way
(Men's Voices)

William Cowper   **William B. Bradbury**

With deliberation ♩=69

1. God moves in   a mys - ter-ious way   His won-ders to   per - form;   He
2. Deep   in un - fath - o - ma - ble mines   Of   nev - er fail - ing   skill,   He
3. Ye   fear-ful Saints, fresh cour-age take;   The clouds ye so   much   dread   Are
4. Judge not the Lord by fee-ble sense,   But trust him for   his   grace;   Be -

plants his   foot-steps in   the   sea   And   rides up - on   the   storm.
treas - ures up his bright de - signs   And works his   sov - ereign   will.
big   with mer - cy, and shall break   In   bless-ings   on   your   head.
hind   a frown-ing prov - i - dence   He   hides a   smil - ing   face.

5. His purposes will ripen fast,
   Unfolding every hour,
   The bud may have a bitter taste,
   But sweet will be the flower.

6. Blind unbelief is sure to err
   And scan his works in vain;
   God is his own interpreter,
   And he will make it plain.

332 Rise Up, O Men of God

(Male Chorus)

William Pierson Merrill　　　　　　　　　　　　　**Frank W. Asper**

With vigor ♩ = 104

Rise up, O men of God! Have done with less-er things. Give heart and soul and mind and strength to serve the King of kings. Rise up, O men of God! In one u-nit-ed throng. Bring in the day of broth-er-hood And end the night of wrong. Rise up, O men of God! Tread where his feet have trod. As broth-ers of the

Used by permission of Presbyterian Tribune.

Rise Up, O Men of God

Son of man, Rise up, O men of God! Rise up; rise up; rise up!

333

Redeemer of Israel
(Men's Voices)

Adapted by
William W. Phelps

Freeman Lewis

Steadily ♩ = 84

1. Re - deem - er of Is - rael, Our on - ly de - light, On
2. We know he is com - ing To gath - er his sheep, And
3. How long we have wan - dered As stran - gers in sin, And
4. As chil - dren of Zi - on, Good ti - dings for us, The

whom for a bless - ing we call, Our shad - ow by day, And our
lead them to Zi - on in love; For why in the val - ley of
cried in the des - ert for thee! Our foes have re- joiced When our
to - kens al - read - y ap - pear; Fear not and be just, For the

pil - lar by night, Our King, our De - liv - er - er, our all!
death should they weep, Or in the lone wil - der - ness rove?
sor - rows they've seen, But Is - rael will short - ly be free.
king - dom is ours; The hour of re - demp - tion is near.

334 Not Now, But in the Coming Years

(Male Chorus)

Maxwell N. Cornelius   James McGranahan

Tenderly ♩=58

1. Not now, but in the com-ing years, It may be in the bet-ter land, We'll read the mean-ing of our tears, And there, some-time, we'll un-der-stand.

2. We'll catch the bro-ken threads a-gain And fin-ish what we here be-gan. Heaven will the mys-ter-ies ex-plain; And then, ah, then, we'll un-der-stand.

3. We'll know why clouds in-stead of sun Were o-ver man-y a cher-ished plan, Why song has ceased when scarce be-gun; 'Tis there, some-time, we'll un-der-stand.

4. Why what we long for most of all E-ludes so oft our ea-ger hand; Why hopes are crushed and cas-tles fall, Up there, some-time, we'll un-der-stand.

Then trust in God through all thy days. Fear not, for he doth hold thy hand; (thy hand); Though dark thy

Not Now, But in the Coming Years

way, still sing and praise; Some-time, some-time we'll un - der-stand.

5. God knows the way; he holds the key;
He guides us with unerring hand;
Sometime with tearless eyes we'll see;
Yes, there, up there, we'll understand.

335 O Home Beloved, Where'er I Wander
(Male Chorus)

Evan Stephens   Joseph Parry

Longingly ♩ = 60

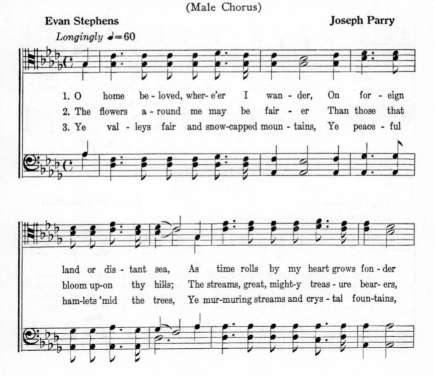

1. O home be - loved, wher- e'er I wan - der, On for - eign
2. The flowers a - round me may be fair - er Than those that
3. Ye val - leys fair and snow-capped moun - tains, Ye peace - ful

land or dis - tant sea, As time rolls by my heart grows fon - der
bloom up-on thy hills; The streams, great, might-y treas - ure bear- ers,
ham-lets 'mid the trees, Ye mur-muring streams and crys - tal foun-tains,

O Home Beloved, Where'er I Wander

And yearns more lov-ing - ly for thee! Though fair be na-ture's scenes a-
More not - ed may be than thy rills; No world re-nown my hum - ble
Kissed by the cool, soft, balm - y breeze, Words can - not tell how well I

round me, And friends are ev - er kind and true, Though joy - ous mirth and
vil - lage Like these great towns may proud-ly claim, Yet my fond heart doth
love thee Nor speak my long-ing when I roam. My heart a - lone can

song sur-round me, My heart, my soul still yearn for you.
thrill with rap - ture When - e'er I hear thy hum - ble name.
cry to heav - en, "God bless my own dear moun - tain home."

336

O My Father

(Male Chorus)

Eliza R. Snow James McGranahan

With contemplation ♩. = 58

1. O my Fa-ther, thou that dwell-est in the high and glo - rious place,
2. For a wise and glo-rious pur-pose thou hast placed me here on earth,
3. I had learned to call thee, Fa-ther, Through thy Spir-it from on high;
4. When I leave this frail ex - ist-ence, When I lay this mor - tal by,

O My Father

When shall I re - gain thy pres - ence And a - gain be - hold thy face?
And with-held the rec - ol - lec - tion Of my form - er friends and birth.
But un - til the **key of knowledge** Was re - stored I knew not why.
Fa - ther, Moth-er, may I meet you In your roy - al courts on high?

In thy ho - ly hab - i - ta - tion Did my spir - it
Yet oft - times a se - cret some - thing Whis-pered, "You're a
In the heavens are par - ents sin - gle? No; the thought makes
Then at length, when I've com - plet - ed All you sent me

once re - side? In my first pri - me - val child - hood,
stran-ger here." And I felt that I had wan - dered
rea - son stare! Truth is rea - son; truth e - ter - nal,
forth to do, With your mu - tual ap - pro - ba - tion,

pp

Was I nur - tured near thy side?
From a more ex - alt - ed sphere.
Tells me I've a moth - er there.
Let me come and dwell with you, and dwell with you.

O Happy Homes Among the Hills

(Male Chorus)

Evan Stephens   Evan Stephens

Happily ♩ = 58

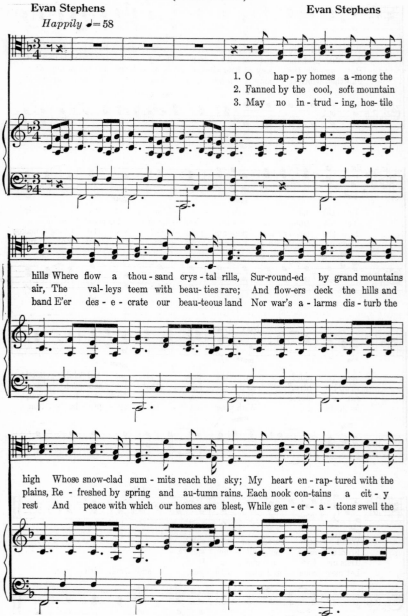

1. O   hap - py homes a -mong the hills Where flow a thou - sand crys - tal rills, Sur-round-ed by grand mountains high Whose snow-clad sum - mits reach the sky; My heart en - rap- tured with the

2. Fanned by the cool, soft mountain air, The val- leys teem with beau- ties rare; And flow-ers deck the hills and plains, Re - freshed by spring and au-tumn rains. Each nook con-tains a cit - y

3. May no in - trud - ing, hos- tile band E'er des - e - crate our beau-teous land Nor war's a - larms dis - turb the rest And peace with which our homes are blest, While gen - er - a - tions swell the

O Happy Homes Among the Hills

sight Cries to the heav - ens with de - light,   God bless and guard our
fair,   Filled with warm hearts who breathe the prayer,   God bless and guard our
throng Of   hap - py hearts   to   sing the   song,   God bless and guard our

moun - tain home.   God   bless   our moun - tain   home.
moun - tain home.   God   bless   our moun - tain   home.
moun - tain home.   God   bless   our moun - tain   home.

338 Come, Lay His Books and Papers By

(Men's Voices)

In memory of Dr. Karl G. Maeser

Annie Pike Greenwood   L. D. Edwards

Slow, distinct, and with feeling ♩=46

1. Come, lay his books and pa - pers by, He shall not need them more,
2. His work is done; no care to - night His tran - quil rest shall break,
3. We feel it, while we miss the hand That made us brave to bear,

The ink shall dry up - on his pen, So soft - ly close the door.
Sweet dreams, and with the morn - ing light, On oth - er shores he'll wake.
Per - chance in that near- touch - ing land His work did wait him there.

His tired head, with locks of white, And like the win - ter's sun;
His no - ble thoughts; his wise ap - peal, His works that bat - tles won;—
Per - chance, when death its change hath wrought, And this brief race is run,

Rit. ad lib.

Hath lain to peace - ful rest to - night,—The teach - er's work is done.
But God doth know the loss we feel,— The teach - er's work is done.
His voice a - gain shall teach, who thought The teach - er's work was done.

339 Oh Say, What is Truth?

(Male Chorus)

John Jaques

Ellen Knowles Melling

Sturdily ♩ = 76

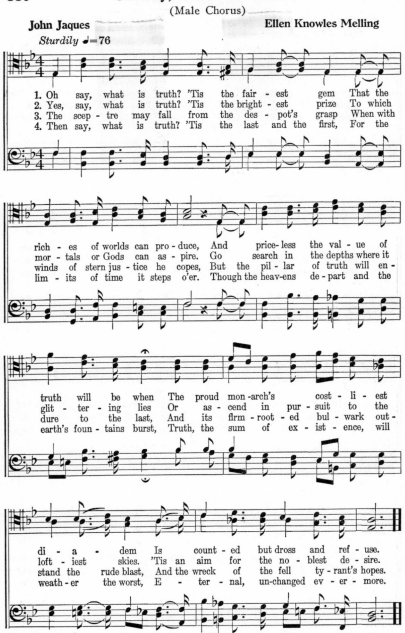

1. Oh say, what is truth? 'Tis the fair - est gem That the rich - es of worlds can pro - duce, And price - less the val - ue of truth will be when The proud mon - arch's cost - li - est di - a - dem Is count - ed but dross and ref - use.

2. Yes, say, what is truth? 'Tis the bright - est prize To which mor - tals or Gods can as - pire. Go search in the depths where it glit - ter - ing lies Or as - cend in pur - suit to the loft - iest skies. 'Tis an aim for the no - blest de - sire.

3. The scep - tre may fall from the des - pot's grasp When with winds of stern jus - tice he copes, But the pil - lar of truth will en - dure to the last, And its firm - root - ed bul - wark out - stand the rude blast, And the wreck of the fell ty - rant's hopes.

4. Then say, what is truth? 'Tis the last and the first, For the lim - its of time it steps o'er. Though the heav - ens de - part and the earth's foun - tains burst, Truth, the sum of ex - ist - ence, will weath - er the worst, E - ter - nal, un - changed ev - er - more.

340 School Thy Feelings
(Male Chorus)

Charles W. Penrose   George F. Root

Thoughtfully ♩ = 66

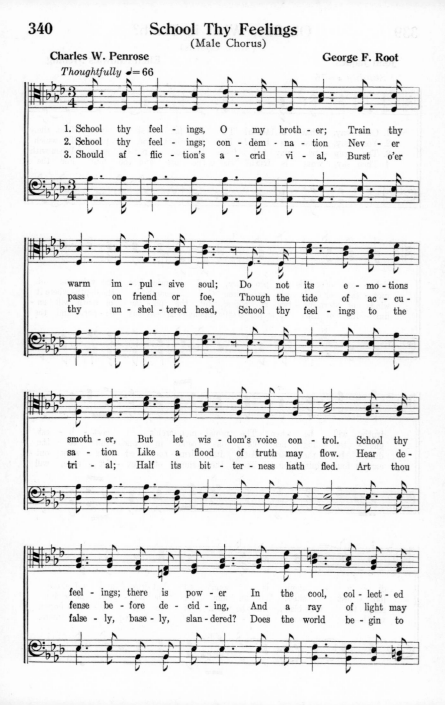

1. School thy feel - ings, O my broth - er; Train thy
2. School thy feel - ings; con - dem - na - tion Nev - er
3. Should af - flic - tion's a - crid vi - al, Burst o'er

warm im - pul - sive soul; Do not its e - mo - tions
pass on friend or foe, Though the tide of ac - cu -
thy un - shel - tered head, School thy feel - ings to the

smoth - er, But let wis - dom's voice con - trol. School thy
sa - tion Like a flood of truth may flow. Hear de -
tri - al; Half its bit - ter - ness hath fled. Art thou

feel - ings; there is pow - er In the cool, col - lect - ed
fense be - fore de - cid - ing, And a ray of light may
false - ly, base - ly, slan - dered? Does the world be - gin to

School Thy Feelings

mind; Pas - sion shat - ters rea - son's tow - er, Makes the
gleam; Show - ing thee what filth is hid - ing Un - der -
frown? Gauge thy wrath by wis - dom's stan - dard; Keep thy

clear - est vi - sion blind.
neath the shal - low stream. School thy feel - ings, O my
ris - ing an - ger down.

broth - er; Train thy warm im - pul - sive soul; Do not

its e - mo - tions smoth - er, But let wis - dom's voice con - trol.

4. Rest thyself on this assurance:
   Time's a friend to innocence,
   And the patient, calm endurance
   Wins respect and aids defense.
   Noblest minds have finest feelings;
   Quiv'ring strings a breath can move;
   And the gospel's sweet revealings,
   Tune them with the key of love.

5. Hearts so sensitively molded,
   Strongly fortified should be,
   Trained to firmness and enfolded
   In a calm tranquility.
   Wound not wilfully another;
   Conquer haste with reason's might;
   School thy feelings, sister, brother;
   Train them in the path of right.

341 Nearer, My God, to Thee

(Men's Voices)

Sarah F. Adams

Lowell Mason

Suppliantly ♩=60

1. Near - er, my God, to thee! Near - er to thee!
2. Though like the wan - der - er, The sun gone down;
3. There let the way ap - pear, Steps un - to heaven;

E'en though it be a cross that rais - eth me:
Dark - ness be o - ver me, My rest a stone,
All that thou send - est me, In mer - cy given;

Still all my song shall be, Near - er, my God, to thee,
Yet in my dreams I'd be Near - er, my God, to thee,
An - gels to beck - on me Near - er, my God, to thee,

Near - er, my God, to thee, Near - er to thee!

4. Or if, on joyful wing,
Cleaving the sky,
Sun, moon, and stars forgot,
Upward I fly,
Still all my song shall be,
Nearer, my God, to thee,
Nearer, my God, to thee,
Nearer to thee.

5. Then with my waking thoughts
Bright with thy praise,
Out of my stony grief
Bethel I'll raise;
So by my woes to be
Nearer, my God, to thee,
Nearer, my God, to thee,
Nearer to thee.

342   See, The Mighty Angel Flying!

(Male Chorus)

Robert B. Thompson   Evan Stephens

Resolutely ♩ = 80

1. See, the might-y an-gel fly-ing; See, he speeds his way to earth, To pro-claim the bless-ed gos-pel And re-store the an-cient faith, And re-store, and re-store the an-cient faith.

2. Hear, O men, the proc-la-ma-tion: Cease from van-i-ty and strife; Has-ten to re-ceive the gos-pel And o-bey the words of life, And o-bey, and o-bey the words of life.

3. Soon the earth will hear the warn-ing. Then the judg-ments will de-scend! Oh, be-fore the days of sor-row Make the Lord of hosts your friend! Make the Lord, make the Lord of hosts your friend!

4. Then when dan-gers are a-round you And the wick-ed are dis-tressed, You, with all the Saints of Zi-on, Shall en-joy e-ter-nal rest, Shall en-joy, shall en-joy e-ter-nal rest.

343 Reverently and Meekly Now

(Male Chorus)

Joseph L. Townsend

Samuel B. Marsh

Quietly ♩=108

1. Rev-erent-ly and meek-ly now Let thy head most humb-ly bow.
2. In this bread now blest for thee, Em-blem of my bod-y see;
3. Bid thine heart all strife to cease; With thy breth-ren be at peace.
4. At the throne I in-ter-cede. For thee ev-er do I plead.

Think of me thou ran-somed one, Think what I for thee have done
In this wa-ter or this wine, Em-blem of my blood di-vine.
Oh, for-give, as thou wouldst be E'en for-giv-en now by me.
I have loved thee as thy friend With a love that can-not end.

With my blood that dripped like rain, Sweat in ag-o-ny of pain.
Oh, re-mem-ber what was done That the sin-ner might be won.
In the sol-emn faith of prayer Cast up-on me all thy care,
Be o-be-dient, I im-plore, Prayer-ful, watch-ful, ev-er-more,

With my bod-y on the tree I have ran-somed e-ven thee.
On the cross of Cal-va-ry I have suf-fered death for thee.
And my spir-it's grace shall be Like a foun-tain un-to thee.
And be con-stant un-to me That thy Sav-ior I may be.

344

Ye Elders of Israel

(Men's Voices)

Cyrus H. Wheelock

Anon.

Gladly ♩ = 63

1. Ye el-ders of Is-rael, come join now with me And seek out the right-eous, wher-e'er they may be: In des-ert, on moun-tain, on land, or on sea, And bring them to Zi-on, the pure and the free.

2. The har-vest is great, and the la-borers are few; But if we're u-nit-ed, we all things can do; We'll gath-er the wheat from the midst of the tares And bring them from bond-age, from sor-rows and snares.

3. We'll go to the poor, like our Cap-tain of old, And vis-it the wea-ry, the hun-gry, and cold; We'll cheer up their hearts with the news that he bore And point them to Zi-on and life ev-er-more.

O Ba-by-lon, O Ba-by-lon, we bid thee fare-well; We're going to the moun-tains of Eph-raim to dwell.

345 Ye Who Are Called to Labor

(Men's Voices)

Mary Judd Page

Anon.

Simply ♩.=46

1. Ye who are called to la - bor and min - is - ter for God,
2. O let not vain am - bi - tion nor world - ly glo - ry stain
3. Then cease from all light speech- es, light - mind - ed - ness, and pride;
4. And while you roam as pil - grims and stran - gers on this earth,

Blest with the roy - al priest - hood, ap - point - ed by his word,
Your minds so pure and ho - ly; ac - quit your-selves like men;
Pray al - ways with - out ceas - ing, and in the truth a - bide;
O do not be dis - cour - aged; with songs of joy go forth;

To preach a - mong the na - tions the news of gos - pel grace,
While lift - ing up your voic - es like trum- pets long and loud,
The Com -fort - er will teach you, His rich - est bless - ings send.
Re - joice in trib - u - la - tion, for your re - ward is sure.

And pub - lish on the moun - tains, sal - va - tion, truth, and peace:
Say to the slum-bering na - tions: "Pre - pare to meet your God!"
Your Sav - ior will be with you for - ev - er to the end.
Re - mem - ber that your Sav - ior like sor - rows did en - dure.

5. Rich blessings there await you, and God will give you faith,
   You shall be crowned with glory and triumph over death,
   And soon you'll come to Zion, and, bearing each his sheave,
   No more shall taste of sorrow, but glorious crowns receive.

346 Zion Stands With Hills Surrounded

(Men's Voices)

Thomas Kelly

A. C. Smyth

Sturdily ♩=92

1. Zi - on stands with hills sur - round-ed— Zi - on, kept by power di - vine; All her foes shall be con - found - ed, Though the world in arms com - bine. Hap - py Zi - on, Hap - py Zi - on, What a fa - vored lot is thine!

2. Ev - ery hu - man tie may per - ish; Friend to friend un - faith - ful prove; Moth - ers cease their own to cher - ish; Heaven and earth at last re - move; But no chang - es, But no chang - es Can at - tend Je - ho - vah's love.

3. In the fur - nace God may prove thee, Thence to bring thee forth more bright, But can nev - er cease to love thee. Thou art pre - cious in his sight. God is with thee; God is with thee; Thou shalt tri - umph in his might.

347 Abide With Me

(Women's Voices)

Henry F. Lyte

William Henry Monk

Reverently ♩=80

1. A - bide with me! fast falls the e - ven - tide; The dark-ness deep - ens, Lord, with me a - bide! When oth - er help - ers
2. Swift to it's close ebbs out life's lit - tle day; Earth's joys grow dim; it's glo - ries pass a - way; Change and de - cay in
3. I need thy pres - ence ev - ery pass - ing hour; What but thy grace can foil the tempt-er's power? Who like thy - self, my

Abide With Me

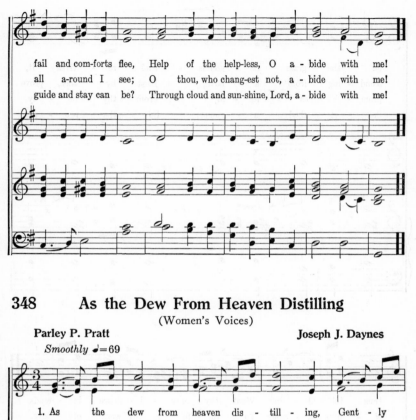

fail and com-forts flee, Help of the help-less, O a - bide with me!
all a-round I see; O thou, who chang-est not, a - bide with me!
guide and stay can be? Through cloud and sun-shine, Lord, a - bide with me!

348   As the Dew From Heaven Distilling
(Women's Voices)

Parley P. Pratt   Joseph J. Daynes

Smoothly ♩=69

1. As the dew from heaven dis - till - ing, Gent - ly
2. Let thy doc - trine, Lord, so gra - cious Thus de -
3. Lord, be - hold this con - gre - ga - tion; Pre - cious
4. Let our cry come up be - fore thee; Thy sweet

As the Dew From Heaven Distilling

on the grass de - scends. And re - vives it,
scend - ing from a - bove, Blest by thee, prove
prom - is - es ful - fil; From thy ho - ly
Spir - it shed a - round; So the peo - ple

thus ful - fil - ing What thy prov - i - dence in - tends,
ef - fi - ca - cious To ful - fil thy work of love.
hab - i - ta - tion Let the dews of life dis - til.
shall a - dore thee And con - fess the joy - ful sound.

349 Bring, Heavy Heart, Your Grief to Me

(Women's Chorus)

Herbert Auerbach

Anthony C. Lund

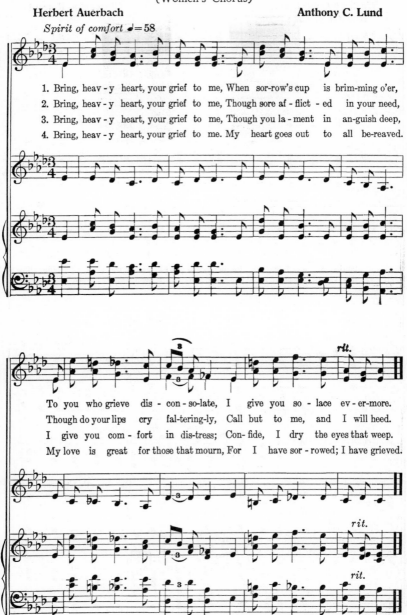

1. Bring, heav-y heart, your grief to me, When sor-row's cup is brim-ming o'er,
2. Bring, heav-y heart, your grief to me, Though sore af-flict-ed in your need,
3. Bring, heav-y heart, your grief to me, Though you la-ment in an-guish deep,
4. Bring, heav-y heart, your grief to me. My heart goes out to all be-reaved.

To you who grieve dis-con-so-late, I give you so-lace ev-er-more.
Though do your lips cry fal-tering-ly, Call but to me, and I will heed.
I give you com-fort in dis-tress; Con-fide, I dry the eyes that weep.
My love is great for those that mourn, For I have sor-rowed; I have grieved.

350 Captain of Israel's Host

(Women's Chorus)

Wesley's Collection

Gioacchino Rossini

Broadly ♩· = 54

1. Cap - tain of Is - rael's host, and Guide Of all who seek the
2. By thy un - err - ing Spir - it led, We shall not in the

land a - bove, Be - neath the shad - ow we a - bide The
des - ert stray, We shall no oth - er guid - ance need Nor

rit. *a tempo*

cloud of thy pro - tect - ing love. Our strength, thy grace; our
miss our prov - i - den - tial way; As far from dan - ger

Captain of Israel's Host

rule,   thy word; Our   end, the   glo - ry   of   the   Lord!
as   from fear, While love, al - might - y   love,   is   near.

351   Cast Thy Burden Upon the Lord
(Women's Chorus)

Felix Mendelssohn

Slowly ♩ = 52

Cast   thy bur - den up - on   the Lord, And he will sus - tain thee. He

Cast Thy Burden Upon the Lord

352 Come, Let Us Sing an Evening Hymn

(Women's Voices)

William W. Phelps

Tracy Y. Cannon

Calmly ♩ = 69

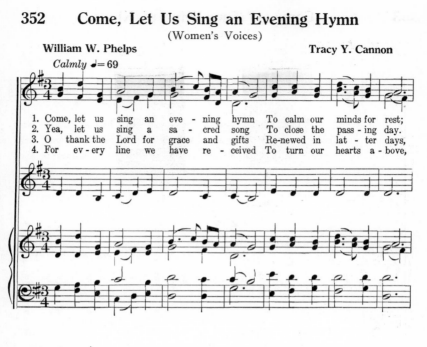

1. Come, let us sing an eve - ning hymn To calm our minds for rest;
2. Yea, let us sing a sa - cred song To close the pass - ing day.
3. O thank the Lord for grace and gifts Re-newed in lat - ter days,
4. For ev - ery line we have re - ceived To turn our hearts a - bove,

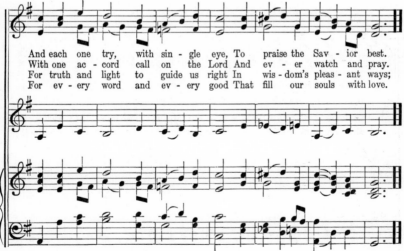

And each one try, with sin - gle eye, To praise the Sav - ior best.
With one ac - cord call on the Lord And ev - er watch and pray.
For truth and light to guide us right In wis - dom's pleas - ant ways;
For ev - ery word and ev - ery good That fill our souls with love.

5. O let us raise a holier strain,
For blessings great as ours,
And be prepared while angels guard
Us through our slumbering hours.

6. O may we sleep and wake in joy
While life with us remains,
And then go home beyond the tomb
Where peace forever reigns.

353   Come, O Thou King of Kings

(Women's Voices)

Parley P. Pratt

Boldly ♩=92

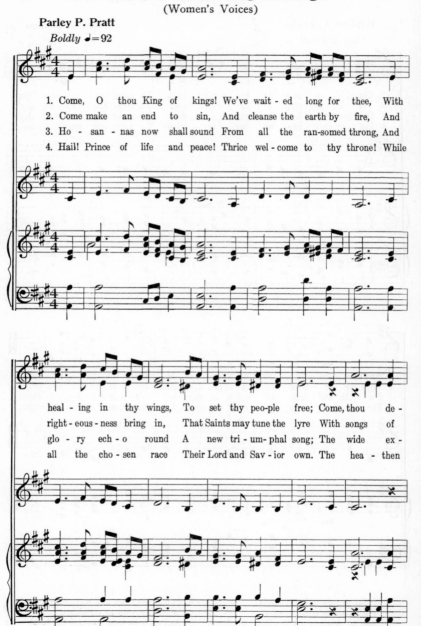

1. Come, O thou King of kings! We've wait-ed long for thee, With
2. Come make an end to sin, And cleanse the earth by fire, And
3. Ho - san - nas now shall sound From all the ran-somed throng, And
4. Hail! Prince of life and peace! Thrice wel - come to thy throne! While

heal - ing in thy wings, To set thy peo-ple free; Come, thou de -
right - eous - ness bring in, That Saints may tune the lyre With songs of
glo - ry ech - o round A new tri - um- phal song; The wide ex -
all the cho - sen race Their Lord and Sav - ior own. The hea - then

Come, O Thou King of Kings

sire of na - tions, come! Let Is - rael now be gath - ered home.
joy, a hap - pier strain, To wel-come in thy peace - ful reign.
panse of heav - en fill With an-thems sweet from Zi - on's hill.
na - tions bow the knee, And ev-ery tongue sounds praise to thee.

354 Earth With Her Ten Thousand Flowers

(Women's Voices)

William W. Phelps

Thomas C. Griggs

Calmly ♩=80

1. Earth with her ten thou-sand flowers, Air, with all its beams and showers,
2. Sounds a - mong the vales and hills, In the woods and by the rills,
3. All the hopes that sweet - ly start From the foun - tain of the heart,

Earth With Her Ten Thousand Flowers

Heav-en's in - fi - nite ex - panse, Sea's re- splen-dent coun - te - nance.
Of   the   breeze and of   the   bird, By   the gen - tle   mur - mur stirred.
All   the   bliss that ev - er comes To   our earth - ly   hu - man homes,

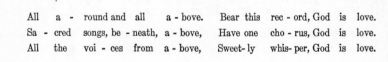

All   a - round and all   a - bove. Bear this   rec - ord, God is   love.
Sa -   cred   songs, be - neath, a - bove, Have one   cho - rus, God is   love.
All   the   voi - ces from a - bove, Sweet- ly   whis- per, God is   love.

355 How Gentle God's Commands

(Women's Voices)

Philip Doddridge   **Hans G. Naegeli**

Gently ♩ = 76

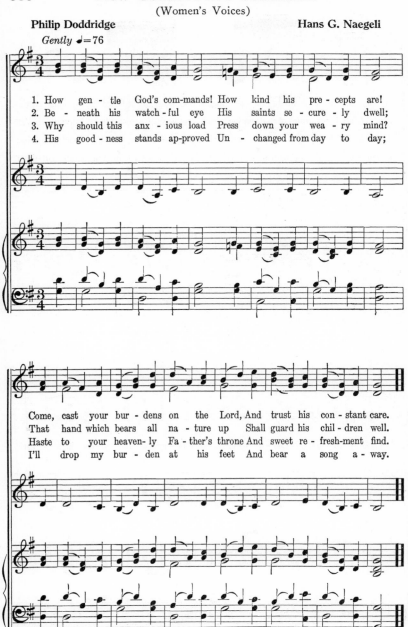

1. How gen - tle God's com-mands! How kind his pre - cepts are!
2. Be - neath his watch - ful eye His saints se - cure - ly dwell;
3. Why should this anx - ious load Press down your wea - ry mind?
4. His good - ness stands ap-proved Un - changed from day to day;

Come, cast your bur - dens on the Lord, And trust his con - stant care.
That hand which bears all na - ture up Shall guard his chil - dren well.
Haste to your heaven- ly Fa - ther's throne And sweet re - fresh-ment find.
I'll drop my bur - den at his feet And bear a song a - way.

356 Far, Far Away on Judea's Plains

(Women's Voices)

James MacFarlane   James MacFarlane

Joyously ♩= 100

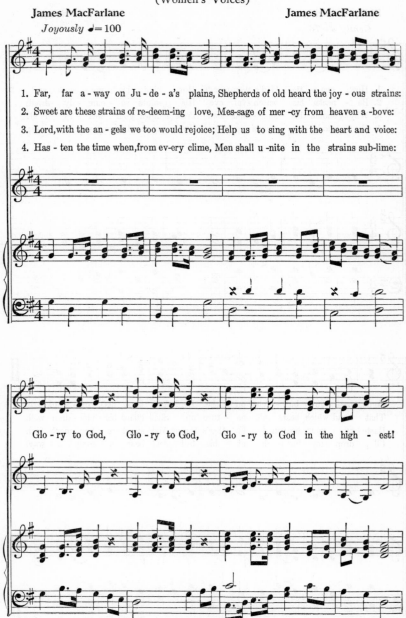

1. Far, far a-way on Ju-de-a's plains, Shepherds of old heard the joy-ous strains:

2. Sweet are these strains of re-deem-ing love, Mes-sage of mer-cy from heaven a-bove:

3. Lord, with the an-gels we too would rejoice; Help us to sing with the heart and voice:

4. Has-ten the time when, from ev-ery clime, Men shall u-nite in the strains sub-lime:

Glo-ry to God, Glo-ry to God, Glo-ry to God in the high-est!

Far, Far Away On Judea's Plains

Peace on earth, good will to men, Peace on earth, good will to men.

357   Gently Raise the Sacred Strain
(Women's Voices)

William W. Phelps   Thomas C. Griggs

Flowing ♩ = 96

1. Gent-ly   raise   the   sa - cred strain,   For   the   Sab - bath's come a -
2. Ho - ly   day,   de - void   of   strife,   Let   us   seek   e - ter - nal
3. Sweet-ly   swells   the   sol - emn sound   While   we   bring   our   gifts a -
4. Hap - py   type   of   things   to   come,   When   the   saints   are   gath - ered

Gently Raise the Sacred Strain

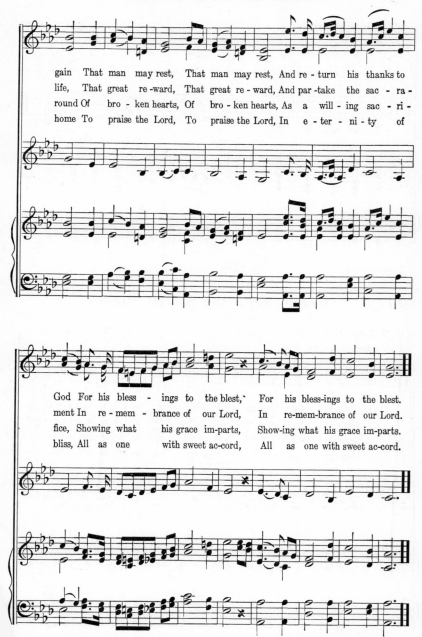

gain That man may rest, That man may rest, And re - turn his thanks to
life, That great re -ward, That great re - ward, And par -take the sac - ra -
round Of bro - ken hearts, Of bro - ken hearts, As a will - ing sac - ri -
home To praise the Lord, To praise the Lord, In e - ter - ni - ty of

God For his bless - ings to the blest, For his bless-ings to the blest.
ment In re - mem - brance of our Lord, In re-mem-brance of our Lord.
fice, Showing what his grace im-parts, Show-ing what his grace im-parts.
bliss, All as one with sweet ac-cord, All as one with sweet ac-cord.

358   How Great the Wisdom and the Love

(Women's Voices)

Eliza R. Snow   **Thomas McIntyre**

Calmly ♩=66

1. How great the wis-dom and the love That filled the courts on high And
2. His pre-cious blood he free-ly spilt; His life he free-ly gave, A
3. By strict o-be-dience Je-sus won The prize with glo-ry rife:"Thy
4. He marked the path and led the way And ev-ery point de-fines, To

sent the Sav-ior from a-bove To suf-fer, bleed, and die.
sin-less sac-ri-fice for guilt, A dy-ing world to save.
will, O God, not mine be done,"A-dorned his mor-tal life.
light and life and end-less day Where God's full pres-ence shines.

5. How great, how glorious and complete
Redemption's grand design.
Where justice, love, and mercy meet
In harmony divine.

6. In memory of the broken flesh
We eat the broken bread,
And witness with the cup, afresh
Our faith in Christ, our Head.

359 Glory Be to God in the Highest
(Women's Chorus)

Evan Stephens

Evan Stephens

Joyously ♩ = 100

Glo-ry be to God in the high - est,
Glo - ry, glo-ry be to God, and peace on earth, and

peace on earth.

1. This was the song the an - gels sang, Beth - le-hem's
2. This is the song re-peat - ed o'er Each hap-py
3. Oh, let us try some aid to lend. These of the

plains a - bove, While near, the bless-ed moth-er held The new-born King of
Christ-mas morn, And bless-ed moth-ers cling a-new To dear ones new-ly
new-born throng, To grow and live so in the end They, too, may join the

love. Born un-to sor-row was the child, Though Lord of life was he
born, Born un-to sor-row as was he, But, oh, how weak and frail,
song With the re-deemed when life is o'er, When all the ran-somed sing.

To die as man, but un-de-filed, Win death - less vic-to-ry,
These lit-tle lamb-kins of our Lord, How prone to err and fail,
There's peace on earth; there's joy in heaven Saved by our Sav-ior King,

Win death-less vic-to - ry,

Glory Be to God in the Highest

Win death-less vic-to-ry.
How prone to err and fail.
Saved by our Sav-ior King, And peace on earth, peace on earth.

360 God, Our Father, Hear Us Pray
(Women's Voices)

Annie Malin   L. Gottschalk

Worshipfully ♩= 72

1. God, our Fa-ther, hear us pray; Send thy grace this ho-ly day;
2. Grant us, Fa-ther, grace di-vine; May thy smile up-on us shine;
3. As we drink the wa-ter clear, Let thy Spir-it lin-ger near;

As we take of em-blems blest, On our Sav-ior's love we rest.
As we eat the brok-en bread, Thine ap-prov-al on us shed.
Par-don faults, O Lord, we pray; Bless our ef-forts day by day.

361   I Know That My Redeemer Lives
(Women's Voices)

Samuel Medley   **Lewis D. Edwards**

Solo *With devotion* ♩=60

1. I know that my Re-deem-er lives, What com-fort this sweet sen-tence gives! He lives, he lives, who once was dead; He lives, my ev-er liv-ing head!

2. He lives to grant me rich sup-ply; He lives to guide me with his eye; He lives to com-fort me when faint; He lives to hear my soul's com-plaint.

3. He lives, my kind, wise, heaven-ly friend; He lives and loves me to the end; He lives and while he lives I'll sing, He lives, my Proph-et, Priest, and King.

4. He lives, all glo-ry to his name! He lives, my Sav-ior, still the same; O sweet the joy this sen-tence gives: "I know that my Re-deem-er lives." He lives, all glo-ry to his

Chorus

He lives to bless me with his
He lives to si-lence all my
He lives and grants me dai-ly

I Know That My Redeemer Lives

love; He lives to plead for me a - bove; He lives my
fears; He lives to wipe a - way my tears; He lives to
breath; He lives, and I shall con - quer death; He lives my
name! He lives, my Sav-iour, still the same; O sweet the

hun - gry soul to feed; He lives to bless in time of need.
calm my trou-bled heart; He lives all bless - ings to im - part.
man - sion to pre - pare; He lives to bring me safe - ly there.
joy this sen-tence gives: "I know that my Re-deem - er lives!"

Jesus, Once of Humble Birth

(Women's Voices)

Parley P. Pratt

From English Chorister

Solemnly ♩ = 69

1. Je - sus, once of hum - ble birth, Now in glo - ry comes to earth. Once he suf - fered grief and pain; Now he
2. Once a meek and low - ly Lamb, Now the Lord, the great I Am. Once up - on the cross he bowed, Now his
3. Once he groaned in blood and tears; Now in glo - ry he ap - pears. Once re - ject - ed by his own; Now their
4. Once for - sak - en, left a - lone, Now ex - alt - ed to a throne. Once all things he meek - ly bore, But he

Jesus, Once of Humble Birth

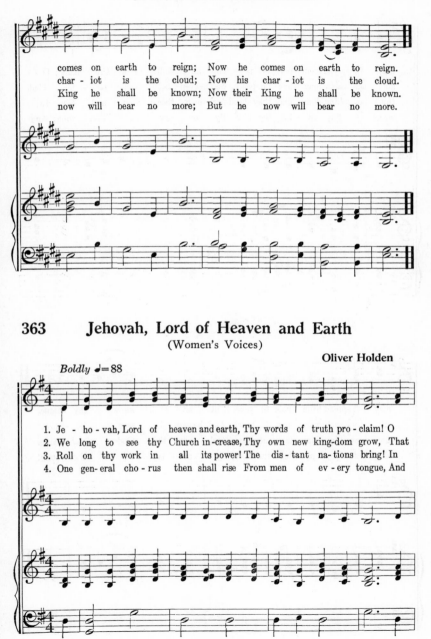

comes on earth to reign; Now he comes on earth to reign.
char - iot is the cloud; Now his char - iot is the cloud.
King he shall be known; Now their King he shall be known.
now will bear no more; But he now will bear no more.

363   Jehovah, Lord of Heaven and Earth
(Women's Voices)

Oliver Holden

Boldly ♩=88

1. Je - ho - vah, Lord of heaven and earth, Thy words of truth pro - claim! O
2. We long to see thy Church in - crease, Thy own new king-dom grow, That
3. Roll on thy work in all its power! The dis - tant na - tions bring! In
4. One gen- eral cho - rus then shall rise From men of ev - ery tongue, And

Jehovah, Lord of Heaven and Earth

may it spread from pole to pole, Till all shall know thy name; O
all the earth may live in peace, And heaven be seen be - low; That
thy new king-dom may they stand And own thee God and King; In
songs of joy sa - lute the skies By ev - ery na - tion sung; And

may it spread from pole to pole, Till all shall know thy name.
all the earth may live in peace And heaven be seen be - low.
thy new king-dom may they stand And own thee God and King.
songs of joy sa - lute the skies, By ev - ery na - tion sung!

364 How Wondrous and Great

(Women's Voices)

Henry U. Onderdonk   J. Michael Haydn

With dignity ♩= 88

1. How won-drous and great Thy works, God of praise! How just, King of
2. To na-tions long dark Thy light shall be shown; Their wor-ship and

Saints, And true, are thy ways! O who shall not fear thee And
vows Shall come to thy throne; Thy truth and thy judg-ments Shall

hon-or thy Name? Thou on-ly art ho-ly, Thou on-ly su-preme.
spread all a-broad, Till earth's ev-ery peo-ple Con-fess thee their God.

365

Jesus, Savior, Pilot Me

(Women's Voices)

Edward Hopper

J. E. Gould

Suppliantly ♩ = 58

1. Je - sus, Sav - ior, pi - lot me O - ver life's tem - pes - tuous
2. As a moth - er stills her child, Thou canst hush the o - cean
3. When at last I near the shore, And the fear - ful break - ers

sea; Un - known waves be - fore me roll, Hid - ing rock and treach - erous
wild; Boist - erous waves o - bey thy will When thou sayest to them, "Be
roar 'Twixt me and the peace - ful rest, Then, while lean - ing on thy

Jesus, Savior, Pilot Me

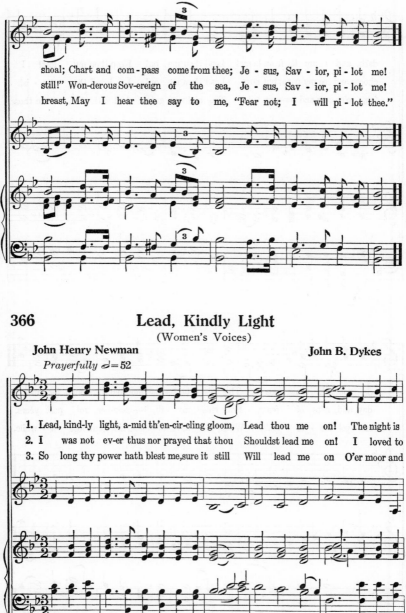

shoal; Chart and com-pass come from thee; Je - sus, Sav - ior, pi - lot me!
still!" Won-derous Sov-ereign of the sea, Je - sus, Sav - ior, pi - lot me!
breast, May I hear thee say to me, "Fear not; I will pi - lot thee."

366

Lead, Kindly Light

(Women's Voices)

John Henry Newman

John B. Dykes

Prayerfully ♩ = 52

1. Lead, kind-ly light, a-mid th'en-cir-cling gloom, Lead thou me on! The night is
2. I was not ev-er thus nor prayed that thou Shouldst lead me on! I loved to
3. So long thy power hath blest me, sure it still Will lead me on O'er moor and

Lead, Kindly Light

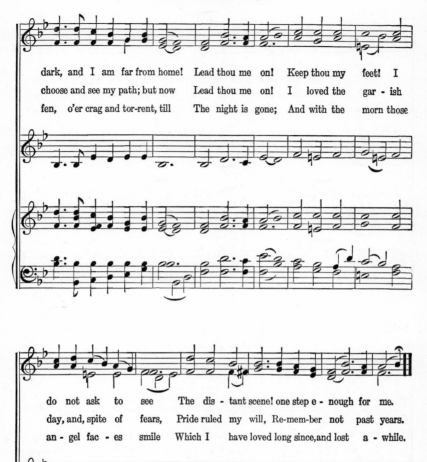

dark, and I am far from home! Lead thou me on! Keep thou my feet! I
choose and see my path; but now Lead thou me on! I loved the gar - ish
fen, o'er crag and tor-rent, till The night is gone; And with the morn those

do not ask to see The dis - tant scene! one step e - nough for me.
day, and, spite of fears, Pride ruled my will, Re-mem-ber not past years.
an - gel fac - es smile Which I have loved long since, and lost a - while.

367   Jesus, The Very Thought of Thee

(Women's Voices)

Bernard of Clairvaux
John B. Dykes

Praisingly ♩=72

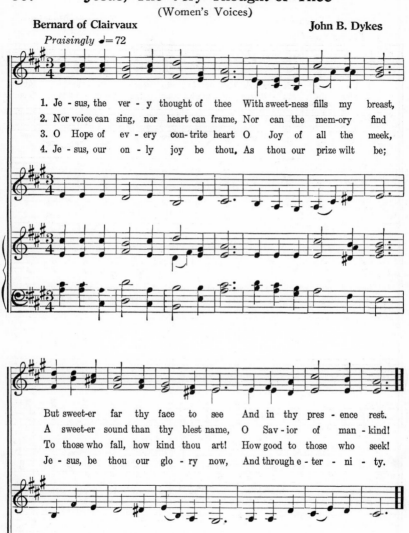

1. Je - sus, the ver - y thought of thee With sweet-ness fills my breast,
2. Nor voice can sing, nor heart can frame, Nor can the mem-ory find
3. O Hope of ev - ery con-trite heart O Joy of all the meek,
4. Je - sus, our on - ly joy be thou, As thou our prize wilt be;

But sweet-er far thy face to see And in thy pres - ence rest.
A sweet-er sound than thy blest name, O Sav - ior of man - kind!
To those who fall, how kind thou art! How good to those who seek!
Je - sus, be thou our glo - ry now, And through e - ter - ni - ty.

368 Let Us Oft Speak Kind Words

(Women's Voices)

Joseph L. Townsend

Ebenezer Beesley

Fluently ♩=63

1. Let us oft speak kind words to each oth-er At
2. Like the sun-beams of morn on the moun-tains, The

home or wher-e'er we may be; Like the war-blings of
soul they a-wake to good cheer; Like the mur-mur of

birds on the heath-er, The tones will be wel-come and
cool pleas-ant foun-tains, They fall in sweet ca-den-ces

Let Us Oft Speak Kind Words

free; They'll glad - den the heart that's re - pin - ing; Give
near. Let's oft, then, in kind - ly toned voic - es Our

cour - age and hope from a - bove; And where the dark clouds
mu - tu - al friend-ship re - new, Till heart meets with heart

hide the shin - ing, Let in the bright sun - light of love.
and re - joic - es In friend - ship that ev - er is true.

368-2

Let Us Oft Speak Kind Words

Oh, the kind words we give shall in mem - o - ry live,

And sun - shine for - ev - er im - part; Let us oft speak kind

words to each oth - er; Kind words are sweet tones of the heart.

368-3

369 Lord, We Ask Thee Ere We Part

(Women's Voices)

George Manwaring

Ebenezer Beesley

Simply ♩=66

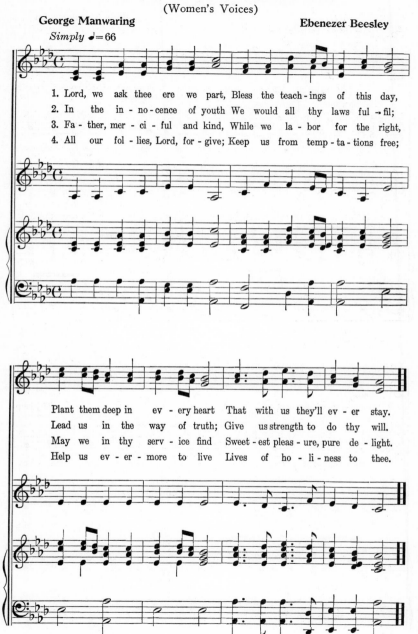

1. Lord, we ask thee ere we part, Bless the teach-ings of this day,
2. In the in-no-cence of youth We would all thy laws ful→fil;
3. Fa-ther, mer-ci-ful and kind, While we la-bor for the right,
4. All our fol-lies, Lord, for-give; Keep us from temp-ta-tions free;

Plant them deep in ev-ery heart That with us they'll ev-er stay.
Lead us in the way of truth; Give us strength to do thy will.
May we in thy serv-ice find Sweet-est pleas-ure, pure de-light.
Help us ev-er-more to live Lives of ho-li-ness to thee.

370   Lift Thine Eyes to the Mountains

(Women's Chorus)

Felix Mendelssohn

Lift Thine Eyes to the Mountains

com - eth from the Lord, the Mak - er of heav - en and

from the Lord, from the Lord, the Mak - er of heav - en and

from the Lord, the Mak - - er of heav - en and

earth. He hath said, "Thy foot shall not be mov - ed. Thy

earth. He hath said, "Thy foot shall not be mov - ed.

earth. He hath said, "Thy foot shall not be mov - ed.

Lift Thine Eyes to the Mountains

Lift Thine Eyes to the Mountains

371 The Lord is My Shepherd

(Women's Chorus)

23rd Psalm

Thomas Koschat

Worshipfully ♩ = 60

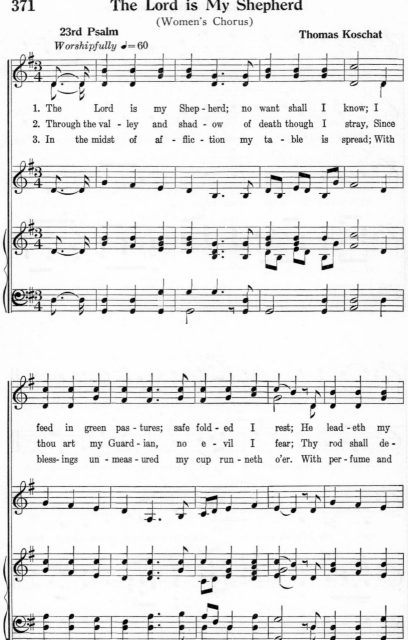

1. The Lord is my Shep-herd; no want shall I know; I feed in green pas-tures; safe fold-ed I rest; He lead-eth my
2. Through the val-ley and shad-ow of death though I stray, Since thou art my Guard-ian, no e-vil I fear; Thy rod shall de-
3. In the midst of af-flic-tion my ta-ble is spread; With bless-ings un-meas-ured my cup run-neth o'er. With per-fume and

The Lord is My Shepherd

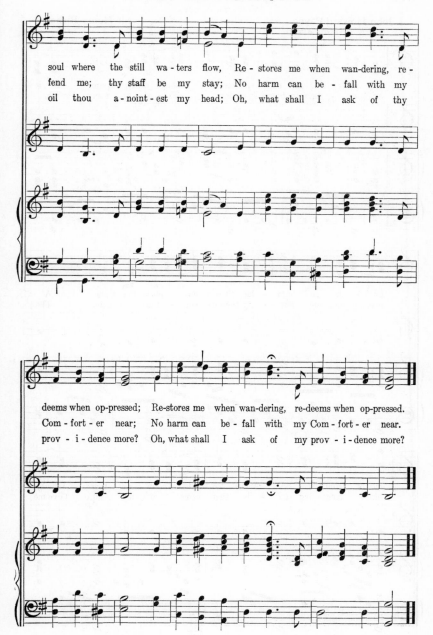

soul where the still wa - ters flow, Re - stores me when wan - dering, re -
fend me; thy staff be my stay; No harm can be - fall with my
oil thou a - noint - est my head; Oh, what shall I ask of thy

deems when op-pressed; Re-stores me when wan-dering, re-deems when op-pressed.
Com - fort - er near; No harm can be - fall with my Com - fort - er near.
prov - i - dence more? Oh, what shall I ask of my prov - i - dence more?

'Mid Pleasures and Palaces
(Women's Voices)

John Howard Payne

Sir Henry Bishop

With devotion ♩ = 46

1. 'Mid pleas - ures and pal - a - ces though we may roam, Be it
2. An ex - ile from home, splen-dor daz - zles in vain; Oh,

ev - er so hum - ble, there's no place like home. A
give me my low - ly thatched cot - tage a - gain, The

charm from the skies seems to hal - low us there Which,
birds sing - ing gai - ly that came at my call; Give me

'Mid Pleasures and Palaces

seek through the world, is ne'er met with else-where.
them, with that peace of mind, dear - er than all.

Home, home, sweet, sweet home! Be it

ev - er so hum - ble, there's no place like home.

373 The Morning Breaks; The Shadows Flee

(Women's Voices)

Parley P. Pratt

George Careless

Triumphantly ♩=92

1. The morn - ing breaks; the shad - ows flee;
2. The clouds of er - ror dis - ap - pear
3. The Gen - tile ful - ness now comes in,

Lo! Zi - on's stan - dard is un - furled. The dawn - ing
Be - fore the rays of truth di - vine; The glo - ry
And Is - rael's bless - ings are at hand; Lo! Ju - dah's

The Morning Breaks, The Shadows Flee

of a bright - er day, The dawn - ing of a
burst - ing from a - far, The glo - ry burst - ing
rem - nant, cleansed from sin, Lo! Ju - dah's rem - nant

bright - er day Ma - jes - tic ris - es on the world.
from a - far, Wide o'er the na - tions soon will shine.
cleansed from sin, Shall in their prom - ised Ca - naan stand.

4. Jehovah speaks! let earth give ear,
   And Gentile nations turn and live;
   His mighty arm is making bare,
   His mighty arm is making bare
   His covenant people to receive.

5. Angels from heaven and truth from earth
   Have met, and both have record borne;
   Thus Zion's light is bursting forth,
   Thus Zion's light is bursting forth
   To bring her ransomed children home.

Nay, Speak No Ill

(Women's Voices)

With contemplation ♩=66

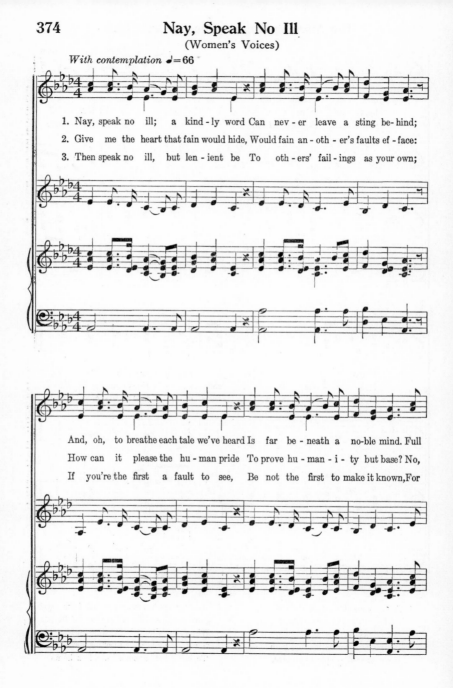

1. Nay, speak no ill; a kind-ly word Can nev-er leave a sting be-hind;
2. Give me the heart that fain would hide, Would fain an-oth-er's faults ef-face:
3. Then speak no ill, but len-ient be To oth-ers' fail-ings as your own;

And, oh, to breathe each tale we've heard Is far be-neath a no-ble mind. Full
How can it please the hu-man pride To prove hu-man-i-ty but base? No,
If you're the first a fault to see, Be not the first to make it known, For

Nay, Speak No Ill

oft a bet - ter seed is sown By choos-ing thus the kind-er plan, For
let us reach a high-er mood, A no-bler es - ti-mate of man; Be
life is but a pass-ing day; No lip may tell how brief its span; Then,

if but lit - tle good is known, Still let us speak the best we can.
ear - nest in the search for good, And speak of all the best we can.
O the lit - tle time we stay, Let's speak of all the best we can.

375 Not Now, But in the Coming Years

(Women's Chorus)

Maxwell N. Cornelius   James McGranahan

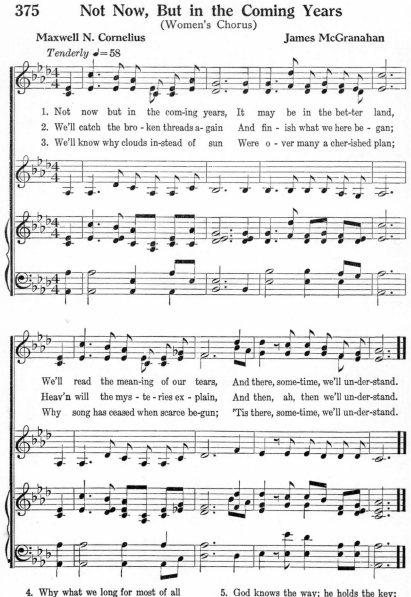

1. Not now but in the com-ing years, It may be in the bet-ter land,
2. We'll catch the bro - ken threads a- gain And fin - ish what we here be - gan;
3. We'll know why clouds in-stead of sun Were o - ver many a cher-ished plan;

We'll read the mean-ing of our tears, And there, some-time, we'll un-der-stand.
Heav'n will the mys - te - ries ex - plain, And then, ah, then we'll un-der-stand.
Why song has ceased when scarce be-gun; 'Tis there, some-time, we'll un-der-stand.

4. Why what we long for most of all
   Eludes so oft our eager hand,
   Why hopes are crushed and castles fall;
   Up there, sometime we'll understand.

5. God knows the way; he holds the key;
   He guides us with unerring hand;
   Sometime with tearless eyes we'll see;
   Yes, there, up there we'll understand.

Not Now, But in the Coming Years

Then trust in God through all thy days; Fear not, for he doth hold thy hand; Though dark thy way still sing and praise; Some-time, some-time we'll un-der-stand.

376 More Holiness Give Me

(Women's Voices)

Philip Paul Bliss

Philip Paul Bliss

Prayerfully ♩· = 50

1. More ho - li - ness give me, More striv-ings with- in; More pa-tience
2. More gra - ti - tude give me, More trust in the Lord, More pride in
3. More pur - i - ty give me, More strength to o'er - come; More free-dom

in suf - fering, More sor - row for sin; More faith in my Sav - ior,
his glo - ry, More hope in his word, More tears for his sor - rows,
from earth-stains, More long - ings for home. More fit for the king - dom;

More sense of his care, More joy in his ser - vice, More pur-pose in prayer.
More pain at his grief, More meek-ness in tri - al, More praise for re - lief.
More used would I be; More bless - ed and ho - ly, More, Sav - ior, like thee.

377 Now the Day Is Over

(Women's Voices)

Sabine Baring-Gould

Joseph Barnby

Solemnly ♩ = 54
pp

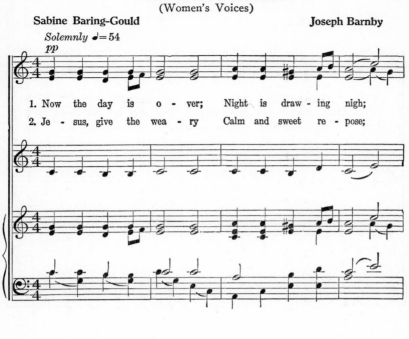

1. Now the day is o - ver; Night is draw - ing nigh;
2. Je - sus, give the wea - ry Calm and sweet re - pose;

Shad - ows of the eve - ning Steal a - cross the sky.
With thy ten - derest bless - ing May our eye - lids close.

378 Oh Beautiful For Spacious Skies

(Women's Voices)

Katherine Lee Bates

Samuel A. Ward

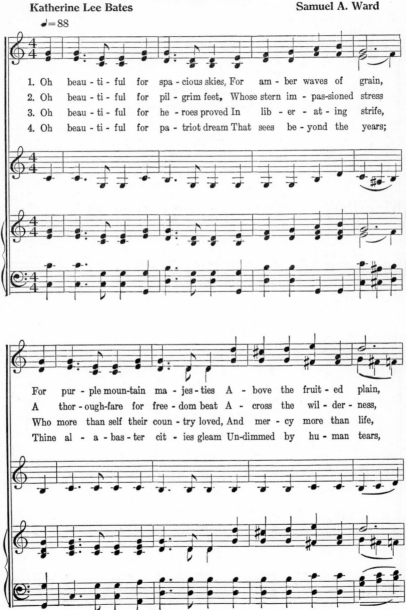

1. Oh beau - ti - ful for spa - cious skies, For am - ber waves of grain,
2. Oh beau - ti - ful for pil - grim feet, Whose stern im - pas-sioned stress
3. Oh beau - ti - ful for he - roes proved In lib - er - at - ing strife,
4. Oh beau - ti - ful for pa - triot dream That sees be - yond the years;

For pur - ple moun-tain ma - jes - ties A - bove the fruit - ed plain,
A thor - ough-fare for free - dom beat A - cross the wil - der - ness,
Who more than self their coun - try loved, And mer - cy more than life,
Thine al - a - bas - ter cit - ies gleam Un-dimmed by hu - man tears,

Oh Beautiful For Spacious Skies

A - mer - i - ca! A - mer - i - ca! God shed his grace on thee
A - mer - i - ca! A - mer - i - ca! God mend thine ev - ery flaw,
A - mer - i - ca! A - mer - i - ca! May God thy gold re - fine
A - mer - i - ca! A - mer - i - ca! God shed his grace on thee

And crown thy good with broth - er - hood From sea to shin - ing sea.
Con - firm thy soul in self - con - trol, Thy lib - er - ty in law.
Till all suc - cess be no - ble - ness And ev - ery gain di - vine.
And crown thy good with broth - er - hood From sea to shin - ing sea.

379 O Lord of Hosts

(Women's Voices)

A. Dalrymple

George Careless

♩ = 56

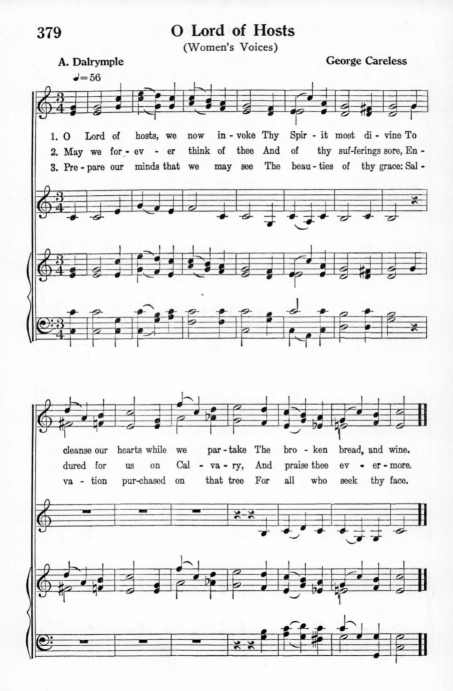

1. O Lord of hosts, we now in-voke Thy Spir-it most di-vine To
2. May we for-ev-er think of thee And of thy suf-ferings sore, En-
3. Pre-pare our minds that we may see The beau-ties of thy grace: Sal-

cleanse our hearts while we par-take The bro-ken bread, and wine.
dured for us on Cal-va-ry, And praise thee ev-er-more.
va-tion pur-chased on that tree For all who seek thy face.

380 Prayer is the Soul's Sincere Desire

(Women's Voices)

James Montgomery

George Careless

Fluently ♩ = 72

1. Prayer is the soul's sin-cere de-sire, Ut-tered or un-ex-pressed, The
2. Prayer is the bur-den of a sigh, The fall-ing of a tear, The
3. Prayer is the sim-plest form of speech That in-fant lips can try, Prayer,
4. Prayer is the Chris-tian's vi-tal breath, The Chris-tian's na-tive air, His

mo-tion of a hid-den fire That trem-bles in the breast.
up-ward glanc-ing of an eye When none but God is near.
the sub-lim-est strains that reach The Maj-es-ty on high.
watch-word at the gates of death; He en-ters heaven with prayer.

5. Prayer is the contrite sinner's voice,
   Returning from his ways,
   While angels in their songs rejoice,
   And cry,"Behold, he prays!"

6. The Saints in prayer appear as one
   In word and deed and mind,
   While with the Father and the Son
   Their fellowship they find.

7. Nor prayer is made on earth alone,
   The Holy Spirit pleads,
   And Jesus, at the Father's throne,
   For sinners intercedes.

8. Oh, thou by whom we come to God,
   The Life, the Truth, the Way!
   The path of prayer thyself hast trod;
   Lord, teach us how to pray.

381 Sister, Thou Wast Mild and Lovely
(Women's Voices)

Samuel F. Smith   John S. Lewis

Somberly ♩ = 88

1. Sis - ter, thou wast mild and love - ly, Gent - le as the sum - mer breeze,
2. Peace - ful be thy si - lent slum - ber, Peace - ful in the grave so low;
3. Dear - est sis - ter, thou hast left us; Here thy loss we deep - ly feel,
4. Yet a - gain we hope to meet thee When death's gloom-y night has fled;

Pleas - ant as the air of ev-ening When it floats a-mong the trees.
Thou no more wilt join our num-ber; Thou no more our songs shalt know.
But 'tis God that hast be - reft us; He can all our sor -rows heal.
Then on earth with joy to greet thee Where no bit - ter tears are shed.

382 Rock of Ages

(Women's Voices)

Augustus M. Toplady   **Thomas Hastings**

With religious fervor ♩ = 58

1. Rock of A - ges, cleft for me, Let me hide my - self in thee;
2. While I draw this fleet - ing breath, When my eyes shall close in death,

Let the wa - ter and the blood From thy wound - ed side which flowed,
When I rise to worlds un - known And be - hold thee on thy throne,

Be of sin the dou - ble cure; Save from wrath and make me pure.
Rock of A - ges, cleft for me, Let me hide my - self in thee.

383 There Is Beauty All Around

(Women's Voices)

Fervently ♩=68

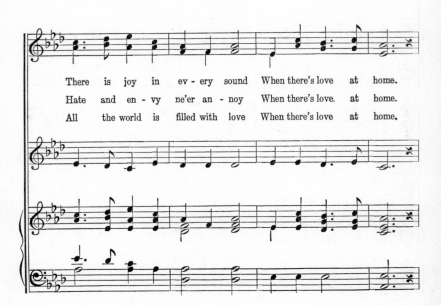

1. There is beau - ty all a - round When there's love at home;
2. In the cot - tage there is joy When there's love at home;
3. Kind - ly heav - en smiles a - bove When there's love at home;

There is joy in ev - ery sound When there's love at home.
Hate and en - vy ne'er an - noy When there's love, at home.
All the world is filled with love When there's love at home.

384 Sweet Is the Work, My God, My King

(Women's Voices)

Isaac Watts John J. McClellan

Worshipfully ♩=84

1. Sweet is the work, my God, my King, To praise thy name, give thanks and sing,
2. Sweet is the day of sa - cred rest; No mor - tal care shall seize my breast.
3. My heart shall tri - umph in my Lord And bless his works and bless his word;
4. But, oh, what tri - umph shall I raise To thy dear name through end - less days,

To show thy love by morn - ing light, And talk of all thy truths at night.
may my heart in tune be found Like Da - vid's harp of sol - emn sound.
Thy works of grace, how bright they shine, How deep thy coun - sels, how di - vine!
Then in the realms of joy I see Thy face in full fe - lic - i - ty!

385 The Wintry Day Descending to Its Close

(Women's Chorus)

Orson F. Whitney

Edward P. Kimball

Calmly ♩= 63

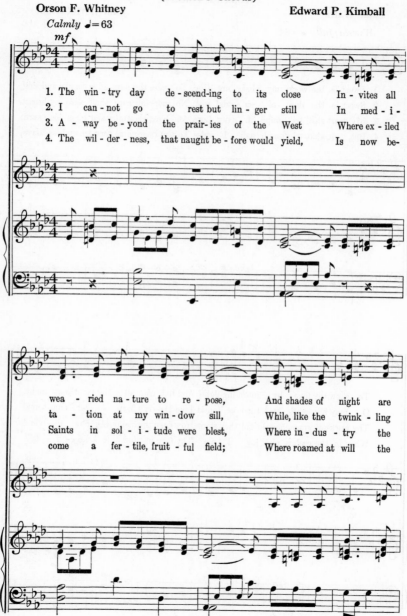

1. The win-try day de-scend-ing to its close In-vites all wea-ried na-ture to re-pose, And shades of night are
2. I can-not go to rest but lin-ger still In med-i-ta-tion at my win-dow sill, While, like the twink-ling
3. A-way be-yond the prair-ies of the West Where ex-iled Saints in sol-i-tude were blest, Where in-dus-try the
4. The wil-der-ness, that naught be-fore would yield, Is now be-come a fer-tile, fruit-ful field; Where roamed at will the

The Wintry Day Descending to Its Close

fall-ing dense and fast Like sa - ble cur - tains clos - ing o'er the
stars in heav-en's dome, Come one by one sweet mem - o - ries of
seal of wealth has set A - mid the peace - ful vales of Des - er -
sav-age In - dian band, The tem - pled cit - ies of the Saints now

past. Pale through the gloom the new- ly fall - en snow Wraps in a
home. And wouldst thou ask me where my fan - cy roves To re - pro -
et, Un - heed - ing still the fierc-est blasts that blow, With tops en -
stand; And sweet re - li - gion in its pur - i - ty In - vites all

The Wintry Day Descending to Its Close

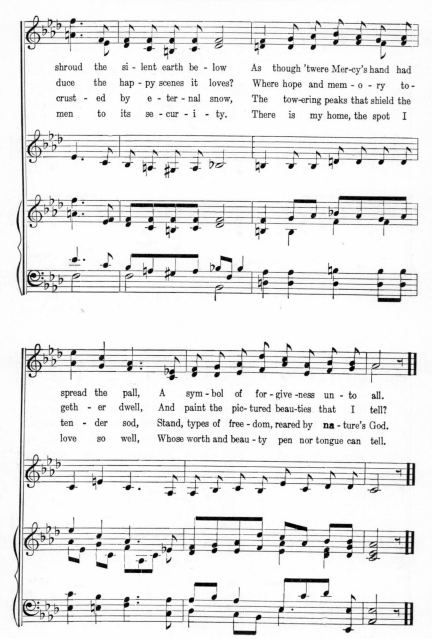

shroud the si - lent earth be - low As though 'twere Mer-cy's hand had
duce the hap - py scenes it loves? Where hope and mem - o - ry to -
crust - ed by e - ter - nal snow, The tow-ering peaks that shield the
men to its se - cur - i - ty. There is my home, the spot I

spread the pall, A sym - bol of for - give -ness un - to all.
geth - er dwell, And paint the pic- tured beau-ties that I tell?
ten - der sod, Stand, types of free - dom, reared by **na** - ture's God.
love so well, Whose worth and beau - ty pen nor tongue can tell.

386 We Ever Pray For Thee

(Women's Voices)

Evan Stephens   Evan Stephens

♩ = 69

1. We ev-er pray for thee, our Proph-et dear, That God will give to thee com-fort and cheer; As the ad-vanc-ing years fur-row thy brow, Still may the light with-in shine bright as now, Still may the light with-in shine bright as now.

2. We ev-er pray for thee with all our hearts, That strength be giv-en thee to do thy part, To guide and coun-sel us from day to day, To shed a ho-ly light a-round our way, To shed a ho-ly light a-round our way.

3. We ev-er pray for thee with fer-vent love, And as the chil-dren's prayer is heard a-bove, Thou shalt be ev-er blest, and God will give All that is meet and best while thou shalt live, All that is meet and best while thou shalt live.

387 Ye Simple Souls Who Stray

(Women's Chorus)

Wesley's Collection

Evan Stephens

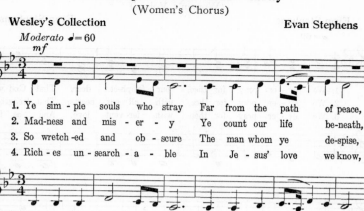

1. Ye sim - ple souls who stray Far from the path of peace,
2. Mad-ness and mis - er - y Ye count our life be-neath,
3. So wretch-ed and ob - scure The man whom ye de-spise,
4. Rich - es un - search - a - ble In Je - sus' love we know,

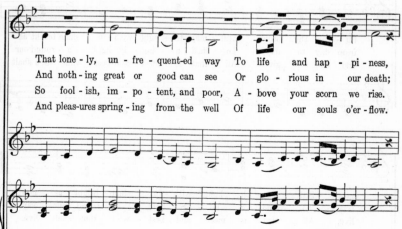

That lone - ly, un - fre - quent-ed way To life and hap - pi - ness,
And noth - ing great or good can see Or glo - rious in our death;
So fool - ish, im - po - tent, and poor, A - bove your scorn we rise.
And pleas-ures spring - ing from the well Of life our souls o'er - flow.

Ye Simple Souls Who Stray

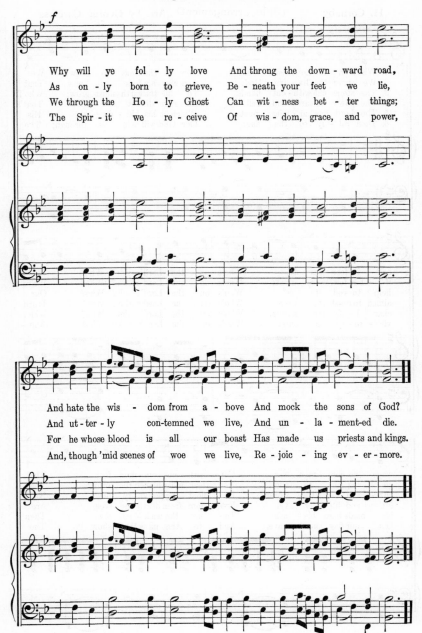

Why will ye fol - ly love And throng the down - ward road,
As on - ly born to grieve, Be - neath your feet we lie,
We through the Ho - ly Ghost Can wit - ness bet - ter things;
The Spir - it we re - ceive Of wis - dom, grace, and power,

And hate the wis - dom from a - bove And mock the sons of God?
And ut - ter - ly con - temned we live, And un - la - ment-ed die.
For he whose blood is all our boast Has made us priests and kings.
And, though 'mid scenes of woe we live, Re - joic - ing ev - er - more.

388 Who's On the Lord's Side?

H. Cornaby   (Solo arrangement)   **Arr. by George Careless**

1. Who's on the Lord's side? Who? Now is the time to show; We
2. We serve the liv-ing God; And want his foes to know That
3. The stone cut with-out hands, To fill the earth must grow; Who'll
4. The pow'r of earth and hell In rage di-rect the blow That's
5. The Lord has ar-mies great Which at his bid-ding go, His
6. Then ral-ly to the flag; Our God will help us through; The

ask it fear-less-ly, Who's on the Lord's side? Who? We
if but few, we're great; Who's on the Lord's side? Who? We're
help to roll it on? Who's on the Lord's side? Who? Our
aimed to crush the work; Who's on the Lord's side? Who? Truth,
char-i-ots are strong; Who's on the Lord's side? Who? When
vic-to-ry is ours: Who's on the Lord's side? Who? Stain-

wage no com-mon war, Cope with no com-mon foe; The
go-ing on to win, Nor fear must blanch the brow; The
en-sign to the world Is float-ing proud-ly now; No
life and lib-er-ty, Free-dom from death and woe, Are
he made bare his arm To lay the wick-ed low, Then
less our flag must wave, And to the na-tions show The

Who's On the Lord's Side?

en - e - my's a - wake; Who's on the Lord's side? Who?......
Lord of Hosts is ours; Who's on the Lord's side? Who?......
cow - ard bears our flag Who's on the Lord's side? Who?......
stakes we're fight - ing for; Who's on the Lord's side? Who?......
is the time to ask Who's on the Lord's side? Who?......
ol - ive branch of peace; Who's on the Lord's side? Who?......

Who's on the Lord's side? Who? Now is the time to show; We

ask it fear - less - ly, Who's on the Lord's side? Who?

389 This Earth Was Once a Garden Place

W. W. Phelps

(Congregation)

Peacefully ♪ = 96

1. This earth was once a gar - den place, With
2. We read that E - noch walked with God, A -
3. Her land was good and great - ly blest, Be -
4. Ho - san - na to such days to come, The

all her glo - ries com - mon, And men did
bove the power of mam - mon, While Zi - on
yond all Is - rael's Ca - naan, Her fame was
Sav - iour's sec - ond com - ing, When all the

live a ho - ly race, And wor - ship Je - sus
spread her - self a - broad, And Saints and an - gels
known from east to west, Her peace was great, and
earth in glo - rious bloom Af - fords the Saints a

face to face, In A - dam - on - di - Ah - man.
sang a - loud, In A - dam - on - di - Ah - man.
pure the rest Of A - dam - on - di - Ah - man.
ho - ly home, Like A - dam - on - di - Ah - man.

INDEX

INDEX OF FIRST LINE

INDEX OF FIRST LINE

INDEX OF FIRST LINE

INDEX OF FIRST LINE

INDEX OF FIRST LINE

INDEX OF FIRST LINE

INDEX OF FIRST LINE

INDEX OF FIRST LINE

INDEX OF FIRST LINE

Note: All hymns that have a meter indicated may be sung to the tune of any other hymn having the same meter letters after it.

TOPICAL INDEX

TOPICAL INDEX

TOPICAL INDEX

TOPICAL INDEX